At the Table

My life and times

By Bob Hamman
with Brent Manley

DBM Publications
Memphis, Tennessee
1994

Dedication

To the chess players who made me realize there had to be an easier game. To the college professors whose classes were so boring I couldn't help but focus on bridge. And to the theorists and promoters responsible for five-card majors and forcing notrumps – they gave many talented opponents weapons they couldn't beat me with.

BH

To Donna, who urged me on, supported me and made the project work. We couldn't have done it without you.

BM

First Edition

DBM Publications
5481 Raleigh-LaGrange
Memphis, Tennessee 38134

First published in the United States, 1994
© Bob Hamman and Brent Manley 1994

Library of Congress Catalog Card Number: 94-67897

ISBN 0-9642584-0-4

Edited by Henry Francis
Cover by Lisa Edwards
Typeset by Donna Manley

Contents

Foreword by Don Krauss

1	Go on to the next hand	1
2	Emperor of the 2-cent game	10
3	A thumb in the eye	22
4	Trials and tribulations	34
5	Escape from New York	46
6	Fired up and burned out	59
7	The promoter	73
8	Moose	86
9	The juggernaut	97
10	Vindication	112
11	Winds of change	125
12	Nemesis	141
13	On the verge of scandal	158
14	Scandal	171
15	Redemption	191
16	Valleys	213
17	Peaks	230
18	Close calls	259
19	Sure things	277
20	A competitive game	297

Postscripts 308
The skins on the wall 311

Thank you

The authors thank the following for their invaluable assistance in this project:

Ron Andersen, Henry Francis, Bobby Goldman, Eddie Kantar, Edgar Kaplan, Bruce Keidan, Don Krauss, Mike Lawrence, Sidney Lazard, Susie Marshall, Dorothy Moore, Joe Musumeci, Al Okuneff, Alfred Sheinwold, John Swanson, Alan Truscott, Fran Tsacnaris and Bobby Wolff.

♣ ♦ ♥ ♠

The publishers thank the following friends for their advice, encouragement and assistance:

Randy Baron, Lisa Edwards, Garland Ergüden, Henry Francis, Rex Germany, Matt Granovetter, Petra Hamman, Harold Katz, Jody Latham, Colleen Manley, Susie Marshall, Larry Ohrberg, Susan Reagor, Frank Stewart – and especially Andy Bernstein.

Foreword

Bob Hamman and I played together for the first time in an IMP game in the fall of 1962. It was a practice match and I was filling in. Our first hand was a great success as we craftily stopped in game on a hand where only a 5-0 trump split could defeat a grand slam in hearts. Our opponents were obviously not amused as we scored up an undeserved 13-IMP swing. On that note, we formed a partnership that was far more rewarding than I ever could have expected.

Bob and I surprised everyone (except Bob, of course) by winning the pair trials for the 1964 Bridge Olympiad, and we became the youngest pair at the time to represent the United States in international play. Since then, Bob has had several partners with whom he has achieved national and international victories, but the successful Hamman-Krauss partnership was the beginning. My association with Bob, however, goes far beyond the game of bridge. That chance IMP game led to a friendship of more than 32 years. I suppose that is why I was asked to offer my thoughts on why Bob became the top-rated bridge player in the world, and why he has stayed on top for so long.

Bob has a great mind for the game. Bridge was the logical next step from the problem-solving he enjoyed as a math major in college as well as his days as an aspiring chess player. His technical excellence is unsurpassed. He is willing to go against the odds in favor of his own flawless judgment and "table feel." Equally important, he has the mental toughness necessary to shrug off the occasional bad result. He plays every hand as if it is the first hand of the game. Bad results instantly disappear from memory.

Another of Bob's strengths is his ability to get the most out of his partners. He has an incredible record playing with partners for the first time. He has won the Blue Ribbon Pairs four times – twice in the 1990s – with four different partners. My personal experience as Bob's partner was fantastic. It was always a comfortable feeling to put down a dummy when Bob was my partner. I never had to worry. If the hand could be made, Bob would make it. All of his partners have felt the same.

Bob's longevity at the top of the bridge world can be attributed to his zest for the game and his competitive spirit. While other bridge experts seem to drift away from the game, Bob rarely passes up a chance to compete. He has missed exactly one National tournament – St. Louis in 1963, when he had mononucleosis. When he comes to Los Angeles on one of his frequent business trips, bridge games seem to instantly materialize. Whatever the stakes, Bob is ready to play.

For all his achievements and his stature in the bridge world, Bob has humility and the ability to look at his mistakes with an open mind. Some years ago, he called to tell me about a 4♠ hand he played that was cold for five. He went down two trying to guard against a foul trump split. He claimed at the time that confession was good for the soul.

Bob is also scrupulously honest. A couple of months ago, he made a claim in a rubber bridge game and later decided the claim was not exactly right. He looked up the players the next day and offered to give back the money he had won on that hand. How many people do you know who would do that?

Bob is serious about bridge, but he never gets down on himself or his partners about losing, and he always seems to be in a good mood. He laughs easily, often at himself. Bob is a great player, but he's also a great human being. In his business, he looks out for his employees first. His acts of kindness and generosity are well known in the bridge world.

One more story. One of the regulars at the Los Angeles Bridge Club in the early 1960s who shall remain nameless considered himself quite a judge of bridge talent. One day, he decided to rate the other players at the club. He was adamant about two young hot-shots he considered the worst of the group. One was Paul Soloway. The other, Bob Hamman. *Right!*

Don Krauss
July 1994

1

Go on to the next hand

IT WAS LIKE starting the second half of a football game down by three touchdowns and having the other guys run the kickoff back for a score. Not the way you want to start your comeback.

It seemed to me that the two young men on either side of me at the bridge table shifted slightly in their seats. No words were spoken, but I felt that they had a sense that – at last – they were going to end the streak. Jeff Meckstroth and Eric Rodwell had just run that figurative kickoff back on us – making a doubled contract that should have gone down – and they were already up by 32 IMPs. Their lead had probably just climbed into the 40s, and they had momentum. What do we do now?

Go on to the next hand, that's what.

The streak – we had won every head-to-head match with Meckstroth and Rodwell since 1982, and this was 1990 – wasn't over until we lost, and I want to hear someone count ten over me before I make an exit. I never celebrate until the win is official – and I don't quit before then, either.

Personal experience has taught me the wisdom of Yogi Berra's truism – "It ain't over 'til it's over."

In the spring of 1966, I was playing with Lew Mathe in the Vanderbilt at the Nationals in Louisville, Kentucky. Our teammates were Ira Rubin and Phil Feldesman. We hadn't played well throughout, but somehow we had gotten to the final against a team led by the great Tobias Stone, half of the famous Roth-Stone partnership. They worked us over pretty good for the first three quarters of the match, and they had a 37-IMP lead with 18 boards to go.

During the break between the third and fourth quarters, Mathe and I were wandering around the Kentucky Hotel, where the tournament was being played, and we happened upon a scene that lit us up. The ACBL photographer was taking pictures of our opponents! He was taking it for granted that we were going to lose.

Now Mathe was a bulldog to start with, and he didn't need much to stir him up. This scene turned him up a couple more notches. We raced back to the playing area to find our teammates and tell them what we had just seen. "Let's make them waste some film," I said.

Mathe and I had a sensational set against Billy Eisenberg and Lenny Harmon. We felt if Feldesman and Rubin were breathing, we had a good shot to win it. When we met to compare, we found that they had played the last quarter with a vengeance, too. We won the set 88-5!

Up to that point, we hadn't played terribly well, but that scene with the camera changed everything. Suddenly, we got tough – we started playing like a team. During our victory celebration, we had a few drinks and got kind of rowdy and called Eric Murray in Toronto at 3 in the morning. He was supposed to be on our team but he hurt his back and couldn't come to Louisville. "We couldn't have won it with you," we joked.

I was so excited I couldn't sleep, and about 3:30 a.m. I wandered out of the hotel. Stone was there, pacing up and down the sidewalk. It was a little out of character for me, but I didn't needle him at all. He looked sad and he said, "Nice game, Bob."

I don't think he ever won another national.

But now it was 1990 in Boston, where the American Contract Bridge League was holding its summer championships. Wolffie and I had sat down against Meckstroth and Rodwell on a Sunday evening in a spacious, carpeted room on the second floor of the Sheraton Hotel. It was the fourth and final quarter of the Spingold Knockout Teams. The Spingold is one of the toughest and most prestigious events on the tournament schedule. It's an event I like to win.

Both teams had fought hard and vanquished some difficult opponents to reach this point – and all of us wanted to be in the winner's circle once again. Some may have wanted it too much.

Our team – we had Chip Martel and Lew Stansby playing at the other table – was at a disadvantage as we entered the final quarter. With 16 deals to play, we were down by 32 IMPs to a strong team playing their best lineup.

Meckstroth and Rodwell – these days a lot of people call them Meckwell – are one of the toughest pairs around, and they were on a roll. Their team had won the Grand National Teams earlier in the week. They are expert players who have won three world championships. Their partnership is as good as they get, featuring solid understandings on virtually every imaginable situation and an aggressive system that they handle with daring and skill. When they are hot, they can carry a team, which they demonstrated – at my cost – a year later (yes, the streak finally ended).

Meckstroth in particular projects the kind of mental and emotional toughness that is rare at the table today. A nice-looking young man, he tends to the heavy side – as I do – and he wears a beard. Sometimes the beard looks more like he just needs a shave, giving him a surly appearance that belies his friendly nature away from the table. When he sits down to play, he is all business and a ferocious competitor. Rodwell describes his partner as the best natural card player he's ever seen. I wouldn't argue with him. Meckstroth is a tiger.

I think of Rodwell, once a serious graduate student at Purdue University, as a mad scientist. He is the creator of what he and Meckstroth call RM Precision – for Rodwell-Meckstroth. The notes on their system take up 400 pages, and the book is still growing. Some of the logic of the system is influenced by the Fibonacci series of numbers. Very esoteric.

Only committed partners could play such a complex bidding system. Although I would like to tinker with our system more than Wolffie will let me, I consider Rodwell's machinations to be extreme. Still, their "forgets" are rare and they handle the system well. No one really likes to play against them.

While we settled into our seats in the ballroom at the Sheraton, Stansby and Martel squared off in the other room against another potent pair – Paul Soloway and Bobby Goldman. Both were teammates of mine back in the 1970s on the famous Aces, the team that grew out of the wonderful experiment by Dallas businessman Ira Corn. Soloway and I played together for a period before the Aces broke up. He is one tough competitor, as is Goldman.

Soloway and Goldman have been a regular partnership for a couple of decades – and they're both former world champions. Soloway is well known as the possessor of more masterpoints than anyone – more than 40,000. Since it takes 300 masterpoints to be a Life Master, that's like making Life Master more than 133 times!

This Spingold final was being played – in a sense – before a live audience. There were two rooms in play: a so-called Open Room and a Closed Room, where we were playing. In the Closed Room, television cameras were focused on the players so that viewers in a ballroom nearby could see facial expressions and watch the players as they made their bids and plays.

They call it a vugraph show, and in such a setup, walkie-talkies and telephones are used to relay the bids and plays to a larger ballroom where an audience is gathered. An overhead projector makes it possible for the audience to see hand and bidding diagrams – and expert commentators keep the crowd going with analyses and wise-cracks on every bid and play. A good set of commentators analyzing a close match can be dynamite entertainment.

Ironically, the lead commentator was Ron Andersen, a member of the team we were playing. He had played the first two quarters with Jim Mahaffey, the team's sponsor, and was sitting out the second half.

Ron is probably the best vugraph commentator around today. He's a veteran professional player – and another former teammate of mine. He knows the players and the systems they play, even the complicated stuff, so he can explain it to the audience as play progresses. What makes him so good, though, is that he's a born showman, a real ham. He loves the limelight and he's a great storyteller with a wonderful memory for anecdotes.

After our inauspicious start, it looked as if it was going to take all of Ron's talent to keep the audience interested in this bridge contest.

This was how we started.

```
Dlr: South        ♠ 10 7 3 2
Vul: N-S          ♥ K 10 8 4
                  ♦ 9 8 6
                  ♣ K 2
♠ A K J 8 6 5              ♠ Q 9 4
♥ J 5 2                    ♥ A Q
♦ A 3                      ♦ J 10 2
♣ 9 7                     ♣ 10 8 6 4 3
                  ♠ —
                  ♥ 9 7 6 3
                  ♦ K Q 7 5 4
                  ♣ A Q J 5
```

WEST	NORTH	EAST	SOUTH
Meckstroth	*Me*	*Rodwell*	*Wolff*
			1♥
1♠	2♥	2♠	3♦
3♥	4♥	4♠	Pass
Pass	Dbl	All Pass	

You may gasp at Wolffie's 1♥ opener, but that's our style. We go out of our way to open four-card majors, even when we have longer suits. We both know our major-suit openings can be on suits that bad and we bid accordingly.

As often happens when you play against Meckwell, the auction on this deal got competitive quickly. Rodwell's bid of 4♠ was a bit rash, even considering the vulnerability. I just don't think he had the hand for it.

I doubled and led the ♦9. I chose this lead because of a couple of inferences from the bidding. First, I suspected that Wolff's heart holding wasn't terribly robust. When we have good trumps opposite a raise from partner, we tend to simply bash into game if we think that's where the hand belongs. The delicate game try by Wolff made me think he wasn't too sure about our trump strength.

Second was his diamond bid, almost certainly from his longer suit. The diamond lead seemed less likely to blow a trick for our side.

Meckstroth put up the jack from dummy and won the ace when Wolff covered with the queen. Meckstroth next took the heart finesse and cashed the ace. He got off dummy with the ♦10, taken by Wolff with the king.

At that point, we had one chance to defeat the contract – to play on clubs. Look what happens if Wolff underleads his ♣A, or plays the ace (I would have to work out that it was right to play the king, but that wouldn't be too difficult). If we play three rounds of clubs at Meckstroth, he has to ruff with the ace, king or jack to keep me from scoring the setting trick right away.

But now he can't avoid a spade loser. Even if he can see all the cards and takes a first-round finesse of the ♠9, he can't pick up trumps and ruff a heart, too. If he ruffs a heart right away, he can't get back to his hand to take the finesse in spades. So he's a goner if we play three rounds of clubs at him.

What happened was that Wolff played the ♦7 and Meckstroth had the perfect counter. He discarded one of the clubs he was going to lose anyway. Now there was no way to beat the contract. Meckstroth could ruff the second round of clubs, ruff a heart low and pick up trumps, which is what he did.

Score up 590 for the other side. We couldn't be absolutely sure of it at the time, but it felt like a loss. In reality, Meckwell had scored another 9 IMPs on us. Stansby and Martel had played 3♠ at the other table, making four for plus 170.

However, it was more than a 9-IMP loss. Had we set the contract, we would have been plus 100 for a 7-IMP gain. So we really lost a 16-IMP swing in a match where we were already down by a substantial margin.

I've seen teams sag in their chairs at developments like this. Sometimes it's almost a physical thing – some guys seem to shrink a little when they're faced with a major reversal. Others toughen up. They hunker down, set their jaws and try harder.

Ira Rubin was the best I ever saw at bearing down. In the Bermuda Bowl in 1977, our team played Rubin's. They had led early but our team had overtaken them and had the match locked up. On the very last deal, I was in a ridiculous 2NT contract, but Rubin spent half an hour trying to figure out how to beat me three tricks. What a competitor!

In my 30-plus years of playing bridge in pretty good competition, I've learned to focus on the hand I'm playing – and only the hand I'm playing. It may be stating the obvious to say that nothing can change the result you just got, but I've seen lots of players make the mistake of dwelling on past history.

If you screw up or partner blows one – or even if the opponents fix you somehow – no amount of recrimination, self-flagellation or excuse-making can change the result. Indulging in such exercises does nothing but distract you from the task at hand – which is the next board you're supposed to play.

Bridge is a highly competitive sport and there's often a thin line between winning and losing. Sometimes it seems like it's a tenth of a millimeter. At many of the championships I've won, if an opponent had been even semi-conscious at some key point along the line we would have lost.

I recall playing the quarterfinals of the Vanderbilt in 1971 in Atlanta against a tough team led by George Rosenkranz, who has won many national championships. Our team was the Aces, and we were ahead by more than 20 IMPs going into the last quarter.

When Mike Lawrence and Bobby Goldman came out after the last set, they said it didn't look good – they had had a very bad match. The reports coming from the other room didn't make the picture any rosier. They were down to the last hand of the event. Rosenkranz, who was playing with Bobby Nail, held this collection:

♠10 6 5 4 ♥J 7 5 4 3 ♦K Q ♣6 5.

Nail opened 1♣, the next player overcalled 1♦ and Rosenkranz, an experienced player and normally a conservative bidder, bid 1♥ instead of making a negative double. It went 3♦ on Rosenkranz's left, pass, pass to him.

Now, if Rosenkranz had passed, his team would have gone on to the next round of the Vanderbilt. He could even have bid 3♠ and taken home the trophy. As it was, he bid 3♥ on that pile of garbage. Nail, with a close decision, bid 4♥ which was doubled. Rosenkranz went for 500 and we won by 4 IMPs. His team had been ahead by 5 IMPs going into the last board.

Our team was one pass away from being knocked out of the event. What made Rosenkranz do what he did? No one will ever know. Of course, I've been on the other side, too – where a different action here or there would have resulted in victory for my team instead of defeat. On this occasion, we were done for if Rosenkranz had made a seemingly routine pass, but we went on to win the championship, destroying the team we played in the final.

The point is that the difference between winning and losing is often as close as one little pass – or even closer. When many elements of the game – such as whether someone passes or bids – are beyond your control, it's folly to give the opponents an extra edge by failing to manage the things that you *can* control.

Consistent winners know how important it is to focus on the problem at hand. The fish that has just had a bear swipe at it in the stream and lost a little bit of flesh had better not be looking back at the bear and thinking, "If I'd only done this or that, I wouldn't have this scratch." You know something? There's another bear just around the curve of that stream, and that fish had better not be worrying about the last bear or it might not be just a scratch the next time.

I think Meckstroth and Rodwell may have lost the proper focus just for a moment in that 1990 Spingold match. After the opening shot that put us further in the hole, I think their vision was on ending the streak. You see, even though we ended up winning the match by 24 IMPs, it wasn't because of any heroics or brilliancies by Wolffie or me – or by our teammates. It was a series of errors by the opposing pairs at both tables that turned the tide. In fact, the 9 IMPs they got on the first board were the only IMPs they won in the entire set. Our total at the end was 65.

On the very next board after we failed to beat 4♠ doubled, Meckstroth pushed to a slam that went down. 13 IMPs to us. The board after that, Rodwell opened a 9-point hand and sat for it when Meckstroth doubled us in 4♠. Wolffie made two overtricks. 12 more IMPs to our side.

Another 12 IMPs came our way when Soloway and Goldman went for 800 at the other table. Two boards later, Rodwell made a passive lead against a vulnerable game and I scored it up. It went down at the other table. 12 more IMPs. Finally, Rodwell went down in a grand slam that he might have made. 14 IMPs. They lost another 4 IMPs on the very last hand to cap our comeback.

Meckstroth and Rodwell had a monkey on their back – the long losing streak to us – and I think it may have influenced their thinking just a little bit, maybe just by that one-tenth of a millimeter. That slam they bid right after 4♠ doubled may have been Meckstroth's attempt to put the match totally out of sight. In fact, it started us on our comeback.

All competitors, especially at this level, want to win, but you can't let that desire drive you crazy. You can't let it interfere with your ability to crunch the numbers. If you're ahead in a match that's tough and close, you can't get yourself in a mindset of wishing the damned contest would end. You've got to get above it. You've got to stay **at the table**.

When I first started playing, I never thought bridge would become such a big part of my life. But the psychological rewards keep me coming back. Now I'm programmed to answer the bell, and I'm going to keep showing up. I'm going to keep trying to win.

My experiences during my playing career have taught me some valuable lessons. I've had some great experiences and met some terrific people. If you enjoy sharing memories of that kind, perhaps you'll join me – at the table.

2
Emperor of the 2-cent game

ON A BRIGHT day in November, 1963, Don Krauss and I boarded an airplane headed for Miami, Florida. We were so excited we felt like we didn't even need the plane. We were going to play in *The Trials*.

In the fall of 1962, Don and I – playing with Eddie Kantar and Marshall Miles – had tied for first in the Reisinger Board-a-Match Teams at the Fall Nationals in Phoenix. That win qualified us to play in the pair trials to determine a U.S. team for the World Bridge Olympiad in New York in May of 1964.

Sixteen pairs would play a round-robin for three days, and the top three pairs would make up the team for the Olympiad.

Although Don and I had been practicing all summer and doing pretty well, we probably would have been picked to come in last if the field had been handicapped. After all, we were relative unknowns in those days and the field included some high-powered players: Sam Stayman, Vic Mitchell, Jim Jacoby, Al Roth, Lew Mathe, Tommy Sanders, Eddie Kantar, Marshall Miles and a host of other top players.

Don and I played klaberjass on the plane for a long time without saying much. Finally, Krauss looked up and spoke.

"You know," he said, "it's really going to be great getting all this experience playing against these guys."

I was appalled.

"Experience – bullshit!" I said. "We're going to win the thing!"

I snarled at him for half an hour over that remark.

I'm not sure when or how the competitive drive in me was kindled, but games – competition – have been a part of my life for as far back as I can remember. I liked card games. I tried poker when I was six or seven.

I was born in Pasadena, California, on August 6, 1938, into a middle-class family in a middle-class neighborhood. When I was still very young, we moved to Canoga Park. I still remember the address of the three-bedroom, two-story brown and white brick house where I grew up – 2119 Galbreath Road.

My father, John S. Hamman Jr., sold business forms for a living. He traveled in his business, but not a lot. He was usually around. My father was a big man. Today I look a lot like he did when I was growing up.

I was the eldest of four children. As a five-year-old, I used to badger my parents to let me in on the game when they played a form of gin rummy with their friends. I played lots of games. Rummy, poker, hearts, board games – you name it.

Although my father wasn't a serious games player, he did like to make a bet now and then. He played poker with his friends and a little bit of chess. One thing I remember in our games playing – my dad hated to lose to me.

At 9 or 10, I learned to play chess. At 13, I became serious about the game. I guess my interest grew out of the fun of competing. I loved to participate in things where you could win, where the reward was simply the pleasure of winning. Incidentally, that hasn't changed one iota.

I became fascinated with chess. I started studying various openings and reading about the game. Chess was the first organized game I ever played. My first chess tournament was around 1954, in a club over the garage behind the home of a fellow named Herman Steiner. He was the best chess player in Southern California and he often had tournaments at his home. It was quite a large garage and there was room for 40 or 50 players.

In the round-robin format one of my games was memorable. At least it was to me. I was matched against the eventual winner, an "old fellow" of 30 named James Cross. He was quite a good player, but he got into some extreme difficulty with time pressure, and he offered me a draw. He made the comment that he thought he had somewhat the better of things in the position but significantly the worst of it on the clock. I accepted the draw, but despite being a bit intimidated by Cross, I told him I didn't agree with his assessment of the position. "Let's play it out after the draw is recorded," Cross said. We did – several times. He won every time. It wasn't the first time, or the last, that I had to eat my words.

After that match, chess became almost an obsession with me. I spent hours and hours each week studying, going over positions, and playing whenever I could. I even read chess books in German. School was secondary. My father died of kidney disease the summer before my senior year in high school and my mother didn't think too highly of my obsession, but she was busy working to support the family. I just kept on and on.

When I wasn't playing chess, I did find time for girls and cars, but I also spent a lot of time on other games like hearts and poker, which I always played for money. My father let me play a little poker when I was a junior in high school, and I kept it up.

I barely staggered to the tape, so to speak, in graduating from high school. Fortunately for me, my lackluster senior year at Canoga Park High School didn't ruin my otherwise good academic record, and I earned a scholarship to Occidental College in Eagle Rock, a suburb of Los Angeles.

I was supposed to be studying engineering, but what I did mostly was play chess and pool. Luckily, the stakes at the latter were fairly small. I wasn't very good. The upshot of all the game playing was that I screwed up my scholarship at Occidental – it was to be cut in half if I returned there in the fall – and by the summer of 1957, I was back home in Canoga Park.

By then, my mother had remarried. My stepfather was a fellow by the name of Ned Randall. He was an insurance salesman for State Farm and an okay fellow, but we didn't see eye to eye on very many aspects of life. He was a religious sort who thought life should be taken ultra seriously. He frowned on my game-playing lifestyle. Ned and I got along, but just barely.

That summer, I had a job at Bendix Pacific, which did a lot of aerospace work. It was still the game plan for me to be an engineer, so I got on with Bendix as part of a program for people studying engineering. I worked in a section with a military contract to develop a part for the AQS-10 helicopter sonar device. Using this device, helicopters supposedly would be able to fly above the surface of the water and detect submarines below.

My experience at Bendix was disillusioning, to say the least. I had always thought that in such settings a lot of smart people would conceive of a design and make their calculations and determine exactly which components would go where and then plug them in and it would work. In reality, they pretty much sat around saying, "Well, let's try this and see if it works."

I used to work with these transistors that cost $35 each – a lot of money at that time – and occasionally I would melt one by over-heating it with a soldering iron. I'd think, "Oh, god, I'm going to be canned. I just blew $35 in three seconds." In truth, Bendix had a cost-plus contract with the government. The reality was probably that the more transistors I burned up the better.

Back then, I was still playing a lot of chess. Several of the Bendix employees were chess players, and we often played during the lunch hour. I quickly established myself as the best player there, but none of the others seemed to mind or resent me for it. My routine in those days was to drag myself out of bed at some ungodly hour like 8 a.m. and go to work, get off at 4:30 and head for Zuma Beach, which was about 40 miles away. We would surf a little bit, flirt with the girls and then go play chess. There were chess clubs all over the area, and some had tournaments that ran for weeks.

All that changed one summer night when I got a phone call from Lloyd Richardson.

Lloyd was a friend of mine from high school. He was an athletic guy – a member of the gymnastics team. Also, he was always up to something. He loved to gamble and drink. I had played some chess with him, and he was more or less a drinking buddy.

"Hamman," he said, "we're going to have a bridge game tonight at Dan Gottlieb's house and we need an extra player."

"Who's playing?" I asked.

"George Soules, Dan Gottlieb and me. You interested?"

"Well," I said, "I've seen you guys play hearts and every other game. Chances are I can beat you at bridge, too. Just give me the rules."

I got hold of a bridge book, studied enough to know the mechanics of the game and drove my '48 Chevy over to Gottlieb's house in North Hollywood that night. The stakes were 1/20th of a cent per point.

I waltzed into the den at Gottlieb's and made a complete fool of myself.

I tried to name trump on every hand and ended up the big loser. Things got so bad I thought every auction ended with "double." I lost $10 that night, and at 1/20th of a cent that's a significant beating. The game broke up about two in the morning. Gottlieb had run out of beer and I had run out of money.

That was the beginning.

Different people have different views of the game. When Krauss and I flew to Miami for the trials, Kantar and Miles were on the plane with us.

Both were big-name players even then – and they presented quite a contrast in character. Kantar is pretty much a no-nonsense type of player, although he has a tendency to tinker with a bidding system to the point of distraction. Miles is a different animal altogether.

Nobody loves the game like Marshall Miles. He's the last true believer. He's an excellent player, but he's a lot more into the aesthetics of the game than most people. Whereas some players would rather stick a figurative thumb in your eye, Marshall prefers the clever play, the brilliant bid, the breath-taking coup.

He could drive you nuts.

At one point during our trip to Miami, Krauss turned to Miles, who was seated nearby.

"Marshall," Don said, "suppose you came to the last round of the trials and you were in contention and the bidding went pass, pass, pass to you and some little voice said, 'If you pass this hand out, Marshall, you will win the world championship.' But suppose you had the perfect weak notrump opener. What would you do?"

Miles considered the question briefly. "I suppose," he said, "I'd open."

After I was drubbed in that penny-ante bridge game at Gottlieb's house, I was set on getting revenge, but I certainly wasn't up to it at my level of expertise. I had to get better.

The next day, I went to the library and got another book on bridge. It wasn't hard to find. Keep in mind that in 1957, bridge was in its heyday. Charles Goren was writing regularly for *Sports Illustrated* and was featured in *The Saturday Evening Post*. There had been an article about John Crawford in *Life*, entitled "Tiger at the Table." It was common for young people like me – I was 18 at the time – to play bridge, much more so than nowadays.

Although I was determined to improve at bridge, I was still into chess competition pretty heavily – and it was because of my chess playing that I decided that summer to switch colleges.

George Soules had been trying all that summer to convince me to transfer to UCLA and play on the "chess team." We weren't really representing UCLA as it turns out, but we called ourselves the UCLA team. We won the Open Flight Teams in the Southern California Chess League in the fall of that year.

When I arrived on the UCLA campus, however, I encountered Kirkhoff Hall, the student center. Almost immediately, there was a dramatic shift in my focus. My first day at UCLA was spent signing up for classes. On day two, however, I discovered the bridge games at Kirkhoff. Throughout the day, there were bridge games going in the men's lounge. People would cut in and out. Some of them even went to classes.

Not me.

I played all day. Most of the games were rubber bridge with stakes of 1/10 or 1/5 of a cent per point. I wasn't any great shakes then, but I had had a whole summer of studying bridge and playing when I could, so I was probably better than most of the Kirkhoff players.

Sometime that fall, I met Ralph Clark, a CalTech dropout who ended up at UCLA. We played together a few times before he introduced me to duplicate. After that, my routine was to go to Kirkhoff and play bridge during the day and go to the duplicate clubs at night. I was playing bridge practically around the clock.

Studying? Attending classes? I didn't do either, but I kept from flunking out by dropping out first. I got to the point where I could drop out of UCLA in 30 minutes, which is probably still a record. It took me five years to complete my sophomore year in college – and I eventually did it at Cal State-Northridge, which was called San Fernando Valley State at the time.

I just wasn't into studying. I was on kind of a negative learning curve. The first time I took Chemistry 1-A at UCLA, I was getting an A when I dropped out. The second time I dropped out, I was getting a B. By the time I finally finished the class, I got a C. What can I say?

My mother, who worked as a telephone operator for Pacific Bell, didn't know I was a dropout. I still headed for UCLA every day even when I was no longer enrolled. I *was* going to school, just not to classes.

In the fall of 1957, Ralph and I found out there was a big national tournament at the Ambassador Hotel in Los Angeles. We had signed up with the ACBL when we started playing duplicate, so we were ready.

Ralph was a weird duck. He was a skinny, red-haired guy with glasses. The two of us must have looked odd, charging into the Ambassador that first night to play in the side game. We found that the side game players back then were a lot worse than we were. Actually, we were pretty good in the sense that we had been playing practically night and day, studying double dummy problems and really working to improve. We did very well that first night, winning the side game handily.

I was highly impressed with the tournament. The crowds were huge, there were tables everywhere. It was tremendous fun. The directors scored up the game and we ended up on top. We didn't care if anyone at the tournament knew that we won. We were going back to gloat to our friends that we had gone to the Nationals and cleaned up.

Clark and I played quite a bit after that. We took up the Kaplan-Sheinwold bidding system with weak notrumps and everything. We were going to every sectional within driving distance. Two years later, we even won a national event – sort of – at the Nationals in Coronado, California. It was the Commercial and Industrial Pairs, open only to pairs who worked for the same company (Ralph and I worked for Douglas Aircraft at the time).

I may have been the reason Clark dropped out of bridge. I played with him in the National Men's Pairs in Dallas in 1964. He had come all the way from California, and we were leading going into the final session and I played like a complete bozo and we fell out of contention. I had won several events with various people before that, and I think the experience was just too much for Ralph.

Anyway, the upshot of my introduction to tournament bridge was to make my craving for the game more intense. I discovered that, unlike chess tournaments, which can drag on for weeks, bridge tournaments are over in a relatively short span of time.

Beyond that, I could see that the scope of bridge was so broad that it seemed immeasurable. It still does. You could play bridge for a lifetime and never master it. But what a challenge to try!

I was already attuned to the thrill of winning. After our experience at the Ambassador, I wanted to win more. I wanted to win all the time. Ralph and I won a significant percentage of the club games, but we didn't do particularly well in the sectionals. In Los Angeles, there's a sectional within driving distance virtually every weekend. We played in them often, and it seemed that the big guys would come out and beat us fairly regularly. That just made us work harder.

Sometimes Ralph and I would start on the double-dummy problems at 7 at night and work on them until 8 the next morning.

It was sometime early in 1958 when I made a discovery that – two years later – had a tremendous influence on my development as a bridge player. I'm talking about the L.A. Bridge Club.

The club was owned by Albert Okuneff and Betty Allen. Okuneff was a pretty fair bridge player. The son of Russian immigrants, Okuneff had been involved in lots of different businesses, including an auto dealership and a finance company. He did the best when he went into business with Betty Allen.

The club itself – a green, one-story wood building – was in the heart of the Jewish section of Los Angeles, just west of Hollywood on Fairfax Avenue near Santa Monica Boulevard. It had originally been someone's home. Okuneff had bought the club from a woman whose husband came into a lot of money, allowing them to retire. The building was a little run-down, but it wasn't a dump like some of the clubs in L.A.

I started going to the L.A. Bridge Club after I heard about it from some of the players I met at tournaments. One of the first people I met was a Swedish guy named Olavi Vare. He was only in his thirties at the time, but he seemed older than sand to me then.

Anyway, Vare was at best an average minus player, but he and his girlfriend, Bertie, loved to play set games for money – and he played them at the L.A. Bridge Club. It was absolutely my idea of Utopia, playing bridge while enjoying a payday.

At the L.A. Bridge Club, players paid a table fee to get into the action. The club was licensed to run card games – gin, pinochle and bridge. The average Joe could play in games for 1/10 of a cent a point, up to 2 cents a point, which was very high stakes for me at the time. There was a 5-cent game, too, but you had to have a special invitation to get in. I had played rubber bridge for money before, but never for stakes like that. Occasionally set games were available, but cut-around games were the norm.

Strictly speaking, I was too young to play at the L.A. Bridge Club. I was only 20 and you were supposed to be 21, but Okuneff and Allen didn't worry about it. They didn't have fights or drunks at their club, so the police pretty well left them alone.

Along about 1960, I became a regular at the club, and I pretty much stopped going to the local duplicate clubs. By then I had moved away from home. I shared an apartment in Mar Vista in the west end of Los Angeles with Ralph and a fellow named Eliot Bean, who had gone with us to the Ambassador for the Nationals. When I wasn't playing at Okuneff's club, I was organizing home games – usually at other people's places. Bridge was what I did – all day, every day.

The best part of my early education as a bridge player started after I became a regular at the L.A. Bridge Club. Playing there was important because it exposed me to some of the best players on the continent. Most of the top players in the Los Angeles area – Morris Portugal, Eddie Kantar, Marshall Miles, Mel Breslauer and Dick Ryder, to name a few – were regulars. Paul Soloway got his start there, too. Another regular was Life Master No. 1, David Bruce, who frequented the 1-cent game. I didn't think he played all that well, but he was no patsy.

I was lucky that I could cut my teeth, so to speak, against some of the best. It was an opportunity that is no longer available to aspiring players. Today, only the largest cities have money bridge clubs. For most players, unfriendly rubber bridge games for high stakes are simply unavailable. Believe me, there's no better way to improve your game. If you want to learn how to play bridge, become wealthy enough to afford the losses and play with better players for stakes that can make losing an unpleasant experience. The other schools of bridge are not nearly as good.

I started out playing in weak ½-cent games at the L.A. Bridge Club and eventually moved up to the 1-cent game. However, there were bigger fish to fry. There were two levels of games with higher stakes – the 2-cent game and the 5-cent game.

The nickel game was pretty much closed to all but a few. Okuneff and an old fellow known as "The Commander" decided who played in that game. The Commander was a retired U.S. Navy officer. If you took a seat in the 5-cent game, it was with his consent. The 5-centers certainly didn't want any young punks like me in the game. Of course, there was also the fact that a nickel a point was an astronomical stake to me in those days. I probably would have played if I had been asked, but maybe it was just as well that I wasn't.

Although I didn't play in the nickel game, I heard lots of war stories about what went on in the game.

One time, a pretty good player named Henry Rose was invited to play. Rose was a professional piano player and an entertaining rascal. Perhaps that was why he got asked to play with The Commander and his group. More likely, they thought he was a pigeon. The only problem for The Commander was that Rose could play.

Well, Rose beat The Commander 31 straight days. The tail wagged the dog, so to speak. Rose took his winnings to San Francisco one weekend and blew the whole bundle. Back in L.A., he finally lost to The Commander – and didn't have the money to pay off. That was the end of his career in the nickel game.

I didn't feel that I missed anything by not playing in the 5-cent game. There were plenty of characters and the competition was quite good in the "lower ranks." Another regular was Jesse Sloan, who won the Vanderbilt in 1952. He had been partners with Roth in the famous Mayfair Club in New York but had sold out and moved West.

Then there was Eddie Burns, a fellow from the Twin Cities in Minnesota. Burns was a guy with a sour disposition who tended to blame luck for his losses. He was constantly whining about bad cards. One day, while someone was dealing the first hand of the afternoon, he looked at his first card and began complaining in his usual whine "I never get any cards" after only one card had been dealt to him. "My god, Eddie," someone said, "*nobody's* got any cards yet."

There were other top-notch card players: Stella Rebner, Duke Dautell, Milton Moss, Warren Blank, Bill McWilliams, and Bill Jones. These were names most players wouldn't recognize today, but they were the cream of the crop back then. It was a magnificent school for me.

David Burnstine, *a.k.a.* David Bruce, played at the club, as did a member of the Austrian team which won the world championship in 1937 – Dr. Edward Frischauer. He was reputed to be one of the greatest dummy players of all time. He had to be because his bidding was so bad.

When Alfred Sheinwold moved to Los Angeles in the 1950s, he wanted to meet Frischauer, about whom he had heard so much. One day Sheinwold came into the L.A. Bridge Club and sat down to kibitz a little. He noticed one of the players right away. The guy bid like a maniac but played like a genius. At the end of one particularly wild hand, Sheinwold tapped the man on the shoulder and said, "You must be Doctor Frischauer."

It was quite a cast of characters.

After I had been playing at the L.A. Bridge Club for awhile, I felt it was time to move up. Since the 5-cent game was closed to me, I set my sights on the 2-cent game.

Morris Portugal was the resident hustler – and a very good bridge player who "owned" the 2-cent game. He was a short guy with dark, curly hair. He didn't exactly welcome me with open arms – the 2-cent game was his private game preserve.

It was an economic move for me, however. In the penny game, the average take was about $15 a session. You could win or lose $100, but only rarely. I wanted to be able to eat at the steak house more than once a week. Even though Pink's Hot Dog Stand was as good as they came, I was beginning to tire of a steady diet of chili dogs.

When I made my move, there was Portugal minding the store. At the L.A. Bridge Club, as the stakes got higher the players got better, but not a lot better. I knew I would be a winner.

One day in the 2-cent game, I had cut into the table where Portugal was playing. We played four hands as partners. It was a disaster. We bid to 6NT that had no play on the first hand, and the others were equally ugly. At my next turn to sit out I started wondering whether I should retreat to the sure profits of the penny game. I thought to myself, "Wow, if I can't even get decent results with Portugal, this doesn't seem to be the percentage game for me."

Finally, though, I said to myself, "Screw it. I'm not backing down." Besides, I'd seen the players in action. I went back in. Pretty soon, it was Portugal's turn to sit out. Apparently, he was doing some thinking, too. I'm sure he was wondering whether he wanted to deal with this clown (me). We had just had a disastrous set playing together and it wasn't particularly pleasing to play against me.

When it was Portugal's turn to cut back in, he declined. In fact, he left the L.A. Bridge Club.

Before that day in 1961, Portugal had practically lived at the L.A. Bridge Club. After that, he would drop by once in a while, but he played infrequently.

You see, Portugal's motivation for playing had not been money. He came because he enjoyed it. He liked being the emperor, so to speak, of the 2-cent game. With me in the game, his previously unchallenged status as "King of the Hill" was being questioned. The respect he had commanded was now somewhat diminished. The enjoyment vanished. I'm not sure whether the episode with me was the final straw for Portugal, but in my eyes it was a dramatic afternoon. The young bull had driven off the old-timer.

The significance of this event was not lost on me. At the age of 22, I was the new emperor of the 2-cent game in the biggest money bridge club in Los Angeles.

3

A thumb in the eye

SOMETIME IN the late 1970s, I was playing with Marvin Rosenblatt of Hartford, Connecticut, against Ron Andersen and Kathie Wei in the Knockout Teams at the Miami regional.

Andersen and Wei were a regular partnership for several years, and at their best they could be quite effective. Besides winning a lot, Andersen and Wei wrote three or four books on the Precision bidding system invented by Kathie's late husband, C.C. Wei. It was through C.C. that Ron and Kathie got together. For a time, C.C. paid Ron to play with Kathie and teach her the game. It worked out well for all concerned.

Kathie's bridge accomplishments, especially considering that she did not take up the game until she was in her thirties, have been phenomenal. She has won several world championships and many national and regional titles. What she has accomplished has been through hard work and determination. It doesn't pay to underestimate this woman. Before their partnership broke up in the early 1990s, Kathie and Judi Radin were among the top women's pairs in the world.

As a partnership, Kathie and Ron were somewhat of a contrast. While Kathie has a dark, Oriental beauty, Ron's appearance is almost boyish at times. He has a fair complexion, somewhat of a baby face, and his hair falls over his forehead in bangs in a hairstyle reminiscent of the Beatles.

At the bridge table, Ron is a fierce, sometimes hot-tempered competitor. He has a great, booming voice and a penchant for histrionics. Ron is an excellent card player, but he's not above gamesmanship if he feels the situation calls for it.

In our knockout match, Ron was in fine form. Each time we finished a board, he would go through an elaborate ritual calculated to annoy me and Marvin.

Ron had two pens in his shirt pocket. There was a blue one for plus scores and a red one for minus scores. In dramatic fashion, he would reach into his pocket, slowly pull out a pen, remove the cap, write down the score and – still going through each overdone step – return it to his pocket.

This got old rather quickly, plus it was slowing down the game. Finally, after he had gone through the procedure just one time too many, I leaned over, reached into his pocket and pulled out the blue pen. "You're not going to be needing this one again," I said as I hurled the pen into a corner of the hotel room we were playing in. Without his lucky pen, Andersen suffered a couple more minuses. The strain was too great – he got up from the table to root around in the corner of the room for the missing pen.

Ron could have called the director and sought a conduct penalty against me. But it would have been like admitting that he couldn't take the needle. He had been dishing it out, and to call the director would have been psychological surrender. It would have signaled that he couldn't take it. He would have won the battle but lost the war.

The point is that in the main event of any competitive endeavor, you had best be prepared to play hard ball – literally in some arenas, figuratively in others. You wouldn't be surprised to get a thumb in the eye on the first play from scrimmage in the Super Bowl – or an elbow to the jaw in the NBA final. Well, bridge is no different.

Nobody's going to punch you or kick you, but the other guy is there to beat you – period. It's fierce competition, not a social situation. The politeness police are not part of the scene. In many settings, such as a local duplicate club, I don't beat up on my opponents because most of them are pleasure players and they are not really challenging me. When I'm in a major event like the Spingold, however, I don't ask for quarter and I don't give it.

At the 1993 Spring NABC in Kansas City, Wolffie and I were playing an underdog team in the Vanderbilt about the third round. One of our opponents – they were two young men – was doubled in 5♦. He overpulled trumps and went down in a cold contract. On the next board they had another accident.

The partner of the declarer on the previous deal opened a 15-17 notrump. The response was 2♦, forcing Stayman. Opener bid 2♠. Responder now bid 4♥, Alerted by opener as a splinter in support of spades. The only problem was that responder had six hearts. He was so rattled that he forgot that 4♥ was a splinter – showing spade support and a singleton or void in hearts – in their system.

Opener bid 4♠. Responder now bid 5♥ and opener passed, a dubious action from the standpoint of what was ethically correct. Had we been using screens – where the responder would not have been privy to the Alert of 4♥ – the 5♥ bid would probably have indicated a void in hearts with slam interest. In other words, opener should have bid more spades. As it was, the guy passed. Wolffie and I could have taken this to an appeals committee and won, I'm pretty sure, but that's not our style.

But when the shaky player's partner suggested they take a brief break so the guy could compose himself, I said, "We're running behind. We've got to keep playing." This certainly doesn't fit in with the scheme of total gentlemanly conduct, and maybe it constituted intimidation. To my way of thinking, that's part of the game. We didn't rough them up over the 5♥ bid, but I wasn't cutting them any slack when it came to a time-out.

The Spingold isn't a tea party. We play hardball there.

I was still learning how to get along in the big leagues – learning the true meaning of hardball at the bridge table – when I had my first confrontation with Lew Mathe.

It was 1960, about three years after I had taken up the game. We were back at the Ambassador Hotel, where Ralph Clark and I had played in our first Nationals. We had long since graduated from side games. Ralph and I had won the Commercial and Industrial Pairs at the Fall Nationals in Coronado in 1959 and early in 1960 we had won a regional pair game.

Along came Los Angeles Bridge Week. It was then and still is one of the biggest annual regionals on the ACBL tournament calendar.

Ralph and I entered the Knockout Teams with Art Fletcher and Richard Cheng – *Dr.* Richard Cheng. What a curious path this studious fellow chose for his life. He had a doctorate in physics and today is a vice president for Hughes Aerospace in Los Angeles. But along the way, he stopped to open a Chinese restaurant. By the way, he had tremendous potential as a bridge player and could have gone a long way if he had chosen to direct his energy that way.

Ironically, Fletcher also ended up marching to the beat of a different drummer. He had a degree in aeronautical engineering, but he eventually went into the pizza business and got rich.

Anyway, in the knockout event our team played well, and although we were relatively inexperienced, we made it to the final. That was where we ran into the big guns – Lew Mathe, Paul Allinger, Meyer Schleifer and Don Oakie.

Schleifer, who died just this year, was an acknowledged master of the game. He played money bridge at the Regency Bridge Club, another of the successful clubs in Los Angeles. Schleifer and Mathe were practically the gods of bridge in Los Angeles back then.

Meyer was an unassuming man who never intimidated opponents – he'd just pick them clean. He'd be killing you and stealing you blind, but you hardly knew he was at the table. When you played against Meyer, you would walk away from the table with empty pockets and say, "Who was that who just creamed me?" Meyer didn't play much prior to his death, but he may have been the greatest card player who ever lived. He played a few sessions at the Spring Nationals in Pasadena in 1992.

Oakie won the Bermuda Bowl in 1954 on a team with Mathe, Billy Rosen, Milton Q. Ellenby and Cliff Bishop. He later became president of the ACBL.

Allinger was an accountant who could have been a real star as a bridge player if he had avoided the gin and tonics. In a way, he was an oddity. When I first saw him he was incredibly skinny, perhaps 120 pounds. Later on he ballooned up to 300. He ended up killing himself in a car crash. At this point, however, he was good enough to join the heralded Lew Mathe on a knockout team.

Mathe, a short, stocky man with a crewcut, was like a caricature of a bulldog. He had a drill sergeant's disposition and was the kind of player who could dominate a game by the force of his personality. He was intimidating, fierce and – and I was to learn later – very hard on partners.

Mathe and his team didn't know much about us, but we knew who they were.

Ralph and I played against Mathe and Allinger. Despite the reputations of our opponents, we were conceding nothing. We figured to be underdogs, but we also believed we could win. Why else would we enter the event?

We played in a large meeting room at the Ambassador. A huge gallery of kibitzers was on hand, adding to the pressure on us. Still, we were eager to play.

Early in the match, I was declarer in 5♣. I took an inferior – not to say hopeless – line of play and went down in a contract I'm certain I should have made. When the hand was over, Mathe turned to me and asked, "Could you have made it?"

The battle lines had been drawn. I could almost feel the smoke curling out of my ears. Mathe's reputation preceded him – he was definitely one of the big guys. But I was never exactly shy and retiring, even in my formative years. I would like to have said something smart back to him, but no fitting rejoinder leapt to mind right away. I just went on to the next board, biding my time. Then came this:

```
Dlr: West      ♠ Q 6 5 4
Vul: Both      ♥ J 8 7 6
               ♦ K 8 4
               ♣ K 3
♠ J 10 9                        ♠ 7 2
♥ A K Q 4                       ♥ 10 9 3
♦ 5 2                           ♦ A Q 10 7 3
♣ 9 8 7 6                       ♣ 10 5 4
               ♠ A K 8 3
               ♥ 5 2
               ♦ J 9 6
               ♣ A Q J 2
```

WEST	NORTH	EAST	SOUTH
Mathe	*Clark*	*Allinger*	*Me*
Pass	Pass	Pass	1NT
Pass	2♣	Pass	2♠
Pass	4♠	All Pass	

Mathe cashed two top hearts, getting the signal from Allinger that he had three hearts. Mathe then switched to the ♠J. From the way he played the hearts, I was pretty sure Mathe had the AKQ. Mathe was a passed hand, so he couldn't have the ♦A. Leading up to the king, therefore, would have been giving up. I needed a different plan.

Here's what I did. I won with the ♠Q in dummy, ruffed a heart and played a top spade from my hand. Then I played four rounds of clubs. Luckily, Mathe had to follow, so I pitched two diamonds from the dummy, reaching this position:

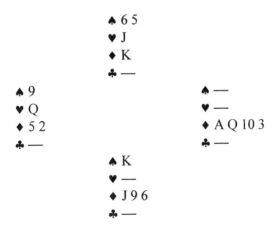

```
            ♠ 6 5
            ♥ J
            ♦ K
            ♣ —
♠ 9                        ♠ —
♥ Q                        ♥ —
♦ 5 2                      ♦ A Q 10 3
♣ —                        ♣ —
            ♠ K
            ♥ —
            ♦ J 9 6
            ♣ —
```

I played a diamond to the king and Allinger's ace. Allinger was stuck. If he played the ♦Q, I could ruff in dummy, play a spade to my hand – pulling Mathe's trump – and claim with the good ♦J. If he played a low diamond, I could put up the jack, pitching the heart from dummy. Then I could play the ♠K. Dummy's ♠6 would be my tenth trick.

Obviously, if Mathe had switched to a diamond at trick three, I would have gone down. As Allinger suffered in silence, I looked at Mathe and asked, "Could you have beaten it?"

Mathe didn't react. What could he say? I had picked my spot. He wasn't in a good position to say anything with a full gallery there watching. If he mouthed off, he would look like a fool.

Yes, the battle lines were drawn. I had made my point. I may have been a young pup in the eyes of these players, but I wasn't backing down.

The match remained close after that and we ended up losing. But I didn't attach too much significance to the loss or to the fact that our relatively inexperienced team had done pretty well considering the caliber of the opposition. What I thought about it was that it was a lot of fun to get in there and mix it up with the big boys.

I was determined to continue playing and trying to earn pocket money playing the game – and getting better. I didn't really think about bridge in the long term. I lived life by waking up in the morning – then worrying about what to do that day. The only planning ahead we did was trips to the Nationals.

It was at the Spring Nationals in Denver in 1961 that I encountered another bridge figure who made a big impression on me. I'm talking about Eric Murray.

Ralph Clark and I had teamed with Cheng, Jim Pestaner and Don Krauss to play in the Vanderbilt, which was a double-elimination event back then. We lost our first match by 80 IMPs. Then we played a team which included Charles Goren and Helen Sobel. We got clobbered again and were out.

After that, we played a few pair games. The other members of the team left for home, but I stayed around to kibitz the Vanderbilt.

The first time I saw Murray, a lawyer from Toronto, he was playing with Charles Coon, a very fine player from New England. From the moment I arrived at tableside, I was impressed with Murray. His square jaw, huge hands, very serious demeanor and of course the gigantic cigar combined with excellent card play and aggressive bidding enabled him to completely dominate all but the toughest and most experienced opponents. He would puff on his huge cigar and absolutely dominate the table with a no-nonsense, all-business atti-tude.

Murray was a force. You could feel it. He wasn't a giant of a man, but at times his opponents must have thought he was eight feet tall. He was not abusive to the opponents in any conventional sense, but he did convey the impression that he was scornful of anyone who would dare to get in his way. You got the idea he was thinking, "What are you doing cluttering up my event? Why are you taking up my time, imposing on me to thrash you and send you home to mother? I mean, go read a book."

I didn't see how he could lose.

Murray did lose in the Vanderbilt that spring, but the impression I had of him never left me. A few players since then have impressed me similarly, but not many.

One day in the summer of 1962, I got a phone call from Eddie Kantar. He and I weren't bosom buddies, but we had gotten to know each other pretty well through tournaments and at the L.A. Bridge Club. We had even teamed up to win a Board-a-Match event at Bridge Week, and he appeared to have some slight respect for my game.

"Here's the deal," Kantar said. "We're going to play a team match at the Regency Bridge Club for money."

The plan was for me to play with Don Krauss. Our teammates would be Harold Guiver and Ron Von der Porten. The opposition would be Kantar and Marshall Miles, Joe Bechely and Steve Geller.

I had never played a hand with Krauss, but I knew him as a capable player, so I agreed. Our proposed teammates were certainly strong. Guiver, known as "Squeezer" for reasons that may or may not be related to bridge, was one of the West Coast's most successful players. A short fellow and a dapper dresser, Squeezer owned a mortgage company and had done very well for himself. Von der Porten, with whom I would later win the Blue Ribbon Pairs, was a very successful bridge pro and a terrific player.

Well, we got to the club that afternoon and I found that the stakes had escalated dramatically. Suddenly we were playing for $5 per IMP per team. Luckily, Guiver had lots of money so he was willing to take most of the risk. Don and I were playing for something like 50 cents an IMP.

Krauss and I discussed our system for 20 minutes and sat down to play. That may have been the luckiest session I ever had – and a long session it was. We played from noon to midnight with barely a break.

The first hand Krauss and I played together set the tone for the entire day. We were playing against Kantar and Miles. Don and I fumbled the bidding terribly and ended up in 4♥. On this deal, even 7♥ is cold if trumps split no worse than 4-1. As it happened, however, trumps were 5-0 and slam was impossible. Naturally, 6♥ was bid at the other table.

It was like that all day and all night. Any bad game or slam we bid was a maker. Any good slam we stayed out of went down. At one point, Kantar was close to despair. "My god," he said after one particularly grueling series, "they're not even falsecarding us any more."

Kantar got to 4♥ on one hand and I underled an ace on the go. Dummy had the K-J in the suit and Kantar went into a trance. "What the hell," he said finally, "play the king. What's one more wrong guess?" Well, he got that one right but our team ended up winning by 128 IMPs on the old scale – that would be like 200 IMPs today.

Before we left, Krauss and I asked Kantar and Miles, "Are you available tomorrow?" We were cocky.

Although that all-day match wasn't earth-shaking, it did pay a dividend, in a way, for me later on.

Not long after that match, I made the decision to go to the Fall Nationals in Phoenix. I figured my car would make it that far. I was going to play with Bill McWilliams, a computer engineer from North Hollywood and a very capable player. He was also quite an entertaining guy. I had met him at the L.A. Bridge Club and we had played together some. He had won several regionals and could have really gone places in bridge. Like some others, however, he was done in by booze.

Anyway, I gave Kantar a call. "Tell you what," I said, "I'll get Bill McWilliams and you and Marshall can play with us in the Men's Board-a-Match Teams and I'll get Krauss and play with you two in the Reisinger."

Kantar just about choked. He and Miles were big names even then. They had won the Spingold the previous summer and they could be choosy about their teammates. On the other hand, my team had just whipped them by 128 IMPs. It just about killed him, but Kantar decided to accept the invitation.

McWilliams and I played reasonably well in the Men's Board-a-Match Teams, but we didn't come particularly close to the brass ring.

In the main event – the Reisinger – we had a tremendous run on the last day of the event and finished in a tie for first. The other team was well known to us – Paul Allinger (Mathe's partner in our confrontation), Mathe, Harold Guiver, Ron Von der Porten, Erik Paulsen and Edward O. Taylor. How sweet it was!

Almost overlooked in the excitement of the moment was the fact that we qualified to take part in the pair trials in Miami the following year. The pair trials! That meant we had a chance to play for a world championship – every player's dream. The top three pairs in the trials would be the team that would represent the United States in the World Bridge Olympiad in New York in 1964. There would be no fooling around. Krauss and I had to practice and get better.

We started playing set games. We played a lot against our teammates – Kantar and Miles. We'd play at someone's home, and I remember using playing cards with cartoon characters on them – Woody Woodpecker and Chilly Willy, the little penguin from the cartoons created by Walter Lantz. They were a giveaway from a movie studio. Don and I both remember that we seemed to bid a lot of slams with the Chilly Willys.

One night when we were playing against Kantar and Miles at Krauss's apartment, things were going badly for them. As was his wont, Marshall was trying to hit a hole in one, so to speak, on every deal. Marshall is the kind of player who likes to create plays for posterity – brilliancies that are written up and admired by future generations.

Well, Don and I were outholding Kantar and Miles – outplaying them, too. At one point Kantar put his cards down on the table and said, "Marshall, would you do me a favor?"

Miles, the most obliging person in the world, responded: "Of course, Eddie, what would you like me to do?"

"Before you make another bid or play," Kantar said, "ask yourself this: 'If I read about somebody else making the bid or play that I'm about to make, would I consider it a brilliant bid or play?' If the answer is yes – *do something else.*"

Don and I played some practice sessions against a character named Sidney Borden, a fellow I'd met at the local duplicate club. Sid was in the insurance business, and he later helped me get into that field – a good move for me since I was married by then and needed a steadier income than I could get playing bridge.

Sid also taught me a little humility, although I can't say I've practiced it much through the years.

The first time I encountered Borden was at the duplicate club early in my playing career. Borden was playing with a guy named Hugh Meloche, a white-haired fellow who was a supervisor at the Schlitz brewery in Los Angeles. He sometimes played as if he had consumed too much of the product. I was declarer in 4♥ and Sid made the opening lead. I was cold for the contract if I played on dummy-reversal lines, but I chose another line of play and should have gone down. Luckily for me, Meloche didn't spot the error that paved the way to beat me, so I made it.

Sid started in on Meloche. "I know you took up the game today," Borden said, "but what time today?" After heaping more abuse on the hapless Hugh, Borden turned to me and snarled. "Don't feel so damned smug," he said. "You chopped it up." I was new, so I just mumbled something like "Yes, sir" and went on.

When Krauss and I needed to practice for the trials, we wanted to go against tough competition, so Sid was one of the players we chose. We played half a dozen games against Borden and Art Fletcher and we probably lost five of them.

Since we had been playing these practice games for money, we needed some pigeons to keep us in spending money. One such arrangement was a set game against a despicable character named Ivan Erdos. He was a Hungarian who had lived in London for a time before coming to the United States. In Los Angeles, he worked as a travel agent and played bridge for money.

Erdos was quite wild and had a dark, gypsy-like quality to him, but he was an expert player. Our set games usually involved Erdos and another former National Champion, a guy named Ollie Adams. We usually played for four or five cents per point. Krauss and I would split the risk, while Erdos was in for one cent, Ollie for the balance. One day we really chopped them up and when it was over we asked if they wanted to play the following week.

Ivan snarled, "We'll never play you guys again for this little."

"You mean," I said, "you'll make Ollie play for nine cents a point so you can play for a penny." We didn't get many more games against the Hungarian, who billed himself as "The Bad Boy of Bridge."

Experiences like these reinforced my growing notion that bridge competition at high levels is not for the faint of heart.

I didn't think it would be any different at the pair trials in Miami – the next challenge. I was ready.

4

Trials and tribulations

I HAD KNOWN Jack Hancock a long time before I heard about *the hand*. To this day, I consider it one of the greatest bridge hands ever played – possibly *the* greatest.

The hand was played by Hancock, who was kind of legendary in Los Angeles bridge circles. In fact, Krauss and I often referred to Hancock as "The Legend" – even though we knew nothing of *the hand*.

Jack was a diminutive, bookish-looking fellow who looked like a teenager until he was 60. A mathematician and a true genius, Jack was building computers in his garage in the 1940s. Surprisingly, his real ambition was to be a farmer.

Hancock was originally from San Francisco, but he lived in Woodland Hills in the L.A. area in the 1950s – when he played *the hand*. He had gone to Los Angeles after graduating from the University of Chicago and was working in the aerospace industry. I nearly collaborated with him on a book once – a book on his ideas about bridge. It would have been great.

Jack played *the hand* with a fellow named Norbert Kaufman in the Knockout Teams at the Los Angeles Bridge Week Regional in 1955 or 1956. At the time, knockout matches were scored by total points rather than IMPs.

The story of this deal was spread by one of Hancock's teammates in the knockout event, the inimitable Sidney Lazard of New Orleans. In fact, it was Sidney who told me about it about 15 years later.

Sidney is one of the most colorful characters in the bridge world – and a terrific player. Sidney is an imaginative, aggressive bidder and a fierce competitor. He also marches to a different drummer at times.

At the world championships in Rio de Janeiro, Brazil, in 1969, Sidney was playing with George Rapée – another of bridge's true characters. Sidney wasn't doing too well and he swore it was the orange juice that was making him crazy.

While the team was in Brazil, Sidney somehow got himself into a poker game where the players were calling out their bets in Portuguese. There were lots of weird local options he didn't quite understand, but Sidney was going with the flow.

Then Sidney found himself holding the KQJ10 of hearts and some other card in a draw poker game. He threw away the little card and suddenly his whole life flashed before his eyes. What if he filled the royal flush? Here he was playing in a no-limit poker game in a foreign country. If he drew the ace or nine of hearts, he imagined someone going up to his teammates the next day to say, "So sorry, your friend has been eaten by a jaguar." Sidney breathed a sigh of relief when he drew the spade seven.

Sidney said that when he heard how Hancock had played this hand, he nearly gave up bridge. Sidney was about 25 at the time and was just starting his long and distinguished bridge career. "I thought," Sidney said, "that if there were people making plays like this, what was I doing playing this game?"

Here's what happened.

```
Dlr: East        ♠ 6
Vul: Both        ♥ J 5 4
                 ♦ A 6 5 2
                 ♣ A 8 7 6 5
  ♠ 9 8 2                      ♠ A K J 10 7 5
  ♥ A 10 3                     ♥ 9 7 2
  ♦ K J 10 4 3                 ♦ 8 7
  ♣ 10 3                       ♣ 9 4
                 ♠ Q 4 3
                 ♥ K Q 8 6
                 ♦ Q 9
                 ♣ K Q J 2
```

WEST	NORTH	EAST	SOUTH
	Kaufman		*Hancock*
		Pass	1NT
Pass	3NT	Pass (1)	Pass
Pass			

(1) Very slow.

The hesitation by East was revealing – to the entire table. This was in the days before weak two-bids and it was obvious that East had a long suit. After East passed, Hancock turned to West and said, "Make your normal lead."

Well, out came the ♠9. Did West take advantage of the information gained from his partner's hesitation? Who knows? Players have been known to do that. In truth, the ethics of the top players today are probably the best they've ever been, but in my time I've seen some pretty ripe stuff, particularly in some of the world championships I've played in.

Anyway, not only did West find Hancock's weak spot, but East – a good player – put in the ♠10 to maintain communication. How could Hancock come up with nine tricks after that? He had only seven tricks – barring the highly unlikely event that someone had the singleton ♦K – and as soon as he played on hearts, West would grab the ace and fire back another spade. So what did Hancock do?

He played a low spade!

What a stunning, totally remarkable play! It was simply light years ahead of its time in terms of comprehension of what's involved in playing bridge. Hancock had to have been thinking in a manner different from other people.

Of course, against a bad player such a play would never work. The bad player would simply cash the ace and king of spades, felling the queen, and then take his other three spade tricks.

In this setting, however, East could not picture Hancock with anything but four spades to the queen. Hancock had worked out that East didn't have the ♥A – he would have opened the bidding with six spades to the AKJ10 and the ♥A.

Anyway, the sand had been thrown in East's eyes. It looked to East as though playing the top two spades would be setting up a spade trick Hancock could never get once he chose to duck.

East switched to a low heart. West got in with the ace and played another spade. East won with the king, but again he switched, grimly refusing to concede that spade trick to declarer.

Hancock now had nine tricks, which he took with gusto.

I wish I had been there to see it.

Don Krauss has been a friend of mine for years. When he and his wife Renee had a son, they named him Robert David Krauss in my honor.

When I first met Don, he was fresh out of Stanford University with a degree in statistics. He was working for Systems Development Corporation in Los Angeles. There were lots of bridge players at that company. Don, a nice-looking, Ivy League sort of fellow, was a very talented bridge player, but I always thought he should have been more of a tiger. In fact, his demeanor at the table drove me nuts sometimes. Still, he was a fine player and we had our days in the sun together.

We also had some bizarre moments at the bridge table.

During a set game in Los Angeles one time against Harold Guiver and Gerald Bare, Don and I were having a very bad run of cards. Finally I picked up a strong 1NT opener.

"Hark," I said sarcastically, "the cannon roars. One notrump."

Krauss, in his benumbed state, thought he heard me say "one heart."

"Two clubs," said Don. It was a natural bid over 1 ♥, but it was Stayman over my 1NT bid.

"Two spades," I said. What did I know?

"Three hearts," said Krauss.

The mystery auction continued as I bid 3NT. I had no idea what Don was doing, but 3 ♥ sounded forcing.

"Four hearts," insisted Krauss.

When we finally realized what had happened, Don was playing a 3-3 fit that might have made game on a good day. Unfortunately, trumps were 6-1 and we went down three vulnerable tricks on a hand where we were cold for 11 tricks in notrump.

In the Spingold in 1963 at the Summer Nationals in Los Angeles, Don and I played with Joe Bechely and Bill McWilliams against Bobby Wolff, Oswald Jacoby, Ira Rubin and Curtis Smith – a very strong team. We had already lost to Charles Goren's team, but it was a double-elimination event back then. Our second chance came against Ozzie and company.

In the first quarter, I suffered one of the worst beatings of my career – playing *with my opponents!* We had all sat in the wrong direction, so Don's and my comparisons were with Rubin and Smith.

On the old IMP scale – where the maximum swing on any board was 15 IMPs, compared to 24 today – Wolff and Jacoby and our teammates, Bechely and McWilliams, had beaten us and our opponents Rubin and Smith by 82 IMPs. Ozzie, a legend in bridge, was near apoplexy. "It was the best game I ever had," he growled.

There was nothing to be done but start over, which we did. We began the fourth quarter at 3 a.m. – and lost again.

When the plane landed in Miami, where we were to play in the pair trials, Don couldn't find his luggage. I hoped fervently that it wasn't an omen. We checked into the Balmoral Hotel, which today is an old folks home. We didn't have the money to stay at the ritzy Americana Hotel, where the trials were being held.

We got in on a Sunday night. Play started the next day.

When Monday morning arrived and we started making our way to the Americana, Don and I had to take a detour. President John F. Kennedy was giving a speech at the hotel that day. The pedestrian bridge between our hotel and the Americana had been sealed off by the Secret Service. That was less than a week before the President was assassinated in Dallas.

In the playing area – the basement of the Americana – each table was cordoned off by curtains hanging on aluminum rods, creating little cubicles for play. This was an important event and security was tight. We were going to play 20 hands against each of the other pairs in the trials. In each matchup, the same hands would be in play – all at the same time. The ACBL didn't want to take any chances that bids or plays might be overheard.

Today, all major championships are played with screens and bid-boxes. Partners never see each other during the bidding, which is completely silent, and they don't really see each other during the play because the screens stay put. The players simply open a sliding door at the bottom of the screen after the auction and the opening lead.

It's a curious setup, but it's necessary to assure that the only information exchanged is done within the rules. It doesn't take long to get used to and it helps ease some of the pressure on the players. It's tough enough butting heads in such high-level competition without worrying about ethical considerations, too.

Don and I had qualified as a team with Kantar and Miles, but we were playing as pairs. There were 16 pairs altogether, so we would play 15 rounds. The scoring would be by IMPs. Our score against each other pair would be compared to an average of all the scores from all the tables – with the high and low scores thrown out.

The comparison would determine how many IMPs we won or lost on each board, with a maximum of 60 IMPs available on each round. When it was all over, the top three pairs would become the U.S. team in the World Bridge Olympiad the following year.

We started off against our teammates – another precaution taken by the ACBL. With everyone on equal footing at the beginning, we would all be trying equally hard. In truth, I guess there *were* possibilities for collusion. Say you were doing really well and were in contention late in the event and played your teammates, who were doing really badly and had no chance to win. If you clobbered them, some might suspect that your teammates took a dive to improve your chances. As I said, strange things can happen when the stakes are high.

So we started off against Kantar and Miles, our teammates and friends. Some wag suggested that Mathe – who had a reputation for shredding partners and opponents – was in no danger of starting off against a friend, but he had to play someone so it might as well be his teammates.

Anyway, we had a great set against Kantar and Miles. If we hadn't been in Miami, I would have checked the backs of the cards to see if they were Chilly Willys.

We finished our 20 boards and we got up to stretch. We overheard Miles say, "I guess it's about even."

Krauss gasped. "What in the hell is he smoking! If this is even I'm going home now."

We beat them 58-2.

Next up were Albert Weiss of Chicago and Russ Arnold of Miami. They went down 60-0. A blitz.

In round three we faced Howard Schenken, arguably the greatest bridge player of all time, and Peter Levintritt. Another blitz.

We had raced away from the field. We played Lew Mathe and Ed Taylor next round and they beat us 31-29, and although I hated losing to Mathe again, it was just a skirmish. We were winning the war. I thought Don performed superbly on this hand against Mathe and Taylor.

```
Dlr: West        ♠ 8 6 3
Vul: None        ♥ 9 3
                 ♦ A K Q 3 2
                 ♣ 6 4 2
♠ 5                              ♠ 9 7
♥ K 7 5 4                        ♥ A Q J 2
♦ 7 5                            ♦ J 10 9 6
♣ A K 10 9 5 3                   ♣ Q J 7
                 ♠ A K Q J 10 4 2
                 ♥ 10 8 6
                 ♦ 8 4
                 ♣ 8
```

WEST	NORTH	EAST	SOUTH
Krauss	*Mathe*	*Me*	*Taylor*
1♣	1♦	1♥	Pass (!)
2♥	Pass	3♥	Pass (!)
4♥	Pass	Pass	4♠
Pass	Pass	Dbl	Pass
5♣	Pass	Pass	5♠
All Pass			

First, Don diagnosed what Taylor was doing – lying in the bushes and hoping we'd be taken by surprise with his 4♠ bid. Taylor must have taken us for rubes. Fortunately, one of us wasn't. Don correctly reasoned that it was always Taylor's intention to bid 4♠ and that he was simply trying to draw a double.

Taylor took the push to 5♠, which was fated to go down one. It wasn't hopeless, however. It could make with a slip by the defense. Krauss cashed a high club and considered his next play carefully. If Don had tried to cash another club, Taylor would have ruffed high, played two rounds of trumps and then four rounds of diamonds, pitching one heart on the ♦Q, ruffing a diamond to establish the suit and then getting back to dummy with a trump to the 8. Another heart would go on the last diamond.

Krauss remembered that I had passed 5♣, however, so he figured I had three of them. A heart switch was indicated, and he played the king first to assure that nothing went wrong. If he had played a low heart to my ace, I would have had a problem. I knew declarer probably had three hearts, but if they included the king, I would need to shift back to clubs in hopes that another one would cash. Don's play of the ♥K took all the pressure off me and we got the plus we deserved.

As we plowed our way through the field, continuing to lead, our confidence was growing and I was observing carefully. There were a couple of incidents that made an impression on me.

Our match against the great Al Roth and Billy Seamon was one of them. Roth was and is a legendary figure. He is one of the great bidding theorists and players of all time. He invented the negative double, played by just about every tournament player in the world, and the unusual 2NT, another popular bidding gadget with tournament players. He and Tobias Stone were the creators of the famous Roth-Stone bidding system.

Roth has a great record in big-time competition. He had already played for the U.S. twice in the Bermuda Bowl before this trials event and he had won many national championships. He would win many more before his active playing days were done.

Although his reputation as a player and theorist were exemplary, his partnership demeanor was worse than dismal. Roth matches his imposing physical presence – he has a great hook nose and an intimidating scowl – with an incredibly sharp tongue and biting wit. He used these assets, if you want to call them that, as weapons against one and all. Partners were especially susceptible to abuse.

Billy Seamon, on the other hand, was a banking executive and a thoroughly likable man, besides being an excellent player. He didn't deserve what happened to him during our match.

Things weren't going well for the two and Roth never shut up. He was chewing up Seamon and jabbering nonstop, which kept Don and me off balance. We clearly weren't playing our best. In fact, we stunk. We played like rank novices. But no matter how bad we were, Roth and Seamon were ever so much worse. We beat them 60-0.

I got up from the table after the set and was utterly disgusted. Under my breath, I said to Don, "This is pitiful. Here is Roth, one of the biggest names in bridge, and it looks as if he's more interested in beating up on Seamon than in winning. Why in hell did he enter the event?" I asked rhetorically.

Well, Harold Guiver was nearby and he overheard what I said. The next thing I knew, Guiver had trotted over to Al Sobel, the Tournament Director in charge, to complain that Roth wasn't trying. There was a minor fuss about it, but nothing ever happened. Roth may have been doing his best, but his heart wasn't in it. No one can play his best in the face of the kind of verbal abuse he was heaping on Seamon – and you can't do well when you're dishing it out either. When you're lambasting partner, your mind isn't truly on business.

With about five rounds to go, we were matched up against Jim Jacoby and Bobby Nail – quite a pair. Jim was the son of the legendary Oswald Jacoby, and a fine player in his own right. We would be teammates on the Aces in later years, and we played together in 1988 when we won the World Team Olympiad in Venice, Italy. After I moved to Dallas to join the Aces, I came to know Jim well. It was a great loss to bridge when he died in 1991.

Nail, on the other hand, is another of bridge's great characters – and one of my favorite people. As a child, he suffered from chronic osteomyelitis and wasn't expected to live past 30. The disease caused him to stop growing at about 4-foot-8, but there's nothing diminutive about his bridge talent. In fact, he and Jacoby had won the trials the previous year and had represented the U.S. in Italy. On this occasion, however, Nail and Jacoby were doing very badly. In fact, they stood last in the field.

That didn't affect Nail's sense of humor, though, and he was still in the mood to do a little needling. Just before our match started, he strode up to the table, looked around and saw some collapsible chairs. He stacked three of them on top of each other, climbed up on them and sat down with a comment aimed at me: "This should make it a little harder for the fat boy to see my hand."

It didn't seem to work, however. We were killing them.

Halfway through the match, Nail got off his stack of chairs and motioned for Jacoby to follow him. Nail stopped as they made it halfway out of our cubicle. Looking up at Jacoby, who was easily more than a foot taller than Nail, Bobby said, "James, are you betting on these boys?"

Jim was flustered and expressed horror at the notion that he would do something so reprehensible.

"Relax," Nail said. "If you were, I just wanted half the action."

A couple of deals later, this little gem came up:

```
Dlr: South      ♠ —
Vul: Both       ♥ A Q 10 8 5 3
                ♦ A
                ♣ A K Q 5 3 2
♠ Q 7 6 4 3                    ♠ A 10 9 8
♥ 2                            ♥ K J
♦ K J 9 2                      ♦ Q 6 5
♣ 10 9 6                       ♣ J 8 7 4
                ♠ K J 5 2
                ♥ 9 7 6 4
                ♦ 10 8 7 4 3
                ♣ —
```

WEST	NORTH	EAST	SOUTH
Krauss	*Nail*	*Me*	*Jacoby*
			Pass
Pass	2♥	Pass	3♥
Pass	7♥	Pass (!)	Pass
Pass			

Nail's 2♥ bid was in the Acol style, showing a strong hand. After Jacoby's raise, I sort of hunkered down, awaiting a long auction. I had been prepared to pass Nail's next bid and I hadn't anticipated 7♥ – or maybe I was suffering from terminal stupidity. I'll never know. Anyway, for some reason I passed.

After that, I decided I might as well entertain myself a little bit. So I thought for what seemed to be a significant length of time and led the ♠A, which I knew was going to be ruffed. Krauss said he thought I was putting on an act of looking green after that, but I'm not sure I would have been that cruel.

Anyway, Nail ruffed a club to dummy and played a low heart off. When Don played the 2, Nail went into the tank. He was thinking and thinking. Finally, I took pity on him and showed him my hand. Jacoby saw it, too.

"Bobby," Jim said, "do you think it would have been a good idea to investigate our trump holding rather than just launching into a grand slam that way."

Without missing a beat, Nail replied: "I thought I would have a better play for seven hearts than I would for five notrump."

Don and I beat Bobby and Jim 54-6. With three rounds to play, we practically had the top spot sewed up. In any event, we were a lock for one of the top three places – and qualification to play in the world championship.

In our final three rounds, we lost to Robert Jordan and Arthur Robinson – considered by many to be the best pair in the U.S. at the time – defeated Erik Paulsen and Paul Allinger and lost to Vic Mitchell and Sam Stayman.

The losses didn't hurt our overall game, however, and we finished first by a rather comfortable margin. Mitchell and Stayman were second, Jordan and Robinson third. Ironically, over the final three rounds, two of the three pairs we played ended up as our teammates for the world championship.

Don and I were elated. It hardly seemed real. I don't know if I really believed that we had won, but it didn't matter. We had traveled a long way – and we hadn't made the trip to lose.

Later that day, a telegram arrived at our hotel. It was from Sid Borden and Art Fletcher, our rubber bridge buddies back in Los Angeles. "Congratulations on your brilliant victory," the telegram said, ending: "Hurry home. We're running short of cash." We laughed and vowed to make them pay for their cheek.

All of a sudden, my view of bridge – and my place in the bridge world – had changed. I began to think of myself as the favorite. I began to think that we were going to win every time. There was no reason why we shouldn't.

When I sat down to play, it was the opponents who had a problem, not me.

5

Escape from New York

MY PARTNER, Don Krauss, tried to murder our team captain at the world championships. It turned out to be one of the few high points of the tournament for us.

We had arrived in New York City a couple of days early, not to see the sights but to have a practice match with our teammates.

Teammates. That word didn't exactly apply to the six of us representing the United States at the World Bridge Olympiad in May of 1964.

After Don and I had won the trials, we sort of shook hands with the others who qualified – Sam Stayman, Vic Mitchell, Robert Jordan and Arthur Robinson – but no one would have mistaken us for the Six Musketeers. We were basically a team of three pairs.

For one thing, Don and I were looked upon somewhat as upstarts. We had whipped them fair and square and won the trials in a walk, but we still didn't have the respect from these guys that we should have. Hell, we were damned good, but they didn't know it as well as we did.

There was also an age gap with at least one of our teammates. Stayman, now famous for the convention named after him, was an older fellow. For reasons we weren't completely sure of, Stayman was somewhat aloof.

One thing we knew, though: Stayman was rich. He owned a wool mill at the time and had the look of a man with money. I think he looked down on the two California jokers who, in his mind, lucked their way onto the team. I didn't think much of his bridge at that time – and I thought even less of it when the world championships were over.

On the other hand, I could relate to Mitchell. Here was a wiry little guy who survived by his wits. He had been a professional gambler and kind of a hustler who played a little bridge for pay and spent the rest of his life at the race track.

Jordan and Robinson were somewhat different themselves. Both were slick – good-looking guys and very good players. In fact, most knowledgeable observers would have rated them as the top pair in the United States at the time. They were certainly the best pair on our team.

Then there was our non-playing captain – Frank Westcott. Frank was a businessman and bridge politician from Massachusetts. For some reason, he had been anointed by the ACBL as the captain of our team. Westcott was an unremarkable sort of fellow with short, black, slicked-back hair, probably dyed. He was short, bespectacled, a bit heavy and always wore three-piece suits.

He attempted to carry himself as a proper gentleman. Don and I thought he was a stuffed shirt.

Finally, there was our coach – Edgar Kaplan. Officially, he was the assistant captain, but he called the shots that related to bridge play. Westcott was for window dressing. Kaplan was the *de facto* captain.

Kaplan was an up-and-coming player – he hadn't acquired *The Bridge World* at that point. He was very ambitious and somewhat frustrated that buffoons like Krauss and Hamman had made it to the world championship and he hadn't.

To be fair to Edgar, he had a job to do as "assistant captain" and he did the best he could. Of course, that didn't lessen the frustration Don and I felt at the way things turned out for us in New York.

As we prepared ourselves for the practice match, we had no inkling of what was to come at the tournament. The truth is, we were looking forward to the practice session almost as much as playing in the Olympiad. The setup was for us to have dinner and then a team game at the Regency Club in New York with John Crawford.

At the time, Crawford was about 50, which seemed ancient to me, but he still cut a dashing figure. He was about 5-foot-9, well-tanned from playing tennis all the time, athletic looking and very rich. He was very dapper – there was never a hair out of place – and he had a great presence. He had been married several times – always to a rich woman. Crawford was a true *bon vivant* – a polished, silver-tongued devil.

He was also a helluva bridge player – a legend in the bridge world. In some ways, Crawford was like Charles Goren as a bridge promoter and a *name*.

John was a consistent winner at the rubber-bridge table, in no small measure because of his skill at reading the kibitzers. He might not get a reaction from an opponent, but his eyes were on the spectators for any hints.

Once, in a high-stakes game, Crawford found himself in 7♣ with eight trumps to the AKQ10 opposite a singleton. It was the last hand of the night and it looked like a pianola.

Crawford noticed, however, that none of the kibitzers had moved. Why? he thought to himself. How could this hand be interesting? Finally, he made a decision based on instinct and experience. Crawford amazed the kibitzers by playing the low club from the dummy and putting in the 10. Sure enough, his right-hand opponent was holding four to the jack. Talk about sharp.

Everyone knew Crawford. He was famous as a bridge teacher and writer. By 1964, he had won 37 national championships. He won three straight Bermuda Bowls in the 1950s. We were in awe of Crawford, as any young players would be.

In our practice match, Crawford played with another giant of the bridge world, Howard Schenken – a man once voted the greatest player of all time. He was on the three Bermuda Bowl teams with Crawford when they won. Schenken also won the Spingold and the Vanderbilt 10 times each and he won the Life Master Pairs five times. These were guys I could look up to. I was thrilled to be in their company. Kaplan, who set up the match, played with Peter Levintritt.

We had a great meal at the Regency Club. When the dinner had ended, Crawford settled back in his chair at the head of the table, looked up at the group assembled before him and said, "You guys didn't really think I was buying dinner, did you?"

He turned to Stayman. "I'm betting you $500 on tonight's match." To Mitchell: "It'll cost you $200." Next was Jordan: "I'm betting you $50," Crawford said.

Don and I and Robinson were the next to fall under Crawford's gaze. "If I take a ten spot from each of you, will you have enough for cab fare back to your hotel?" We gulped and nodded assent.

Sure enough, Crawford, Schenken and company took our money.

The Olympiad was played at the Hotel Americana on New York City's West Side. Despite losing the money and the match to Crawford's team, we got back to the hotel full of hope and excitement. The world championship was in the offing and we couldn't wait.

The Fall Nationals had taken place in Miami just after the team trials that Don and I won, and our team – Kantar and Miles, Don and I – came in third in the Reisinger. That was the event we had won the previous year to qualify for the trials.

But the Nationals had been in the fall of 1963 and that disappointing tournament was all but forgotten as we had landed at the airport in New York in May of 1964. I had never been to New York, but I can't say I noticed much about the place despite all I had heard. I was there to play bridge – it might as well have been Beaumont, Texas.

I *do* remember the hotel, however. It was an impressive structure, cutting across the New York City skyline like a huge wedge. The odd-looking building was a block long and seemed thin, if you can call a hotel thin, almost like a giant pack of playing cards sticking out of the ground. It looked as if it might fall over at any time. When we arrived, the hotel was crawling with foreigners – and they weren't all bridge players. The 1964 World's Fair was going on in New York at the same time we were playing for a world championship.

Of course, many of the out-of-towners *were* competitors or friends and associates of players. They were literally from all over the world – France, Australia, Brazil, Italy, Thailand, Poland, Lebanon – you name it. One of the teams was from the Netherlands Antilles. We didn't even know where that was.

Egypt – actually the United Arab Republic – was represented at the Olympiad and Omar Sharif was their playing captain. Although his famous film *Doctor Zhivago* didn't come out until 1965, Sharif was still well known as a screen actor. We were anxious to know if he was a good player. Don and I thought we might get a chance to find out, since our team would play each of the other 28 teams in a qualifying round-robin heat.

It seems kind of complicated, but it was really pretty simple. We played 18 deals against each other team. IMPs were converted to Victory Points, with a maximum of 7 VPs available each round. A close match, for example, might end 4 VPs to 3, whereas a blowout would be 7-0 for the winning team.

The top four teams at the end of the round-robin would go into a semifinal, where there were no more Victory Points. The team with the most IMPs was the winner – period.

The playing area was a huge room with plenty of space between the tables. There were no screens or bid-boxes in use then, but there were several tables in pits so that spectators could see the matches of most interest. It all seemed very exciting – and the tension was increased by the knowledge that spectators were going to be watching the action.

Another way people could watch was on a gizmo called Bridge-O-Rama, a big board with hand and bidding diagrams on it so viewers could see what was happening board by board.

Our team was one of the favorites, no doubt because of the reputations of Jordan, Robinson, Stayman and Mitchell. Not many of the world's bridge cognoscenti had heard of Hamman and Krauss. The real favorite, however, was Italy. The Italians had won world titles in six of the previous seven years – and they had the superstars – Benito Garozzo, Giorgio Belladonna, Pietro Forquet. Those were names that, for me, would become synonymous with anguish in years to come.

At the World Bridge Olympiad in New York City in 1964, however, I had a different view. This was to be my first chance to do battle with the dreaded Italian bridge machine. At least, I *thought* it was.

Even before the tournament started, things didn't go well for Don and me. For one thing, Westcott didn't approve of the two young whippersnappers and our liking for the demon rum. One day during the Olympiad, we had the evening off – in fact, we weren't supposed to play again until 4:45 the next afternoon – so we went to the hotel bar and found a couple of friendly locals to share a whisky or two with us.

Somehow, our debauchery got back to Frank and you would have thought we had shot the Pope – or worse. Imagine, drinking with only 20 hours until the next match.

Our view was that we were young and durable. Chances are a drink or two wouldn't have had a major impact on our game – the next day.

That cut no mustard with Frank, however, and we got a stern lecture. Truthfully, that episode might have been the peak of our relations with Frank Westcott, which is what led up to Don's attempted homicide.

Let me set the scene. The Olympiad was in full swing and Don and I were in against Mexico about midway through the round-robin. We were kind of annoyed that Kaplan and Westcott were holding us out against the really good teams. For example, we didn't touch a card when our team played Great Britain. It really steamed us to know they didn't think we were good enough.

Anyway, Don and I were playing against a couple of guys named F. Diez Barroso and Constant Fua. Belladonna and Garozzo they weren't. Jordan and Robinson were at the other table.

Westcott was right at my elbow in the closed room. Now, Frank was a man with a history of heart trouble and, as we learned in the episode with the drinks at the hotel bar, a person who was excitable at times.

We had played 13 of the 18 deals and seemed to have matters well in hand, but it's a mistake to take anything for granted.

If I say that Board 14 took a couple of years off my life, think about what it did to Frank. I was South and this was my hand:

♠K 8 5 3 ♥10 7 4 3 ♦Q 2 ♣10 9 3.

This was the auction:

WEST	NORTH	EAST	SOUTH
Barroso	*Krauss*	*Fua*	*Me*
		2♣ (1)	Pass
3NT	Pass	4♣	Pass
4♦	Pass	4♥	Pass
5♦	Pass	5♥	Pass
7♣	Dbl	All Pass	
(1) Strong.			

I started to sweat. Most often, when partner doubles a voluntarily bid slam it's because he wants a certain lead, usually because he has a void. I asked myself what Don could mean by the double? What was I supposed to lead? Could it be a diamond, dummy's first bid suit? I hemmed and hawed, trying to figure what was happening. Meanwhile, Frank was also going through the tortures of the damned. He was probably thinking, "What sort of travesty are these two perpetrating now?"

Finally, I led the ♦Q and this hand hit in dummy:

         ♠A 7 6   ♥A   ♦A K 10 9 8 7 5 3   ♣6.

Declarer won dummy's ace – and Don didn't ruff. Oh, brother. Dummy looked even stronger than I had envisioned in my wildest nightmares. The auction sounded like East had about 14 clubs. How were we going to beat this contract? I was staring in horror at dummy, but I could see Frank out of the corner of my eye starting to squirm.

Fua led a club from dummy to the jack in his hand. I'm thinking: Crap! Why doesn't this guy claim and get it over with? Frank was practically apoplectic. Then Fua played another club – to Don's ace!

Don looked at me kind of sheepishly. He knew I had been sweating bullets worrying about the doubled grand slam. Don said: "Sorry to catch you in the crossfire, Bob, but I had to do it for Frank. I thought you could stand it better than he could."

I could hear Frank grinding his teeth beside me.

This was the entire deal:

```
Dlr: East        ♠ Q J 10 9 4 2
Vul: None        ♥ 6 5 2
                 ♦ 6 4
                 ♣ A 5
♠ A 7 6                          ♠ —
♥ A                              ♥ K Q J 9 8
♦ A K 10 9 8 7 5 3               ♦ J
♣ 6                              ♣ K Q J 8 7 4 2
                 ♠ K 8 5 3
                 ♥ 10 7 4 3
                 ♦ Q 2
                 ♣ 10 9 3
```

Subconsciously, Don might have been getting even with me, too, for a hand that we had played against the Philippines early in the competition. In a way, it was kind of funny – if you weren't in Krauss's seat. This was the deal:

```
Dlr: North       ♠ K Q 5
Vul: N-S         ♥ A 9 8
                 ♦ K
                 ♣ A K J 10 7 2
♠ J 10 9 4                       ♠ 6 2
♥ Q 7 6 4                        ♥ J 10 5
♦ A Q 9 8                        ♦ 10 6 5 4 3
♣ 5                              ♣ Q 9 6
                 ♠ A 8 7 3
                 ♥ K 3 2
                 ♦ J 7 2
                 ♣ 8 4 3
```

WEST	NORTH	EAST	SOUTH
Krauss		*Me*	
	1♣	Pass	1♠
Pass	3♣	Pass	3NT
Pass	4♠	Pass	5♣
All Pass			

I led the ♥J, taken by North with the ace. Declarer played three rounds of trumps, putting me on play, and I brainlessly led the ♥10. Declarer took it in dummy and played a spade to his hand. On the run of the clubs, Don had to make five discards and he was squeezed in three suits. He could pitch three diamonds and a heart pretty easily, but on the fifth round of clubs, he couldn't find the right pitch from ♠J 10 9 ♥Q ♦A ♣ —.

He finally threw away the ♥Q, but when declarer cashed his good ♥9, Don was squeezed again. Making an overtrick for plus 620 when Jordan, at the other table, had been held to 10 tricks in the same contract.

In the discussion of this board later, Krauss was telling everyone, "Well, Hamman led the jack of hearts and, being the good partner that he is, got in with the queen of clubs and continued with the ten of hearts. He then left for the men's room and allowed me to defend the rest of the hand by myself."

I was glad he was a friend – and that he had a good sense of humor.

There was another hand from the Olympiad that I'll never forget, partly because of my history at the time with 6-6 in the black suits. Don and I were playing against Jamaica – do you think we'd be in against anyone any good? – and I picked up this little number:

♠A Q J 10 6 5 ♥ — ♦4 ♣K Q J 8 3 2.

Not bad, but all it did was bring to mind the *other* time I found myself holding twelve black cards. It was a rubber bridge game at Sid Borden's house in Encino. That game was for money and I was playing with Hugh Meloche against Borden and Art Fletcher – not the way I would have lined things up if I could have helped it. Pretty soon, this hand came up:

♠K Q J 6 5 4 ♥5 ♦ — ♣K Q 10 9 5 2.

I was the dealer. They were vulnerable. I opened 1♠. Fletcher, on my left, passed, as did Hugh. Sid was in there with a 3♥ bid. Undeterred, I bid 4♣. Fletcher bid 4♥. It went pass, pass, and I bid 4♠. Fletcher doubled with a vengeance.

Now, out of Meloche's mouth fell the words, "Five diamonds." What! Hugh couldn't keep the bidding open over 1♠ and now he's bidding diamonds at the five level? Of course this bid was doubled loudly.

It didn't look good, but I tried to stay calm and think straight. I thought to myself, "It's very important to play in the right black suit. If I get tapped out of one of my suits it's going to be horrible."

So I selected the sophisticated bid of 5♥, hoping to get Hugh to realize that I wanted him to show even a slight preference for clubs. Naturally, 5♥ was doubled. Hugh's eyes were now glazed over. He passed 5♥ doubled and I recognized that unquestionably the correct technical call was "redouble" to try once again to get him to take his pick of the black suits. But I also realized that I ran the very great risk that I would be playing 5♥ redoubled – down nine. I didn't have that much money, so I retreated to 5♠ and took my minus 1300.

That was my first experience with 6-6 in the black suits. Now I had my second chance. Here's my hand again:

♠ A Q J 10 6 5   ♥ —   ♦ 4   ♣ K Q J 8 3 2.

This was our auction:

WEST	NORTH	EAST	SOUTH
	Krauss		*Me*
		Pass	1♣
1♦	4♥	Pass	4♠
Pass	5♥	Pass	Pass
Dbl	Pass	Pass	5♠
Dbl	All Pass		

There's more here than meets the eye. Don and I had recently installed a new gadget to our system. We had agreed that when one of us opened 1♣ and the other bid 4♥ or 4♠, a new suit by opener was asking for controls in the suit bid. When Don bid 4♥ on this hand, I thought, "Whoopee! Isn't this wonderful?" Well, I decided to make the "asking bid" of 4♠. If I was lucky, his response would be 5♣ and I could pass. Naturally, he bid 5♥, showing no control in spades. I passed because 5♠ would have been another asking bid.

When 5♥ got doubled, I thought it prudent to run and the only reasonable choice was 5♠. Good grief! Were we about to reprise the

Hamman-Meloche debacle? No, not this time. Take a look at the full
deal:

```
Dlr: East        ♠ 8 2
Vul: Both        ♥ A J 10 9 7 6 5 4
                 ♦ 8 6
                 ♣ 6
♠ 9 7                              ♠ K 4 3
♥ K Q 8                            ♥ 3 2
♦ Q J 7 5 2                        ♦ A K 10 9 3
♣ A 9 5                            ♣ 10 7 4
                 ♠ A Q J 10 6 5
                 ♥ —
                 ♦ 4
                 ♣ K Q J 8 3 2
```

West led the ♦Q, which was overtaken by East, who played
another diamond. I ruffed and played the ♣J. Amazingly, West
ducked. Now it was all over. I followed with the ♣K and ruffed out
West's ace. With the club suit breaking 3-3 I had no trouble making
11 tricks for plus 850. Technology won . . . sort of.

That was another of the high spots for Don and me at the
Olympiad. We certainly had our lows. One of them was losing to the
Netherlands Antilles. That didn't help our standing with Westcott and
Kaplan, our two captains.

We got off to a rocky start, but Don and I warmed up as the
tournament wore on. In fact, Don and I were solid in the semifinal
match against Canada – a win that got our team into the final against
Italy.

Despite the embarrassment of losing to the Netherlands Antilles in
the round-robin, we qualified third, ahead of Canada. Great Britain
was first in the round-robin, followed by Italy. The four teams drew
lots for pairings and we ended up with Canada, leaving Italy and Great
Britain to fight it out. Italy beat Great Britain by 6 IMPs. We beat
Canada 133-117. Don and I felt good about how we played against the

Canadians and we were looking forward to challenging the great Italians.

It didn't happen.

Westcott and Kaplan kept the other two pairs in the final the entire match. We didn't touch a card. It was the captain's decision and we had no recourse, but I can tell you we were plenty upset. Sure, we were rookies in the sense that we had never played in a world championship before then, but we had lots of experience. We had played thousands of hands against good players. It wasn't your garden variety six years of experience. Not only that, we had won the Team Trials. By a mile!

What made it worse was some of the shenanigans by the so-called "experienced" guys who were in there against Italy. It turned my stomach. Take a gander at this gem against Walter Avarelli and Belladonna:

```
Dlr: West        ♠ A Q 10 7 3
Vul: None        ♥ A J 8 6
                 ♦ 4 2
                 ♣ A 9
♠ K J 9 6 5                      ♠ 8
♥ 10 5 4 2                       ♥ K Q 3
♦ —                             ♦ A K Q 9 8 5 3
♣ 7 6 3 2                        ♣ J 8
                 ♠ 4 2
                 ♥ 9 7
                 ♦ J 10 7 6
                 ♣ K Q 10 5 4
```

WEST	NORTH	EAST	SOUTH
Mitchell	*Belladonna*	*Stayman*	*Avarelli*
Pass	1♥ (1)	2♦	Dbl
2♠	Dbl	Pass	Pass
Redbl (2)	Pass	2NT	Dbl
All Pass			

(1) Canapé style – four-card suits are opened before longer suits.
(2) Help!

Stayman's bid of 2NT was terrible after the penalty double of 2♦, warning Stayman that diamonds weren't running. He should have taken a small minus by bidding 3♦. In fact, if South had led a heart against 3♦, Stayman would have gone down only one. 2NT was bloody, and Stayman finished down four after South led a spade.

I had the pleasure of watching this on Bridge-O-Rama. It wasn't just that board that made me disgusted. On another hand, Stayman went down in a cold vulnerable slam that was made at the other table. He balanced, vulnerable, after the opponents had a misfit auction and went for 800.

I could understand that Westcott and Kaplan thought Don and I were inexperienced, but to keep us on the bench when this kind of crap was going on was too much. We had to say something to Westcott. Frank hemmed and hawed when we asked when we were going in, but he never said yes or no. It wasn't hard to figure out what was going on.

Well, when the dust settled we still hadn't played a board in the final and our team was beaten, 158-112. The United States was second in the Olympiad. Of course, Don and I didn't feel like we had finished second in anything.

The next day, Don was checking out of the hotel feeling kind of low and here comes Westcott trotting across the lobby. I guess he was trying to make amends, because he went up to Don and said, "Well, it was a pleasure having you fellows on the team. You played really well against Canada." Don exchanged a few reluctant pleasantries with Frank, and as Westcott turned to leave, he looked at Don and said, "It was really nice to have gotten to know you, Bob."

When Don told me about it, all I could do was shake my head. We were happy to be leaving New York.

6

Fired up and burned out

L EW MATHE. That name still evokes a mixture of emotions in
me.

Lew was my partner in one of my finest hours – when we
won the Blue Ribbon Pairs in a walk. Lew and I were partners the
night we made the ACBL waste some film – when we won the final
set of the Spingold 88-5 after everyone had figured the other team
couldn't lose.

But I also have memories of Mathe's miserable partnership manner, of his superior attitude and of bitter confrontations at the table
when I let him goad me into them.

Lew and I shared the thrill of playing in a world championship
together. As short as our partnership was, I probably had more truly
crushing sessions with Mathe than anyone else.

On the other hand, our partnership became so dysfunctional that in
1966 we finished last – dead last! – in the Bermuda Bowl Team Trials
in Pittsburgh.

Once our partnership ended, we got along passably for the most
part, even playing an odd session or two without incident.

Yet, in one of our last encounters – years after our partnership
broke up – I threatened to push his head through the wall. And I meant
it.

It was a rollercoaster ride all the way.

I had known Mathe for years before we ever played. You might say his reputation preceded him.

Lewis L. Mathe was a real estate appraiser and broker – a man destined to become a member of the Board of Directors of the ACBL and president of the ACBL. He also achieved high rank with the World Bridge Federation, as a player and as a politician.

There is no question that Mathe was an excellent card player. He was on the winning team in the Bermuda Bowl in 1954 and played for the Bermuda Bowl title four times in all – once with me. Lew won lots of national championships – pairs and teams. He was feared as an opponent – and as a partner.

Mathe was a short, bulldog-like man with a crewcut like a drill sergeant and a disposition to match. He had a square jaw, an imposing countenance and a relentless determination to win. Had Lew been able to harness that energy in a way that didn't destroy partnerships, he might have won twice as much as he did. He was just too hard on partners for any of them to take it for very long. I lasted with him about three years.

Lew and I made our first date to play during the summer of 1964. We had faced each other at the table many times and had even played on some teams together. In fact, in the spring of that year, Don and I won the Vanderbilt playing with Mathe, Eddie Kantar, Howard Schenken and Peter Levintritt.

Mathe ran through partners like a hot knife through butter, so I wasn't particularly surprised when he suggested that we play. At the time, I thought Mathe was a better player than I was, so I looked on the prospective partnership as an opportunity to learn and improve my game. At the time, Mathe was one of the best despite his reputation for being a terrible partner. I had seen first-hand that he could be overbearing and obnoxious, but I had a lot of respect for his bridge ability.

Lew and I played in a regional in San Francisco over Labor Day in 1964 and seemed to get along well. When he had first asked me to play, Mathe said, "I want to see if you're as bad as everyone says." He was joking, of course. Things went smoothly for us initially – the honeymoon period, you might call it.

Lew and I made a date for the Blue Ribbon Pairs after I learned that Don, my regular partner, wouldn't be available to play in the Fall

Nationals at all. In those days, the pair trials for the world championships were played in the same city as the Nationals right before the big tournament began.

Don and I had a date for the trials, but Don had just started a new job and knew ahead of time he couldn't stay for the Nationals. We had qualified for the trials by winning the 1964 Vanderbilt.

So I booked Ralph Clark for the Men's Pairs and Mike Gilbert to play with me in the Reisinger. Mike, whom I had known at UCLA, had just gotten out of the Army. He was a capable player back then. Today, he is a proposition poker player in Gardena – that is, he doesn't pay fees to play. He plays poker as a fill-in and plays for his own account.

Our teammates in the Reisinger were Mathe and a 30-ish fellow named Michael McMahan. This other Mike was a good player, too, probably a little better than Gilbert. McMahan eventually went into the furniture business. As good as he was, he didn't have a dispensation from Lew's abuse. Mathe was an equal opportunity haranguer. In fact, Lew went through partners so fast that he tended to recycle them on occasion.

Anyway, because we knew Don was leaving Dallas after the trials, Lew and I decided to try the Blue Ribbon Pairs – the most prestigious pairs event on the ACBL calendar and certainly one of the toughest events in the world. I was ready to play.

Now Mathe didn't care if he got respect. He wanted results. If he thought his partner was getting in the way of his good results, there was hell to pay. He held nothing back in lambasting partner. No insult was beneath him.

We started out well in the Blue Ribbon, a six-session event – two qualifying sessions, two semifinal qualifying sessions and two final sessions. Lew and I qualified comfortably the first day and things were going well. We were as happy as a couple of clams.

The smiles turned to frowns on the second day, however, as our results weren't nearly as good and the honeymoon ended. Mathe was on me like a dog on a bone – both sessions. I felt we hadn't qualified, so when I went to the bar after the second session I told someone, "If I'm ever caught playing with Mathe again, someone should immediately call the men in the white coats."

Well, we qualified somehow and "never again" was the next day. Some nevers come quicker than others. I can't honestly say I regretted it – that time.

In the afternoon, Mathe was awesome – he was right on every hand. It was the most incredible performance of walking through the raindrops I have ever seen. He was tuned in to everything and making no mistakes. We had two bad boards in the afternoon, one of them preventable if I had listened to my partner.

A mixed pair were heading for our table and Lew called me aside and said, "This pair never blows a trick on opening lead. Never."

I kind of got the drift of what he meant, but not fully, as events proved. I opened 1NT and Mathe bid 3NT. The opening lead was the ♦2. Dummy had the ♦KQ984 and I had the ♦A6. I put in the 8 and my right-hand opponent played the jack. I won with the ace and returned a diamond to dummy's 9, expecting to pick up the whole suit. I wanted to vomit when RHO played the ♦10.

When the round was over, Mathe was bristling. "You simple sonofabitch," he said. "What did I tell you?" There wasn't much I could say. He didn't say the pair seldom blows a trick on opening lead – he said *never*.

We were leading the field by a small margin after the first final session. That night, Mathe was unconscious again and we were working the opponents over as if they were children.

With three rounds to go, Mathe and I went for coffee and I said, "Well, Lewie, do you think we've got it locked up?"

"Don't think, stupid," Mathe growled. "Just play your normal game."

So we went back to the table and I was thinking about what my normal game was when I picked up this hand:

♠Q J 8 7 5   ♥6   ♦A 8 7 6 5 3   ♣Q.

This was the bidding.

WEST	NORTH	EAST	SOUTH
Me		*Mathe*	
Pass	Pass	2♥	2NT
Pass	3NT	All Pass	

Now Mathe's weak two-bids were not known for their solidity, so I had to consider whether leading his suit was right. After all, I couldn't lead it again and we could lose a tempo if I didn't start my own suit – and all he needed was some honor in spades. Finally, I put the ♠7 on the table. This was the dummy I saw:

♠4 3 ♥A 10 ♦10 2 ♣K 7 6 5 4 3 2.

When declarer called for a low spade, Lew produced the 9. I was cringing and clutching my guts and praying I wouldn't see the 10 from declarer's hand. Mercifully, he won with the ace. But the good news ended there. Declarer played the ♣A, felling my queen, and cashed the jack. Mathe followed with the 8 and the 9. Declarer then crossed to dummy with the ♥A and played the ♣K. Mathe's ♣10 hit the table with a thud that, in my mind, shook the whole building. Declarer made two overtricks.

I could almost see the smoke coming out of Mathe's ears. If I had led his suit – he held the ♥KQ – dummy and that long club suit would have been stone dead and declarer would probably have finished down three. I had turned a top into a near-zero.

Now, anything I've accomplished in bridge in the intervening 29 years is probably a result of what I did next.

What I did next was very simple. I shoved my hand back into the board and pulled out the next one. I did not show my hand to Mathe and look for sympathy. That would have been like sticking my hand into the jaws of an alligator and asking it not to bite. I did not make an excuse for not leading his suit. I simply went on to the next hand.

The mistake I had made was done. It couldn't be taken back. I didn't dwell on it – and I hoped Lew wouldn't.

I've learned over the years that there is a process many players go through when they are confronted with bad fortune at the bridge table. Translation: they butchered the play, mangled the defense or bid like a moron.

Say you go down in a contract, and relatively trivial analysis demonstrates that there was an alternative line of play that would have succeeded. One popular approach is the face-saving ploy. You say something like, "I thought the heart hook would work because he opened the bidding . . ." or "I thought he had six spades because . . . blah, blah, blah . . ."

My advice if you've ever tried this: don't. Save your energy. Nobody gives a flip what you thought or why you thought it. To listeners, if there are any, you're babbling. What you say doesn't matter. This face-saving maneuver is hopelessly transparent. You're conjuring up reasons for your bonehead play that were no more on your mind than the man in the moon. They might be reasonable afterthoughts, but they weren't what you were thinking at the time.

This is the reality of the situation: nobody cares why you did what you did. Forget about it.

Then there's Option No. 2 – the beat-your-partner-to-the-punch dodge. You say, "Oh, I chopped it up." Now partner can't jump on you for chopping it up because you've already said you chopped it up.

Well, maybe you did and maybe you didn't. Whether you did or not is totally immaterial. What you've got to do is look at what happened very clinically. Later. After the fact.

When the session is over – you weren't thinking about the error on the next four boards, were you? – you ask yourself key questions. Was my methodology sound? If someone else did this – someone whom I could observe dispassionately – if someone else did what I did, what would my real opinion of it be? *That* should be your opinion of what happened. Don't make the mistake of babbling to save face or trying to get the drop on your partner.

So, what is all this leading up to – and why did I relate it to going on to the next board when I was playing with Mathe in the Blue Ribbon Pairs?

This is why: when you're playing bridge, your objective is to win. To do that, you've got to be ready to expend the requisite amount of energy to play at some high percentage of your capacity. Most people don't even come close to playing at their full capacities. Why not? Why, time after time, do they make mistakes that are totally within their grasp to avoid?

Because they're not thinking about what they're doing. They're thinking about the last hand, or the hand before that – or something else altogether. They're not sticking to business. It's very difficult to do more than one thing at a time, particularly if one of the things you're doing has to be dead right the first shot, which is true to a great degree in bridge.

You know something? When you're done with a hand, it's over. I'm not aware of any technique of time travel that would permit you to go back and reverse the process – to take back what you did. The only way to have an effect on what happened is to achieve results so good that you overcome the adversity created by your mistake. You certainly don't improve your position by allowing the error to diminish your capacity to function downstream.

You can become a winner at bridge by developing good habits. Get used to thinking only about the next board – not the last three. What you can do for your partner is simple: shut up. Just shut up. If partner says, "Would you have done it the same way?" answer in this fashion: "I haven't thought about it. Save your energy. Worry about it later. Let's play this one."

I didn't have to say that to Lew Mathe. He knew the importance of focusing on the hand he was playing. When we first started playing together, he would snarl a lot, but if I ignored him there wasn't any problem. Where we started to break down was when I let him trap me into a dialogue.

I had one more scare with Mathe before the Blue Ribbon Pairs ended. Lew was still stewing about my bad lead against 3NT when we got to the table against another good pair. It was late in the session and I still felt we had a comfortable lead.

Mathe opened 1♥ and I held this sorry collection:

♠J 9 4 3 ♥K 6 5 ♦7 3 ♣J 10 5 4.

Now I knew that Lew would bid game on any 13 cards if I raised, so I said, screw it – pass!

The hand got passed out and he made five. Still nothing was said.

Well, the last session finally ended and we won in a breeze. It wasn't even close. Jubilation prevailed and all was forgiven.

Winning the Blue Ribbon Pairs got Mathe and me into the Team Trials. Once again, I was going to have a chance to play for a world championship.

The previous year, Don Krauss and I had finished fourth in the trials qualifying in Dallas, missing out on a chance to play in two

straight world championships. It might have been just as well because
the North American team – Howard Schenken-Peter Levintritt, B. Jay
Becker-Dorothy Hayden (later Truscott) and Ivan Erdos-Kelsey
Petterson – were annihilated by the dreaded Italians in the Bermuda
Bowl in Buenos Aires, Argentina. The other way to look at it, of
course, is that if Don and I had been in Buenos Aires things might
have turned out differently.

Anyway, the 1965 Team Trials – for the 1966 Bermuda Bowl –
were in San Francisco right before the Fall Nationals, and Mathe and I
came in second, easily making the team that would play in St.
Vincent, Italy, the following spring.

Our team was Ira Rubin and Phil Feldesman of the East Coast;
Mathe and me, and Eric Murray and Sami Kehela, both from Toronto.
Of course, they were well-known to me – Murray had already made a
big impression on me.

Although Mathe and I did well in the trials, we didn't play
together once the Nationals began. By then, the wheels were already
coming off the partnership. The trouble was that my view of my
station in life had changed. I was no longer the student sitting at the
great one's feet, absorbing wisdom. I was no longer applying for
Rookie of the Year honors, and that didn't go over well with Lew. I
was becoming less and less tolerant of Lew's haranguing. I was
beginning to give it back to him.

Somehow, though, Lew and I held it together. I guess we weren't
about to blow our chance to play in a world championship, no matter
what we thought of each other. We were off to Italy to challenge the
great Italian bridge machine again.

The tournament was played at St. Vincent in Northern Italy, a
beautiful little town nestled on a hillside with the towering Alps in the
background.

Most of the players stayed at the Hotel Billia, a grand old building
that had the look of a palace, but I stayed at the du Park Hotel. The
playing site was the festival hall of the Casino della Vallee.

The trip to St. Vincent was my first time in Europe and I should
have been impressed with the picturesque countryside, the springtime

blooms and the grand atmosphere of the most important bridge tournament in the world.

All I could think of was beating the Italians. They had run roughshod over the field in Buenos Aires and they were favored in St. Vincent. Naturally, they were comfortable playing at home, so to speak – and there were sure to be thousands of rabid fans on hand to provide moral support. Throughout my bridge career, I have found that when I was playing against Italy anywhere outside the United States, there was no doubt who the crowd was cheering for. Some of that still rankles.

Although the Italians were favored, our team was given a good chance to unseat the reigning world champions. Interestingly, one writer's comment about the tournament that produced our team was that the San Francisco trials had "gone very much according to form. Two or three powerful pairs had finished just out of the money and for once no dark-horse pair had come out of the field to saddle the non-playing captain with a pair that he must consider was not the equal of the others and that would need to be played only in spots."

Of course, one of those "dark-horse pairs" the author was referring to was Hamman and Krauss, the unknowns who took the Miami trials by storm. What bunk.

Nowadays, the Bermuda Bowl field numbers 16 and the early competition is round-robin style with top qualifiers earning their way to the quarterfinals. In 1966, the Bermuda Bowl field was five teams – North America, Italy, Venezuela, the Netherlands and Thailand. The entire event was a round-robin. The winner was the team that won the most matches or scored the most IMPs if the match wins were even.

Each teams would play 140 boards against each of the other teams in sessions staggered to provide a break for each team after every fifth round.

Venezuela, the Netherlands and Thailand had never before fielded Bermuda Bowl teams, so we were given the best shot to defeat Italy.

Once again, bitter disappointment was our lot.

I have always found it interesting to note that the great Italian juggernaut included some relatively weak players. Of course, players like Benito Garozzo, Pietro Forquet and Giorgio Belladonna earned their reputations – and their records speak for themselves. They are world-class players by any yardstick.

But the Italians also fielded the likes of Massimo D'Alelio and the characters who were caught playing footsie in Bermuda in 1975 – Facchini and Zucchelli. They weren't good enough to clean the ashtrays for players like Garozzo and Belladonna.

In St. Vincent, the Italian team was Garozzo and Forquet, probably the strongest pair on the team; Walter Avarelli and Giorgio Belladonna, another tough partnership, and Camillo Pabis-Ticci and D'Alelio.

This was the team that won the previous year in Argentina – and they were playing on home turf. Defeating this bunch would be difficult, to say the least. It turned out to be impossible. We trampled the other three teams – the Netherlands, Venezuela and Thailand – by an average margin of 162 IMPs.

Italy, meanwhile, was winning by even bigger margins against the weak field. They beat Thailand by more than 300 IMPs.

We played Italy a much closer match, losing by 57 IMPs – but it might as well have been 500. It was still a loss. They got us down, 41-17, after the first 20 boards, and we never recovered. We won the fifth set by 44 IMPs, but by then the match was out of reach.

Bridge is a game of mistakes, with some luck thrown in. Here's a case in point.

```
Dlr: South      ♠ 9 8
Vul: E-W        ♥ Q 10 8 3 2
                ♦ 6
                ♣ J 10 7 5 3
  ♠ J 10 7                      ♠ A K 5 2
  ♥ A 7 6 5 4                   ♥ J
  ♦ Q 10 7 3                    ♦ A J 9 4 2
  ♣ 8                           ♣ A Q 9
                ♠ Q 6 4 3
                ♥ K 9
                ♦ K 8 5
                ♣ K 6 4 2
```

WEST	NORTH	EAST	SOUTH
Me	*Forquet*	*Mathe*	*Garozzo*
			Pass
Pass	Pass	1♦	Pass
1♥	Pass	2♠	Pass
4♦	Pass	4NT	Pass
5♦	Pass	6♦	All Pass

This was a good contract that just happened to be doomed. Garozzo led a trump, which Mathe won in hand. He played the ♣A and ruffed a club, then he played a trump from dummy. When North showed out, Mathe went up with the ace, ruffed his last club in dummy and took the spade finesse. Down one. Tough luck.

At the other table, the Italians were lucky – and good.

WEST	NORTH	EAST	SOUTH
Avarelli	*Murray*	*Belladonna*	*Kehela*
			Pass
Pass	1♥	Dbl	Redbl
2♦	2♥	3♥	Pass
4♦	Pass	5♦	All Pass

I say the Italians were lucky because Murray's psychic opening bid in third seat might have had a devastating effect on the East-West pair. Instead, the auction developed in such a way that it was obvious that Murray had psyched – and the Italians were good enough to use that information to their benefit.

When Kehela redoubled to show good values over Belladonna's takeout double, it didn't take Albert Einstein to figure out that something was amiss. Belladonna knew the redouble showed something in the neighborhood of 10 high-card points. He was looking at 19 himself – and Avarelli was over there making a forward-going bid. That left Murray with precious little.

Belladonna and Avarelli, therefore, were able to diagnose that most of the missing high-card points lay over the strong East hand, making slam a dubious prospect. They duly settled in game. Unimpeded, the Italians no doubt would have reached the good slam, too.

That was the way it went for us. Of course we also shot ourselves in the foot. Here's Mathe helping the Italians to a 7-IMP gain.

```
Dlr: West        ♠ 6 4 2
Vul: Both        ♥ A J
                 ♦ A 9 7 5
                 ♣ K 4 3 2
♠ A K J 8 3                      ♠ 7
♥ 10 7                           ♥ K Q 9 5 4 2
♦ K 10 4 3                       ♦ 8 2
♣ 9 6                            ♣ J 8 7 5
                 ♠ Q 10 9 5
                 ♥ 8 6 3
                 ♦ Q J 6
                 ♣ A Q 10
```

When Murray and Kehela (North-South) played against Avarelli and Belladonna, the board was passed out. Not Hamman and Mathe.

WEST	NORTH	EAST	SOUTH
Me	*Forquet*	*Mathe*	*Garozzo*
1♠	Pass	2♥	Pass
2♠	All Pass		

My opening bid wasn't the greatest, but it was reasonable. I had a good suit and two and a half quick tricks. Over my 1♠ opener, anyone else would have bid 1NT. Not Lew. His 2♥ bid was a killer. I couldn't pass – he might have had a rock-crusher – but I didn't have the tickets to bid 3♦. My only choice was to rebid my five-card spade suit. We would have been better off if Mathe had bid hearts again, but that was begging for more trouble after his questionable decision to respond at the two level on 6 high-card points.

Forquet led a trump and I could take no more than five tricks. Down three – minus 300 – against a passout at the other table.

An amusing situation developed as the match progressed. Mathe and I were the main men on the team. In fact, we ended up playing six of the seven sets against Italy.

Our team captain was Julius Rosenblum and our coach once again was Edgar Kaplan. After four sets, we were down 217-127, and Rosenblum and Kaplan decided it was time to change the lineup. So they benched Murray and Kehela in favor of Rubin and Feldesman. In the fifth set, Lew and I got hot and we won 64-20. With 40 boards to go, we were down by only 46 IMPs. We still had a chance to win.

Rubin and Feldesman were mediocre in that set, so Rosenblum and Kaplan decided to bench *them* and put Murray and Kehela back in. We lost anyway, but Rubin and Feldesman were offended that they had been benched for the last 20 boards. I couldn't help smirking when they accused Kaplan and Rosenblum of being anti-Semitic!

Lew and I had played fairly well in Italy, but the wheels had started coming off the partnership before that – and the process accelerated as 1966 wore on. We were like the Hatfields and the McCoys. It was a constant feud.

At the Summer Nationals in Denver, Lew and I were playing with Don Krauss and Paul Soloway, Howard Schenken and Peter Leventritt. We were playing against a very mediocre team and were leading with one quarter to go, when Mathe doubled one of the opponents in 4♣ for no good reason and they rolled it. All of a sudden, those guys were sitting up straight and thinking they could beat us. They did.

I was really disgusted with Mathe – and I would have done myself a favor if I had followed my instincts and declined to play with him in the trials in Pittsburgh that fall. But I played with him anyway – to my regret.

Despite the fact that we just didn't get along any more, Mathe and I were leading the trials early on. Just like that, we went into a tailspin and could hardly do anything right. We were at each other's throats every time something went wrong. Each of us was out to prove the other was a dumbbell. We were opponents, not partners. Lew and I finished dead last in that event – my swan song with him in any serious bridge endeavor.

I decided in Pittsburgh that I was going to try to form a partnership with Eddie Kantar.

Once Lew and I decided not to play, the pressure was off and we kept a date we had previously made to play in a money bridge tournament in Las Vegas in the spring of 1967. We played well together and won, but we had no delusions about playing together again seriously.

Lew and I were cordial to each other thereafter, but you can't take back hard words – and I think both of us let some of the bitterness linger.

After I had moved to Dallas to join the Aces, I returned to Los Angeles one summer to play in the Bridge Week tournament with a friend out there – a guy by the name of Milt Levison. Milt, who was in the carpet business, lived in Sacramento.

Well, Milt and I were playing and Mathe happened by our table. He stopped to watch a hand or two. I psyched on one of the hands, and we got a good result. When the round was over, Mathe decided he was going to play bridge cop.

"I'd like to talk to you for a minute," Mathe said to me.

I joined him away from the table.

"How often does this happen?" he asked.

I nearly clubbed him right there, but I restrained myself. I got right in his face and with all the intensity I could muster, I said, "Get out of my life, Lew. I'll push your head through the wall if you come back here with any of this horseshit." He knew I meant business. I would have beaten him up. He was getting personal with me, and I had long since stopped taking anything off of Lew Mathe.

I started working on the partnership with Eddie Kantar in the spring of 1967. It was a new beginning. A fresh start.

It was also the year that I would meet a man who, although not immediately, would have a significant impact on my life.

I'm talking about Ira Corn.

7

⊘he promoter

BOBBY WOLFF tells a story about Ira Corn from the early
1970s that sums up the scope of Corn's ambition and his
capacity for dreaming the big dream.

Wolff and Corn were out walking one day in Dallas when
Corn suddenly said, "I'd like to write a book about backgammon."

Wolff was incredulous. Corn was a rich and successful man, the
head of a conglomerate of far-flung companies called the Michigan
General Corporation. He was the founder of the Aces, at the time the
first and only team of professional bridge players to win a world
championship.

For all his wealth and power, Corn didn't know the first thing
about backgammon except that a lot of people seemed to like to play
it. How could he write a book about backgammon?

"You write it," Corn said to Wolff, "and we'll get it published by
one of the Michigan General companies."

Wolff said, "But Ira, you don't even know how to set up the
pieces . . . and you're going to be the backgammon guru?"

"Bobby," said Corn, "you don't understand. That's what makes it
so great."

In the summer of 1967, I found myself sitting next to Eddie
Kantar in a private dining room at the posh Queen Elizabeth Hotel in
Montreal. As the waiters trod lightly in and out serving us, we could

hear glasses clinking and muffled conversations from other parts of the hotel restaurant.

Eddie and I had gone to Montreal to play bridge at the Summer Nationals. We had started working on our partnership after I quit playing with Lew Mathe.

In the ritzy setting at the Queen Elizabeth, we felt a bit out of place. Although we were serious about bridge, Eddie and I were basically a couple of happy-go-lucky Californians.

It hadn't been that long ago that my days consisted of a little bit of work at the Bendix plant before I headed to Zuma Beach for surfing and ogling the girls. That took care of the afternoon. At night, it was rubber bridge for money. To this day, Eddie prefers activities that allow him to wear shorts.

Eddie and I looked at each other and then at our host, a very large man with sideburns and dark, slicked-back hair. As he talked, this 350-pound behemoth wearing an expensive black suit smoked a cigar that was two feet long if it was an inch.

There sat Ira G. Corn Jr. – businessman, multi-millionaire, bridge player and a man with a dream. His plan was to put together a team of players who would work and train and play against the best – and win a world championship.

The man projected determination and enthusiasm. Although Corn was a relatively recent convert to duplicate bridge, he had an evangelist's fervor in describing his project and his vision.

"The Aces," he said. "That's what we'll call the team." Corn, presiding Buddha-like over the meeting, looked around the table for reactions. Also at the table were Bobby Wolff and Jim Jacoby. It was Bobby who had done most of the recruiting for Corn.

Describing my reaction to Corn and his pitch is easy. I was impressed by this gigantic person. Of course, I knew a little about him before I went to the dinner meeting.

Corn came from Arkansas. He grew up during the Great Depression. Most people he knew, including his father, lost everything. But with faith, hard work and a positive attitude, the Corn family rebounded – lessons well learned by young Ira.

Corn was educated at the University of Chicago. He started work in the New York office of General Electric right out of college. He traveled quite a bit in his job. One day, he found himself in Dallas. He called up the business school at Southern Methodist University and, in typical Ira fashion, told them he was ready to come to work.

"I'd like to be a professor," Corn told the dean of the business school, a man named Fleck. The dean said, "We usually start off as instructors here."

"Well," said Corn, "that's not satisfactory. You have a lower-ranked professorship, don't you? Plus a higher one?"

"Yes, assistant professor."

"I'll start as an assistant professor," Ira said.

"What school did you graduate from?" Fleck asked.

"The University of Chicago," said Ira.

"Come right out and see me," said Fleck.

It was the perfect job for Corn, who really wanted to be in business for himself, not working for other people. With lots of free time, he started forming companies. He made a substantial sum in an Indianapolis apartment project which he parlayed into several other deals prior to acquiring Michigan Abrasive Company, which was the initial piece of the Michigan General Corporation conglomerate. Michigan General eventually became a consortium of companies primarily concentrated in manufacturing.

By the time we met Corn, he had acquired considerable wealth.

Also by that time, Corn was on a crusade to bring a world championship in bridge to the United States.

Corn's formative years were spent in a strict Baptist environment. He didn't even know what playing cards were until he was 20 years old. His first brush with bridge was in junior college, when he spotted some people playing and stopped to watch. After a while he realized that bridge was remarkably similar to Rook, a game he had played at home. Rook was all right for Baptists because the deck doesn't have "evil" pictures – it's all numbers. Also in Rook, there are different colors – red, green, yellow and black, like suits – and tricks are taken. You might call Rook "Baptist bridge." Corn was asked to fill in one time after kibitzing the bridge game and took it readily.

He was introduced to tournament bridge in 1961 by Dorothy Moore, who eventually became his girlfriend. Later on, she became an executive with Corn's Michigan General Corporation. At that time,

Dorothy was one of the best woman players in Texas. As a bridge player, she was hungry – and a good competitor. On occasion, she earned some money playing bridge professionally.

Dorothy had considerable enthusiasm and a real gift for organization. Once the Aces had been formed and had started on the quest for a world championship, Dorothy's understanding of Corn's game plan made her extremely valuable as a sounding board for team members.

At the best of times, Corn was a difficult man to talk to. In fact, this was his idea of democracy – when there was an issue to settle, he would outvote the team one to six and get on with doing things his way. Well, Ira's way wasn't always best, and Dorothy helped some of the team members figure out how to approach him.

Anyway, once Dorothy got Corn into bridge and he discovered duplicate, he took the plunge completely. He was so enthralled with the game that he took a year off from work at one point to devote himself entirely to learning and improving.

Corn's idea for the Aces was born in New York City during the World Team Olympiad – the one where our team made it to the final but Don Krauss and I didn't get to play. Corn was in New York, watching the whole thing. No detail escaped his notice, and he was especially impressed with the Italians.

The partnerships on the Blue Team, he saw, were practiced and smooth as silk. The Italians were truly a team, not just a collection of talented individuals. The Blue Team was a well-oiled machine.

But there was more. Team members, Corn observed, were likable, outgoing – in other words, "personalities." At least, that was true for three of them – Garozzo, Belladonna and Forquet.

He admired the way the Italian bridge machine dominated a reasonably strong North American team, and Corn longed to see the United States duplicate that success at the bridge table. He could also see a suave, personable group of American players as key figures in the marketing of Aces products – card tables, books, you name it. To an extent, Corn had dollar signs in his eyes when he thought of the possibilities.

While the businessman in Corn salivated over the marketing opportunities, the patriot in Corn had a grand vision for American bridge. He longed to see the United States assemble a group of expert players and put them in a structured environment where they would work and practice and work and practice until they reached, even exceeded, the Italian standard of play. The Americans would be tough as nails and vanquish all comers – a juggernaut rolling to a world championship.

In Corn's dream, the players would dig in and practice playing bridge the way football teams practice screen plays and traps, the way basketball teams practice fast breaks, the way shortstops and second basemen practice double play drills. Corn's team would be a unit, with everyone working toward the same goal, willing to sacrifice egos for the good of the mission. In Corn's vision, the project would culminate with a scene where the Americans, not the Italians, hoisted the Bermuda Bowl trophy over their heads.

If it happened, it would be the first time in the history of bridge that such a team ascended to the pinnacle.

Of all the people who might have dreamed such a dream, Ira Corn had the wherewithal – and the determination – to make it happen.

Dorothy Moore, who got Corn into bridge, also led him to Bobby Wolff and the first discussions of the Aces. Dorothy was a friend and contemporary of Wolff, who was living in San Antonio at the time. Wolff and a fellow by the name of Joe Musumeci were running a bridge club and playing bridge professionally. It was Musumeci – "Moose" to most of his friends – who would become pivotal in the success of the Aces.

A year before our dinner meeting in Montreal, Dorothy had introduced Corn to Wolff in Pittsburgh. Just before the Summer Nationals in 1967, Corn and Wolff met again at a sectional tournament in Texas and had their first discussions of *The Team.*

Wolff had been around in the bridge world by then and he knew the talented players. Corn asked Wolff to put together some sketches of players he thought would be good candidates for his grand scheme.

That was how Eddie and I came to be having dinner with Corn, Wolff and Jacoby. Bobby and Jim had played against Kantar and to a lesser extent me over the course of several years at national and regional tournaments. I assume that their decision to approach me was based on something other than the Spingold match in 1963 in California.

Anyway, there we were, having dinner with Corn, listening to his pitch for us to join the Aces. At that point, besides Eddie and me, Corn had targeted Wolff and Jacoby as the cornerstones of his planned team. Bobby Goldman, Billy Eisenberg, Mike Lawrence, and a few others were viewed as possible recruits.

The concept of a full-time professional bridge team really appealed to me, but there were aspects of his plan that made me leery.

First of all, I didn't think Corn had the right lineup to make the concept work. With Wolff's advice, Corn had initially asked an entirely different set of players. One was Chuck Burger, a terrific player from Michigan, but he was just getting started in a law practice in Detroit and didn't want to take a chance on the Aces. Corn also had approached Sami Kehela, who, with Eric Murray, was half of Canada's most celebrated pair. Kehela did not want to leave Canada, however, so he also declined.

So Corn was assembling a team which included some second choices. Wolff was a first-class player, but I was dubious about the rest of them. I had played with Lawrence in California and I knew he had talent, but I thought he was somewhat of a project. Goldman and Jacoby, in my mind, weren't good enough. Eisenberg had many skills but was also a bit of a project. In other words, I thought Corn was starting with only one solid, first-round draft choice – Wolff. I didn't think the Aces – if, indeed, the team ever became a reality – had enough horsepower.

Then there was the Eddie Kantar factor. I had hedged a bit with Corn on joining the team, but Kantar outright vetoed the idea. Corn wanted all the players to move to Dallas so they could train together every day. Kantar was happy in California and had no desire to live in Texas.

By the summer of 1967, Eddie and I had been working on our partnership for several months and had just gotten to the point where we were functional. I thought about how hard we had worked to get to that point. If I up and left for Texas, all that work would be down the drain.

Another thing – I had just gotten started in the insurance business. I had married in 1966, and my wife Barbara wasn't particularly opposed to moving to Texas. She was a free spirit and the move would have suited her just fine. But I was still learning the ropes in the insurance trade – Sid Borden had helped me get started – and I was worried about giving up what was looking like a decent livelihood for Corn's iffy proposition.

As much as I liked Corn's style and panache, by the time the Fall Nationals in New Orleans rolled around, I gave Corn my answer: thanks but no thanks. Still, I thought I ought to keep my eye on the Aces just in case.

After I gave Corn my decision, he did not look elsewhere for another player. Corn decided *he* would play. The Aces would be a team of two threesomes – Corn-Jacoby-Wolff and Goldman-Eisenberg-Lawrence.

On Feb. 1, 1968, the experiment officially began as the team members arrived for work. Jacoby already lived in Dallas. Wolff had moved there from San Antonio. Goldman had thrown all his belongings into a car and driven in from Philadelphia. Eisenberg – "Broadway Billy" to some – came in from New York. Lawrence, from San Francisco, was the lone California representative on the team.

They all had contracts. The single men – Lawrence, Goldman and Eisenberg – were paid $800 a month. The married Aces, Jacoby and Wolff, were paid $1000 a month.

The "work" of being a member of the Aces entailed several duties. The first was to show up at the "office" – Corn's house – at least five days a week. The partnerships were to work on their agreements, fine-tuning where necessary, and practice their bidding. Corn didn't care what system team members played as long as they played something. He insisted that each partnership have a written system with supplementary notes which covered the set of agreements as to general philosophical procedures. Partnerships were expected to work on their systems diligently. They were required to know what they were doing.

Team members would play against each other and in special matches with strong teams that Corn would fly in. Once a month, the Aces would go to a tournament. Corn hired stenographers to record all the bids and plays the Aces made. The first part of the week following a tournament or practice match was spent going over each hand, analyzing virtually every card that was played. Players were given performance ratings after each session, be it a tournament, special match or just practice.

Corn provided the Aces with tape recorders, copying machines and access to a $2 million SDS 940 computer.

Corn believed it toughened the Aces to have them play against the best competitors. In one of the special matches, Corn flew in a team which included Marshall Miles, my old friend and Kantar's former partner. Marshall said, "This is my idea of dying and going to heaven – play bridge, eat and then go over the hands."

Wolff, Jacoby and Corn played a Strong Club system, while Goldman, Eisenberg and Lawrence played Eastern Scientific. It didn't take long for Corn to catch on to the fact that he wasn't going to realize his dream of a world championship if he continued to play. He was a reasonable player, but it's too difficult to take up bridge in your forties and expect to compete at the world level. It just can't be done. So the Aces quickly became a five-man team.

Wolff actually broached the subject of Corn's quitting for the good of the team. "Okay," said Corn, "but you better win, goddamit."

While Corn was the boss – he signed the paychecks, after all – he also knew he didn't have the bridge knowledge or experience to actually coach the team. That duty fell to Monroe Ingberman, a Chicago resident who was known mostly for his bidding theory. Corn liked him, however, possibly because he was a fellow alumnus of the University of Chicago, and Ingberman became coach of the Aces.

After a couple of months, the Aces went on tour, playing exhibition matches in various cities. Corn had them dress in matching orange blazers. He was spending big bucks on this project and he wanted to project an image that would garner some publicity for himself and the team. Truthfully, the idea of the Aces was so novel that the team was an item at most of the stops on the tour.

There were newspaper and magazine write-ups everywhere. Besides the novelty of the concept – and the fact that someone was still trying to pull it off – there was the nationalistic notion that it was time the Italians were divested of their hold on the world championship.

Unfortunately, although they looked snazzy in their matching blazers, the Aces weren't showing much in the bridge department.

At the Spring Nationals in New York City in 1968, the Aces got to the Round of 16 in the Vanderbilt, but they were knocked out by a team led by George Rosenkranz, who had a decent squad but by no means a powerhouse. My team – Eddie and me, Ira Rubin and Jeff Westheimer – came in second to Edgar Kaplan, Norman Kay and company.

Eisenberg and Goldman did win the Life Master Pairs at the Summer Nationals in Minneapolis later that year, but in my view the Aces were still a pretty underwhelming group.

Part of the problem was that, with the exception of Goldman, the work ethic Corn had hoped for was not exactly a fire burning in the bellies of the Aces. I wasn't on hand at the outset, of course, but from stories I've heard it was common practice for the Aces to show up at Corn's house, have someone utter the word "bridge," and then adjourn to the home of another wealthy bridge aficionado – Malcolm Brachman – for tennis and the swimming pool, maybe a little backgammon or ping pong. The Aces were approaching their new jobs in a decidedly casual fashion.

That may be an exaggeration, but you can be sure that the discipline needed to win a world title was not there initially.

I got a first-hand look at the Aces during 1968 when they hit Southern California for an exhibition match. The Aces were playing in a three-way round-robin event that was part of the Omar Sharif Bridge Circus, a traveling bridge show featuring the film star.

Sharif's team was himself, Giorgio Belladonna and Benito Garozzo of the Italian Blue Team; Claude Delmouly, a French bridge star, and Leon Yallouze, a very good Egyptian player. The other two squads were the Aces and my team, which was headed by Lew Mathe.

The four-day match, complete with vugraph, was staged at the Sportsman's Lodge in Studio City. For political reasons, it seemed like everyone on the planet was playing on Mathe's team. When the Aces played against the mugs on our team, the boys from Dallas did reasonably well. When we put our top lineup in, we had no trouble with the vaunted Corn Dream Team.

The Aces experiment was six months old and I had seen nothing to make me believe it was anything but a hopeless project. I congratulated myself for turning down the offer and thought no more about the Aces.

Until Atlantic City.

For years, it had been the custom for the world championship team trials to be held in the same city as the Fall Nationals, right before the big tournament started.

In 1968, the Fall Nationals were in Coronado, California (near San Diego) in late November. The team trials were in Atlantic City in late October.

As usual, the field was star-studded. The 16 pairs included Edgar Kaplan-Norman Kay, George Rapée-Sidney Lazard, Ira Rubin-Jeff Westheimer and B. Jay Becker-Dorothy Hayden (now Truscott). Eddie Kantar and I were there by virtue of our second-place finish in the Vanderbilt that year, as were our teammates, Rubin and Westheimer.

Four of the Aces were also among the competitors – Goldman-Eisenberg (for winning the Life Master Pairs) and Jacoby-Wolff (for coming in second in the same event). Until I went to Atlantic City to play in the trials, I still didn't think much of the Aces.

Everyone knew from the start that this was going to be the last trials that would be played as a pair event. In 1969, the trials would be between the winners of the Vanderbilt and the Spingold. The change was being made mostly for political reasons having to do with Edgar Kaplan, but that was neither here nor there to me at the time. All I knew was that the 1968 trials was going to be a grueling event.

There would be 24 sessions – 462 boards – played against some of the toughest competitors in the bridge world at the time. Scoring was on IMPs converted to Victory Points. There would be luck involved, certainly, but we expected the pairs playing the best to come out on top.

What I saw in Atlantic City made me sit up and take notice – especially what I saw of Eisenberg and Goldman. I had played against them several times since they joined the Aces, and I had been quite unfavorably impressed.

But in Atlantic City, the two guys who had been buffoons before were suddenly tough as nails. Eisenberg and Goldman started poorly, but they rallied strongly and easily made it to the final rounds – the top 10 pairs from the qualifying sessions played a round-robin of 28 boards against each of the other pairs. Also in the final: Wolff and Jacoby.

Kantar and I had started strongly and had a big lead. In fact, after nine of the 15 qualifying rounds, Eddie and I were nearly 100 Victory Points ahead of second. Our score after nine rounds would have been average for all 15 qualifying rounds. We finished as the qualifying leaders and took a carryover of 126 IMPs into the final.

Eddie and I finally came down to earth, but our carryover helped us to a third-place finish and a berth on the team that would play for the Bermuda Bowl in Rio de Janeiro, Brazil. Rapée and Lazard were first.

In second place were . . . Eisenberg and Goldman. All I could say was "Wow!" It wasn't as if they had trotted off to some regional to beat up on the weak sisters. They had knocked off some of the best bridge players around. Catch this action from their match against Kaplan and Kay in the final.

Kaplan and Kay were hot early in their match with Eisenberg and Goldman. After 10 boards, they were nearly 100 IMPs ahead. The two Aces didn't give up, however.

```
Dlr: West        ♠ 6 4 2
Vul: N-S         ♥ 7 2
                 ♦ Q 10 5 3
                 ♣ K 9 7 2
♠ Q 10 9 7 5                      ♠ J
♥ K 9                             ♥ 6 3
♦ K 9 6 2                         ♦ A J 8 7 4
♣ 10 8                           ♣ A Q 6 4 3
                 ♠ A K 8 3
                 ♥ A Q J 10 8 5 4
                 ♦ —
                 ♣ J 5
```

WEST	NORTH	EAST	SOUTH
Eisenberg	*Kay*	*Goldman*	*Kaplan*
Pass	Pass	1♦	4♥
All Pass			

Eisenberg showed remarkable discipline over Kaplan's 4♥ bid. At every other table, West bid – 4♠ or 5♦. Obviously, 4♠ has no chance. 5♦ makes only on double-dummy lines.

Eisenberg led a low diamond against 4♥. Kaplan ruffed and tried to cash the top spades. Goldman ruffed and returned a trump. Kaplan finished down three for minus 300. Eisenberg's excellent decision to pass gained his side 30 IMPs in the scoring method used (each pair's result on a board was compared and IMPed against the results at all the other tables; the score was determined by totaling the plus and minus IMPs).

More bad things happened and Kaplan-Kay were on the ropes when this deal arose.

```
Dlr: East        ♠ A 10
Vul: E-W         ♥ A K Q 6
                 ♦ 8
                 ♣ A Q 10 7 6 5
♠ Q 7                            ♠ 6 5 4 3
♥ J 7 3 2                        ♥ 10 9 8 5
♦ A J 10 6 2                     ♦ Q 7 4
♣ K 8                            ♣ 4 2
                 ♠ K J 9 8 2
                 ♥ 4
                 ♦ K 9 5 3
                 ♣ J 9 3
```

WEST	NORTH	EAST	SOUTH
Eisenberg	*Kay*	*Goldman*	*Kaplan*
		Pass	Pass
Pass	1♣	Pass	1♠
Pass	2♥	Pass	2♠
Pass	4♠	All Pass	

Eisenberg got off to the diabolical lead of the *eight of clubs!* What could Kaplan do? This looked like a singleton. Finessing at trick one was tantamount to giving up on the contract. So Kaplan rose with the ace, played the top three hearts, pitching clubs, and played a diamond to the king.

Eisenberg won the ♦A and coolly returned the ♠7, taken in dummy with the 10. Now Kaplan ruffed dummy's last heart with the ♠8, ruffed a diamond in dummy with the ace and then ruffed a club with the ♠9. Kaplan must have grimaced when he saw the ♣K appear from Eisenberg's hand. Kaplan, whose trump suit was down to the K-J alone, got out with a diamond. Goldman won and returned a trump. The debacle was complete when Kaplan put in the jack and lost to Eisenberg's singleton queen.

That gained Eisenberg-Goldman another 14 IMPs and they won the match, 58 VPs to 26, after being down by nearly 100 IMPs at one point.

When it was all over, I looked at the final standings: Rapée-Lazard, 552.5; Eisenberg-Goldman, 516.5; Hamman-Kantar, 504.5.

Then and there, I made a decision. I said to myself, "Methinks I better jump aboard the Aces ship because I want to play bridge. I want to win myself a world championship."

I knew I would be seeing Ira Corn in Coronado in about a month. I knew that I was going to talk to him about joining the Aces. What I didn't know right away was how and why the Aces had become so tough all of a sudden.

The answer, I found out later, was simple. The difference was a retired Air Force lieutenant colonel named Joseph Musumeci. Moose had made his presence felt.

8

Moose

If I were asked to select the one most important reason for the team's success in the past year, I would have to go with our performance analysis system. Not because it is so great, not because it is without fault, but because it hits you where home is.

You are made uncomfortable for your sins at the bridge table. Rationalize all you want to, you are not kidding the group. You might kid me. You might kid yourself. But you're not kidding the group!

Lazy performance, impulsiveness – all the sins – there they be for everyone to see. You don't like it. You are not supposed to like it. You would be masochistic if you did like it! Hate it if you must. But at least accept it for what it is intended to be: a system whose only aim is better team performance.

– From a memo to the Aces by Joe Musumeci.

One night during the summer of 1968, Joe Musumeci got a call at his home in San Antonio. It was Bobby Wolff telephoning from Dallas. Also on the line was Ira Corn. During parts of the conversation with Wolff and Corn, Musumeci had trouble hearing over the noise in the background from the Dallas end.

It was the Aces arguing with each other.

"We want you to come to Dallas and coach the team," said Wolff.

Musumeci thought they were kidding, but he accepted anyway. Practically before anyone could say "boo," Musumeci had arrived at

Corn's mansion in Dallas to introduce himself. At Ira's suggestion, Joe met with each member of the team. No one outright blackballed Musumeci, so he was hired as the team's coach. It was just what Corn wanted – and just what the team needed.

In the pre-Moose days, the Aces were disorganized. Things were pretty loose and the team had no real direction. Goldman and Eisenberg, who viewed the Aces as an opportunity, worked hard on their partnership. Wolff and Jacoby, however, played what you might call American go-as-you-please – about what you might play if you went into a rubber bridge club somewhere and cut a partner. It wasn't a system they had to work hard at.

Monroe Ingberman was nominally coach of the team, but he lived in Chicago and his activities were pretty much limited to flying down to Dallas once in a while to give the team a quiz or a pep talk.

Corn was often busy with his companies, but he was no dummy. He could see that the Aces needed help, particularly in the area of discipline. Corn wanted Wolff to assume the role of team disciplinarian, but Wolff didn't want it. When Corn insisted that the team needed someone, Wolff thought of Musumeci, his longtime associate.

Wolffie and Moose had met while Musumeci was stationed in San Antonio during his 21-year career in the U.S. Air Force. Musumeci was a tough-looking, bald-headed Italian with a good understanding of how to win at bridge. He was also hard-nosed with just the right people skills for the Aces – he didn't kid around, and if he took a job he was serious about it.

Musumeci was born and raised in Brooklyn. He was attending Brooklyn College when war broke out in Europe in the late 1930s. Moose had aspirations to be a pilot, but he made a big mistake during his physical for flight school – he told a doctor he had fainted once as a child. His dreams of flying airplanes ended right there.

Still, he had a long and successful career as an officer, and when he retired in 1960, he was a lieutenant colonel. He settled in San Antonio, and he and Wolff bought a bridge club. They had met during the early 1950s in San Antonio – during a bridge game, naturally – and had been friends ever since.

Wolff knew that Musumeci – a no-bullshit kind of guy – was just the man to take charge of the floundering Aces.

From the moment Moose showed up in Dallas, things changed for the Aces. All of a sudden, the training routine was structured. From the beginning, the players had been expected to show up for bidding practice or skull sessions, to work on their bidding systems and agreements. Musumeci made sure they did.

The players didn't always like the changes, and sometimes Moose had his hands full, but they responded. They might have groused about the discipline, but deep down they knew he was right. They knew he was teaching them a winning philosophy.

One remarkable aspect of Musumeci's accomplishment is that he turned the Aces around without being their superior – even their equal – as a bridge player. Moose was – and is – a good bridge player, but he wasn't in the same league as the players he was managing. If he had been, he would have been on the team. What Musumeci had was a plan – and the will to execute it.

The single most important element of Moose's plan was the system he devised for performance review – as he put it, "accurate measurement of performance." In other words, how could the Aces identify weaknesses, take steps to eliminate the weaknesses and provide incentive for maximum effort?

It all revolved around sessions involving the Aces themselves – sessions they would have after practice matches or tournaments. With no one else involved, except maybe Corn or the venerable Oswald Jacoby on occasion, the Aces would meet for hours. Every hand that was played – and often every card of certain hands – would be reviewed.

During those sessions, team members assessed each other demerits – called "charges" – for bids and plays that didn't work out – that lost IMPs for the team.

Charges came in three colors – black, white and gray. A black charge was assessed for some bid or play that everyone – all the other Aces, that is – considered unreasonable. Getting a black charge was not good. A white charge came when IMPs were lost but everyone said they would have done the same thing. All the other charges were gray – in between reasonable and foolhardy or just plain stupid.

For example, if one of the Aces doubled 4♠ and the contract made and IMPs were lost, someone got a charge. If it was a rash, impulsive double, the player might get a black charge. If the doubler's partner goaded him into it with a bad bid, the doubler's partner might get the charge. Even if it was a perfectly reasonable double that didn't work out, the doubler would get a white charge – an acknowledgment that reasonable bridge was played. But at the very least it was on record that some IMPs got away.

A record of the charges and who got them was kept on a blackboard for all to see during the team meetings. Naturally, with the Aces themselves voting on charges against their teammates, egos could be bruised and tension sometimes mounted. Moose was there to make sure things didn't get out of hand.

"Charges" weren't the only things listed on the board. There was also a list of Musumeci's "Seven Deadly Sins" and the names of Aces who had committed one or more of them. This was one of Musumeci's innovations for assuring that the Aces engaged in sound bridge practices at all times.

It was his idea that the team would function best if the members policed themselves – if they were their own toughest critics. He reasoned that if each player had to take responsibility for his actions and justify them to the team if they didn't work out, the result would be much less freelancing and much more team play.

It sounds almost facetious to describe the principles as the Seven Deadly Sins, but it was a very serious aspect of the Aces' regimen. These were the sins:

The Seven Deadly Sins
1. Bidding without values.
2. System violations.
3. Unilateral actions.
4. No-win declarer play.
5. No-win defensive play.
6. Impulsive plays.
7. Mechanical errors (pulling the wrong card, revoking, etc.).

Avoiding the first three sins was very important for maintaining partnership confidence and harmony. Moose never let the team forget this principle.

Moose stressed the importance of team members being physically fit, well-rested and alert when it was time to do battle. He especially preached against overeating. Joe believed that too much food before a session clouded a player's mind and fostered errors of all kinds, particularly mechanical errors.

In a letter describing this philosophy, Musumeci once wrote, "One player who had gorged himself on food and chocolate mousse broke the record for black charges at one evening session. Light meals are not only better for your health, they also help your game."

Musumeci made sure that drinking was strictly regulated when the Aces were in competition. No player could drink alcohol within eight hours of any session – that was an inviolate rule. After a night session, a player could have a maximum of two single drinks. If any player broke the rule, he was fined $50 for the first offense. The second offense brought a 30-day suspension.

It was the same with curfew. Players were to be in their rooms by 2 a.m. Violations were very serious offenses.

The Aces felt like they were in boot camp, and that wasn't far from the truth. After I joined the team, there was even an attempt to have us engage in physical training. At one point Moose had us out jogging around a track. That didn't last long, as you can imagine. You've never seen so many "bad knees" and "sore backs." We were not your basic fitness nuts. Nuts, yes, but not in a fitness sense.

I'm sure Musumeci traded on his experience as an Air Force officer in deciding how things would be with the team. Soldiers and sailors are trained on strict discipline and the concept of team play – all for one and one for all. That's not just a cliché. It's a principle with profound importance in many settings.

It is worth noting that Moose didn't get his notions strictly from his Air Force days. He was also a veteran bridge player with enough experience to know what it takes to win consistently. It wasn't as if Corn had hired some grizzled old war veteran who didn't know beans about bridge. Musumeci knew what it would take to turn a disparate group of individuals into a winning team. He had the courage of his convictions and the backing of the boss man – Ira G. Corn, the guy who was paying the salaries.

So there they were – the new, improved Aces. The team I wanted to join. When Corn and I had another discussion at the Fall Nationals in Coronado, he invited me to join the team. Since Jacoby and Wolff had paired up and Eisenberg and Goldman were also a regular partnership, Lawrence had been the odd man out for most of the time the Aces had been together. It was natural that the newest partnership on the team would be Hamman and Lawrence.

After Barbara and I discussed my joining the Aces – she thought it was a fine idea – I broke the news to Eddie Kantar. I was sorry to be dissolving what was turning into a pretty good partnership, but I had never viewed bridge partnerships as the key component of winning at the highest level. The first seven times I played in world championships, I had seven different partners.

Anyway, in January of 1969, Barbara and I stuffed our meager possessions – mostly clothes – and our 16-month-old son, Chris, into our 1969 Ford and headed for Texas. I was still selling insurance, so when we rented a three-bedroom apartment in Dallas I got a separate business line so I could continue the insurance work. I was supposed to be at the Aces' "office" to work on bridge starting at noon each day, so I spent my mornings trying to build up my insurance business.

The Aces' office was Chateau Corn, a mansion on Forest Lane in an exclusive section of Dallas. We started out in his big living room, where there were tables and a copying machine. At one point the workplace was moved to an actual office on Sherry Lane a few miles from Corn's house, to another office in North Dallas and eventually back to the Corn home, to which he had added a wing for the Aces meetings.

When I showed up for work at Chateau Corn, I felt at ease right away. I knew all the players from seeing them at tournaments and playing against them. Corn had flown me in on occasion to practice against the Aces, so I knew the house pretty well. And I had met Musumeci about a year before in California.

I knew before I joined the team that something had changed the Aces from wimps to tigers, but I didn't know how it had been achieved.

The gloves-off sessions, managed by Musumeci, were the key. We reviewed the hands that we played in special matches, regionals or just practice. Moose had his chart and he would start off with a lecture about "losing practices." It wasn't long before someone was targeted for having committed some bridge sin or other – sometimes more than one.

It was interesting to observe the personalities of the other five members and how they handled the peer pressure and being roughed up verbally by their teammates. I was a natural for these sessions because I'm a born needler and I have a pretty thick skin. Also, I don't mind admitting when I've done something dumb. I can take abuse for my crimes.

Two of the Aces – Wolff and Jacoby – didn't like it when the mistake spotlight turned on them. Jacoby was basically lazy, although he was a strangely effective player. He had more talent than anybody ever acknowledged and he was a very tough competitor. On the other hand, he had curious blind spots. Sometimes he would lapse into a rote approach to the game – and he didn't like to be criticized. When he was the target in one of the Aces' meetings, he often reacted emotionally. If he got a "charge" for some offense, he might react by retaliating with a "black charge" against his accuser later in the meeting. Since Jacoby was often leading the pack in criticizing some-one, he often was the target himself.

Wolff, a naturally gifted player, also was uncomfortable when he was the target of criticism. He did what he could to keep the sessions from turning into dogfights, especially if he was going to be on the receiving end of some of the abuse.

Eisenberg, on the other hand, was big on pontificating. His errors, he sometimes argued, were "errors in judgment arising from extremely high-level considerations." Billy felt that he looked at situations differently than the rest of us. Of course we didn't let him get away with such balderdash.

When Billy was arguing that leading the queen from AQxxx in a suit was the right lead even though he caught partner with a singleton king in the suit, we would shout him down. Once we convinced him that these "high-level considerations" seldom created good results, he improved tremendously. He cut down on his errors by a greater percentage than any other member of the team.

Lawrence was tall and lanky with an air of boredom that masked a terribly shy person. Although he was a very talented card player, Mike didn't say much and he disliked being in the criticism spotlight.

Lawrence will be the first to tell you, however, that his experience with Corn and the Aces made his career in bridge.

He wrote his first book, *How to Read Your Opponents' Cards*, at Corn's urging. The book remains a classic in bridge literature. Lawrence also learned to relate to people better as part of his experience with the team.

Then there was Goldman. In his own way, Bobby is as interesting a character as Corn. Years after the breakup of the Aces, Goldman remains one of the top professional players on the circuit. He and Paul Soloway form one of the best partnerships in the world.

At the time he was recruited for the Aces, Goldman was playing rubber bridge in Philadelphia and operating a business that imported women to work as maids. He was having some trouble with the government at the time, so you might say he was ripe for a change in career. Beyond that, however, Goldman was perceptive enough to see the Aces as a great opportunity. Goldman saw that Corn's environment would give him a chance to become the kind of player others only dream of.

Like many of the Aces, Goldman had dropped out of college – Drexel University in Philadelphia – after learning bridge. Always an athletic person, and still an avid tennis player, Goldman has boyish good looks that conceal his age.

When Corn conceived the idea of the Aces, he had never heard of Goldman. But Wolffie talked Corn into recruiting Billy, and Billy brought Goldman's name up. In fact, it was Eisenberg who sold Corn and Wolff on Goldman for the team.

It turned out to be a great move. In many ways, Goldman was the heart and soul of the group therapy sessions in which the Aces tore each other apart. While they were bashing each other, they also laid waste to all the flimsy excuses that were offered by the perpetrators for their bad bridge. At times, the sessions were gut-wrenching. There were occasions when there were five people yelling as they honed in on the sixth person to convince him that a play or bid he made was stupid or sloppy – or just plain crazy.

It was Goldman's drive for perfection that helped make the Aces' team meetings work so well. Bobby was a truth-seeker and a relentless analyst. When an issue remained unresolved, Goldman would not let the group move on to a new topic until we had worked out a solution.

He wasn't particularly interested in proving that his view was correct. He was interested in the truth, even if it proved that his original position was wrong. Bobby was like a dog with a bone – he would chew an issue until there was nothing left.

Goldman, who was familiar with computers, wrote a program to deal hands for bidding practice. He also used that skill to analyze certain bidding situations – he would spend hours working with the computer trying to find an answer.

His theory on what the Aces should do concerning bidding systems came up during a team meeting. There was a heated exchange, with Goldman and Eisenberg on one side and Wolff and Jacoby on the other.

Wolff and Jacoby complained that Goldman and Eisenberg, playing a rather complex variation of Eastern Scientific, were having a lot of accidents in the bidding. Goldman and Eisenberg complained that Wolff and Jacoby had *no* system, that they were more interested in getting to their backgammon games. Goldman and Eisenberg didn't think Jacoby and Wolff were taking things seriously enough.

The argument got pretty heated before Goldman took the floor.

Addressing Wolff and Jacoby, Goldman began, "If our objective is to win a tournament of some kind next month, then you guys are right. Doing what Billy and I are doing, taking two steps forward and one step back, is not a winner for the short term.

"If, on the other hand, our objective is to win a world championship a year from now, the question is, 'How can we be playing our best bridge a year from now?' I think we have to go into it very deeply and suffer the bad results that inevitably occur when complex approaches to problem solving are utilized. If we are willing to pay our dues by using this complex approach to our problems, after a period it will all sort out. At that stage, we'll be bidding as well as we can."

Corn, swayed by that argument, eventually insisted that Wolff and Jacoby quit their go-as-you-please approach. That was when they started playing a strong 1♣ system.

Occasionally the Aces would have late-night meetings in Ira Corn's bedroom. The meetings were informal in a way, but Corn didn't object if anyone wanted to bring up anything serious. It was a good place for team members to air their gripes.

Corn enjoyed watching the team work and progress, and he liked taking part in the discussions, sitting on a king-size bed in his red bathrobe. One night, the team had been meeting for hours and everyone was ready to call it a day. Someone said, "Well, I guess that's it."

That was when Goldman pulled several sheets of paper out of his back pocket. "I've got a few things I'd like to bring up," Bobby said to a chorus of groans. He got to say his piece, though.

The peer pressure generated during the Aces' meetings was remarkably effective. You couldn't get away with some bullshit excuse for doing something lazy or stupid when five guys were ganging up on you. Sometimes we were pretty tough on the offender.

"What was going through your alleged mind on *that* play?" one of us might say to an offender who had committed the deadly sin of no-win declarer play.

I discovered that my talent for needling was very handy during the sessions. I was good at giving it to a team member in such a way that I made my point without getting him overly upset.

One of my biggest gripes was about players not bidding their games.

Through the years I have formed a theory about the importance of bidding game. For one thing, it puts a lot of pressure on the opponents. If you're playing 2NT and the defense gets sloppy and lets you make an overtrick or two, it usually doesn't mean much. But if you're in 3NT and they misdefend, suddenly they're looking at a minus position – maybe 10 or 12 IMPs. By bidding game, you're making the defenders play for higher stakes. That kind of pressure can wear some players down.

Look at it this way: If you beat a guy in a game he overbid to, you don't feel like you've gained all that much. But if he overbids to game and you let him make it, you know there's a big potential loss. You feel worse than just the IMPs you lost.

Anyway, it seemed like Goldman and Eisenberg were forever bidding all the way to *two* notrump and making three. During the team meeting, I'd be on their case. "I'm so tired of you guys missing game I can't stand it," I said one time after they had scored 150 for about the eighth straight time in 2NT. "Are you aware there's a bonus for bidding game?"

Of course I got some of that back from time to time, but it was part of the program as far as I was concerned. Those sessions were not picnics, and they weren't meant to be. They were designed to make us tough, to help the Aces eliminate thoughtless, stupid errors.

In general, team camaraderie was good, even if we were at each other's throats much of the time. In general, we rooted for each other and had a sense that we truly were a team. After all, Ira had done a good job of selling us on the concept of the Aces, and there weren't any among us who didn't hunger for the chance to win the big one.

By the summer of 1969, the team was beginning to gel. The losing practices were slowly but surely being abandoned. The partnerships were really humming. When Corn brought in good teams for us to practice against, we absolutely dismantled them. They never had a chance against us. We were defeating teams composed of top players by 100 or more IMPs.

The overwhelming success we had against these good teams made us more determined to get the most out of our training and practice sessions. We could see where the hard work was taking us – and it felt good. It was an awesome feeling to be a member of the Aces during that period.

We showed everyone that the Aces were for real at the Summer Nationals in Los Angeles. That was when we won the Spingold the way no other team ever won the event – before or since.

9

The juggernaut

LATE ON A Sunday night in August of 1969, I was standing outside a ballroom at the Ambassador Hotel in Los Angeles. Yes, this was the same hotel where, more than 10 years before, Ralph Clark and I had played in our first Nationals. It was one of the events that started everything for me. It felt so good to win, even if it was just a side game, that I never wanted to stop.

Now, here I was, along with my teammates – the Aces – and Moose, our non-playing captain. Basically, we were twiddling our thumbs along with 20 or 30 other people. All of us were interested in what was going to happen next in the Spingold Knockout Teams.

It was the Summer Nationals and our team had rolled to the semifinals of the Spingold. But there had been a foul-up in the third quarter and all four semifinal teams had played the wrong boards. Now we were cooling our heels while a tournament committee decided what to do. We were playing a four-man squad whose captain was Maury Genud. The Aces had run roughshod over them and they weren't in a particularly good humor to find that the third quarter probably wouldn't count.

I eyed Genud with interest. He was a strange bird. He started out as a little fat guy and ended up as a little skinny guy – and he was always lecturing people about their weight. He had the evangelical fervor of a reformed alcoholic. Naturally, he was on my case occasionally about the virtues of a slender physique.

Genud lived in Los Angeles, where he was a child psychologist and a teacher. He was a pretty good bridge player, too, and a fairly likable fellow despite his skinnier-than-thou temperament. In the Spingold, he was playing with a fellow named Ron Garber, a biochemistry professor. Ron and I always got along pretty well even though we needled each other quite a bit when we played as opponents. One of my biggest laughs in tournament bridge came at Ron's expense a few years after the Summer Nationals in Los Angeles.

I was playing in a Bridge Week Knockout with Ron Von der Porten against Garber and a partner I don't remember. Garber always kept up a running commentary during the play – usually designed to annoy the opponents – and on this occasion he landed a few figurative jabs and chalked up a few IMPs on the first four or five boards.

Then Von der Porten and I perpetrated an auction that landed us in a grand slam – we obviously didn't know what we were doing. Well, Garber, on lead with an ace, chose not to table it – for whatever reason. As luck would have it, I had 13 tricks when he didn't cash the ace. Well, now it was our turn at bat, and Von der Porten and I decided to give Garber some of what he had been dishing out earlier.

"You know, Ron," I said to Von der Porten, winking, "at least we know these guys don't have lead signals."

An eerie silence fell over the table. I turned to Garber and asked to see his hand. I spotted the ace and said to Von der Porten, "I take that back. We don't know that these guys are honest – just that they're stupid."

"Hey," Garber protested to his partner, "I trusted them."

"Well," I offered, "the proof is in the pudding." The match was much more enjoyable after that.

But back to the 1969 Spingold. Going into the event, we were feeling some pressure. We had lost in the Vanderbilt and we were fearful that if we didn't do well in the Spingold, Ira might scrap the whole experiment. Not that he had said anything to that effect – just the opposite. For all his foibles, Corn was magnificent in defeat. When we lost the Vanderbilt, he didn't whimper or whine or make excuses – he simply said, "We'll get 'em next time." But we still felt that Corn's patience might be wearing thin. We felt that we needed to win in Los Angeles.

By the time we got to the semifinals, however, any pressure we felt had long since dissipated. In fact, we weren't even worried about what the tournament committee would do regarding the fouled-up third quarter. To that point, we had owned the Spingold and all the competitors in it. Going into the semifinals, we had won every match by more than 100 IMPs. In every contest, we had taken our opponents apart with disdain, as though they were cluttering up our event. And I'm not talking about dogmeat here – the Spingold has always attracted a strong field.

In the quarterfinals, we played a team led by the legendary Waldemar von Zedtwitz. We destroyed them. Our margin of victory was 109 IMPs, an incredible sum against competition of that caliber.

At the halfway point of our match against Genud – who was playing with Garber, Henry Bethe and Mike Ledeen – we were leading by more than 100 IMPs.

In the third quarter, we battered them some more and then gathered to compare scores.

That was when we found out about *The Accident*.

The two semifinal matches had been going on simultaneously – ours and the match between the teams captained by Ira Rubin and Howard Schenken. Maury Braunstein, the tournament director who was running the Spingold had been called away to confer with Al Sobel, the chief director, so one of Maury's assistants made the board exchanges halfway through the third quarter. He passed them to the wrong tables!

Nowadays, teams in national events play the same sets of hands when they get to the late stages, so a mistake like that would not be a big deal. In 1969, however, everyone shuffled and dealt their own hands. So when the director brought boards to our table – I was playing with Mike Lawrence against Genud and Garber – the boards we got were from the Rubin-Schenken match. Similarly, Rubin-Schenken got their boards from our match.

Naturally, when we compared with our teammates, the results made no sense. ("Four hearts!! How could they make four hearts?!? We had 10 hearts between us!!") We quickly discovered what had happened.

A tournament committee, trying to decide what to do, met for an hour and a half before reaching a decision. Ironically, the same thing had happened in the Vanderbilt at the Spring Nationals in Cleveland earlier that year.

While we waited, Phil Feldesman of the Rubin team compared results with Eisenberg and Goldman, who had played the boards Feldesman's teammates were supposed to have played. I got a kick out of the fact that Feldesman was annoyed at Goldman and Eisenberg, who weren't even his teammates, for getting a bad result on a board Feldesman thought he had won.

Anyway, it was after midnight by the time the committee made a decision.

Braunstein sheepishly approached the milling crowd and said, "You're going to have to replay the third quarter," he said.

Genud blew his stack. "YOU can play them," he said to Braunstein. "We quit."

It was hard to blame them. Genud and his teammates had already endured three quarters of being pasted by the Aces. If they replayed the third quarter and then played the fourth, that would be *five* quarters of being drubbed. Genud, Garber, Bethe and Ledeen were demoralized, tired and already beaten. They didn't want any more.

Now Sam Stayman, a member of Rubin's team, started moaning. "This isn't fair," he whined. "Now they (meaning us – the Aces) are going to be rested. They can go to bed."

Well, I thought, what are we supposed to do when our opponents quit? Go out and run five miles? Heck, Stayman and his crew hadn't even won their match at that point, so he was taking quite a bit for granted. Actually, Stayman's team did defeat Schenken after starting the third quarter *again* at 1 a.m. My heart bled for Sam.

Anyway, the upshot of the whole silly episode was that the final was postponed half a day.

The next day, the Aces were sitting around waiting to get started when we heard a knock on the door. When I opened the door, there was a bellhop with a package.

The package was white butcher paper with one word on it – written in red lipstick: "Kill." We found out later it had been sent by Mike Shuman's wife, Kay, who was a fan of ours.

I opened the package and found a big hunk of raw meat. I thought, 'What the hell?' I took a chunk out of the meat with my teeth. Then I passed it to the next Ace. I don't remember how many of them ate with me that day, but it seems like most of them were kind of squeamish.

The symbolism was appropriate, however. The Aces were out to devour the opposition – which we did.

The Aces defeated the No. 1 seed – Ira Rubin, Sam Stayman, Phil Feldesman, Vic Mitchell, Bill Grieve and Jeff Westheimer – by 95 IMPs. They were never in the match.

We were up by 29 IMPs after one quarter and Rubin, who had been playing with Westheimer, decided to make a switch and play with Feldesman. They hadn't played together in two years, but Rubin was trying to create some action, trying to do something to turn the tide.

It didn't work.

Here is one of the early deals. It was a small swing, but it set the tone.

```
Dlr: West      ♠ K 4
Vul: N-S       ♥ K Q 10
               ♦ J 9 6 2
               ♣ Q 8 6 3
♠ A J 10 9 6              ♠ 7 5 3
♥ 8 6                     ♥ J 7 5 3 2
♦ A K 8 7                 ♦ 5 3
♣ A 9                     ♣ J 7 4
               ♠ Q 8 2
               ♥ A 9 4
               ♦ Q 10 4
               ♣ K 10 5 2
```

At one table:

WEST	NORTH	EAST	SOUTH
Goldman	*Feldesman*	*Eisenberg*	*Grieve*
1♠	Pass	Pass	1NT
Pass	2NT	All Pass	

Goldman led the ♦K and switched to the ♠J, taken in dummy by the king. Grieve then played a diamond to his queen, and Goldman took full advantage of the error. Bobby won the ♦A and played the ♠A and ♠10, driving out the queen. Goldman and Eisenberg thus had six tricks (three spades, two diamonds and the ♣A) before Grieve could get eight.

Here's what happened at our table:

WEST	NORTH	EAST	SOUTH
Rubin	*Lawrence*	*Westheimer*	*Me*
1♠	Pass	Pass	1NT
2♦	Pass	2♠	Pass
Pass	2NT	All Pass	

Rubin led the ♠J and I won the king in dummy. Instead of attacking diamonds, however, I worked on clubs. I was virtually certain Rubin had the ♣A, and since Rubin had shown at least nine cards in spades and diamonds in the bidding, I also figured he was short in clubs, possibly a singleton.

So I played a heart to my hand and a low club toward the table. Rubin hopped up with the ace, cleared spades and waited with his diamond entries. He had to wait, however, until I had cashed my eight tricks.

It was only a 6-IMP pickup – not that you should sneeze at 6-IMP gains. A pile of medium-sized gains like that can add up to a blitz just as easily as bombs like game and slam swings. This was the story of the Aces. We outgunned the competition in every phase. If we had to, we could IMP them to death.

Here was a swing of the large variety:

```
Dlr: North        ♠ J
Vul: Both         ♥ Q J 9 7 6 5
                  ♦ J 8 5 3
                  ♣ 7 3
♠ K Q 10 5 4 3                        ♠ 6
♥ 3 2                                 ♥ A 10
♦ 9                                   ♦ K Q 7 6 2
♣ J 9 8 6                             ♣ A Q 10 5 4
                  ♠ A 9 8 7 2
                  ♥ K 8 4
                  ♦ A 10 4
                  ♣ K 2
```

WEST	NORTH	EAST	SOUTH
Goldman	*Feldesman*	*Eisenberg*	*Grieve*
	Pass	1♦	1♠
Pass	Pass	2♣	All Pass

Eisenberg had no trouble making 3♣. Plus 110 to the Aces.
The auction was much more interesting at our table.

WEST	NORTH	EAST	SOUTH
Rubin	*Lawrence*	*Westheimer*	*Me*
	Pass	1♦	1♠
Pass	Pass	Dbl	Pass
Pass	2♥	Pass	Pass
2♠	Pass	3♣	3♥
Pass	4♥	Dbl	All Pass

Westheimer's decision to reopen the bidding with a double – in case partner was lying in wait with a spade stack over me – was what turned the course of the auction in our favor. Mike couldn't sit for the double and he had a decent heart suit, so he introduced it. When the bidding heated up, I was happy to raise hearts with my hand, so Mike decided to try for the vulnerable game.

Westheimer was outraged that we were stopping in a partscore one moment and were in game the next. He doubled furiously and emotionally. Allowing emotion to cloud his judgment cost his team dearly. Had he led the ♦K, Mike would have gone down. Westheimer could win the first round of hearts, cash the ♦Q and give his partner a ruff. The ♣A would have been the setting trick.

But Westheimer, not thinking clearly because of his rage over our bidding, led the ♥A and continued with a heart, trying to reduce the number of ruffs in dummy. That was plus 790 for the Aces and a net gain of 14 IMPs.

Not everything was rosy for our team. We lost a few IMPs here and there, but you know things are going your way when you screw up and still gain IMPs. Mike and I had a bidding misunderstanding on these cards:

Me		Mike
♠ J 2		♠ A K 6
♥ 3		♥ A Q 9 7 6 2
♦ A J 9 8 7		♦ K Q
♣ A J 10 7 6		♣ 5 2

Me		Mike
1♦	(1♠)	2♥
3♣		3♦
Pass		#@!!??

Obviously, Mike thought 3♦ was forcing. When he put dummy down, he said sarcastically: "I think you'll make it." Although both red suits broke 5-1, I still took 11 tricks. At the other table, Mitchell and Stayman bid the same hands this way:

Vic		Sam
Pass	(1♠)	Dbl
3♦		4♥
Pass		

The 5-1 heart split doomed Stayman's silly contract, so the Aces gained 5 IMPs despite the missed game. After all my ranting and raving about missing games, this board was a hot topic when we had our team meeting back in Dallas. The fact that we won the event took a little of the sting out of the jibes I took.

We had a 46-IMP lead going into the fourth quarter. Not a tremendous edge – and certainly not insurmountable for a team of Rubin's caliber – but we were confident. As it happened, the boards were flat. Our margin increased to 95 IMPs by the time it was over because Rubin and his gang were trying to create swings where there weren't any. We got 20 IMPs on crazy games bid by Rubin – all of them down. On another board, Stayman played for a swing by trying to drop a singleton king offside with three cards out. The king was onside – doubleton.

The biggest swing occurred on the last board of the match.

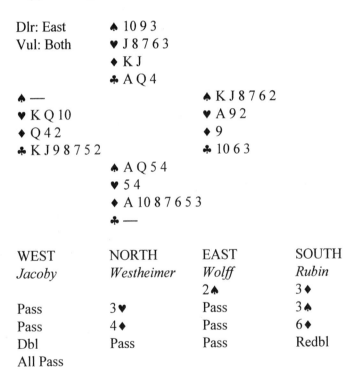

WEST	NORTH	EAST	SOUTH
Jacoby	*Westheimer*	*Wolff*	*Rubin*
		2♠	3♦
Pass	3♥	Pass	3♠
Pass	4♦	Pass	6♦
Dbl	Pass	Pass	Redbl
All Pass			

Rubin's redouble was another attempt to create IMPs out of thin air. It was as futile as the other shots. Jacoby led the ♥K and continued with a heart to Wolff's ace. A spade switch was ruffed and Rubin was down 1000.

At our table:

WEST	NORTH	EAST	SOUTH
Stayman	*Lawrence*	*Mitchell*	*Me*
		2♠	3♦
Pass	3♠	Pass	5♦
Dbl	All Pass		

What a difference an opening lead can make! Look what happened when Stayman tracked a low club instead of the ♥K. I put in the queen, pitching one heart, and cashed the ace, pitching my other heart. This was followed by a heart ruff to my hand and a low diamond to dummy's jack. I cashed the ♦K, ruffed another heart to my hand and cashed the trump ace. Now it was easy to cash my ♠A and concede two spade tricks. Mike's 10 and 9 of spades were great cards, allowing me to avoid three spade losers.

Plus 750 at one table and plus 1000 at the other was worth 18 IMPs.

We knew we were the best team going in. Winning the Spingold proved we were right, especially the way we won it. Ira was beside himself with joy – and we were feeling pretty good, too.

It was the most impressive win by the Aces so far – and it solidified our position as the team to beat in any match of more than a few boards. As they say in betting circles, when the Aces were playing, we were "the chalk" – the absolute favorites.

To the Aces, the most important aspect of the Spingold victory was that it put us in the trials to represent North America in the 1970 Bermuda Bowl in Stockholm, Sweden. It would be the Aces against the team that had won the 1969 Vanderbilt in Cleveland – Dick Walsh, Gerald Hallee, Paul Soloway and John Swanson. We had a date with them in Phoenix in late October for a 180-board match, winner take all. We couldn't wait.

Looking back, there is considerable irony associated with the whole issue of trials and selection processes in that time period. I laugh when I think about it.

Throughout the history of the trials to pick U.S. or North American teams for international competition, the selection process has changed constantly, from team trials to pair trials and many variations in between, including direct selection. From 1962 through 1968, the team was made up of the top finishers in a pair trials – like the one Don Krauss and I won in 1963.

But 1969 was going to be different. No more pair trials – just a head-to-head match between the winners of the Spingold and the Vanderbilt.

How did this come about? Well, that's what's so amusing.

In the late 1960s, Edgar Kaplan had put together a pretty strong team. The squad was Edgar and Norman Kay, Eric Murray and Sami Kehela, Robert Jordan and Arthur Robinson.

In his mind, Edgar had the best team. I'll grant that they had a fine team – and they had a record to prove it. Getting that whole team qualified in a pair trials, however, was too great a task. All three pairs might qualify for a pair trials, but the odds were greatly against their finishing one-two-three in the standings.

No matter how you run it, a pair event is much more random than a head-to-head team match. Luck is much more of a factor. For example, in a pair trials, you might lose a lot of IMPs if your opponents bid an insane game that happens to make on a lucky lie of the cards. That's strictly bad luck. It doesn't take many hands like that to put you out of contention.

In a long match, however, luck tends to even out and the better team usually wins. Opponents who bid like maniacs may nick you for a few IMPs here and there, but crazy bidding loses in the long run and you'll bury them if your team is sound.

Anyway, Edgar was not above trying to manipulate the trials format so that his team would have a better chance of participating. As it happened, he had the ear of a very influential bridge politician of the time – Julius Rosenblum.

Rosenblum, a former president of the ACBL, was due to be elected president of the World Bridge Federation in 1970.

It's important, Rosenblum argued, to have good team camaraderie. You can't have that when your "team" is composed of three pairs who might hardly know each other. There were other arguments about the randomness of the pair trials.

Translation: Edgar Kaplan had the best team and this was now going to be his event. Surely Kaplan and company would win the

Vanderbilt or the Spingold and stroll into the team trials. Next stop: the Bermuda Bowl.

The change to team trials suited Ira Corn just fine. In fact, Corn couldn't have asked for a sweeter setup, especially considering how dominating we had become. In effect, Kaplan used his influence, which was considerable, to lobby for just what Corn and the Aces wanted.

You see, Kaplan didn't reckon with the Aces. True, Kaplan had a fine team, but there was a big difference between them and us. We were working full time at getting better. They all had other pursuits – jobs, mostly – that got in the way.

It was excellent planning by Kaplan, but he didn't reckon with Ira G. Corn, smoking his cigar and riding his armadillo in from Texas. Kaplan fixed the race but forgot to show up. His team didn't even get out of the Spingold qualifying heats.

In Phoenix, we were anxious to play the Swanson team. They had beaten us in one of our exhibition matches early on and again in the Vanderbilt in the spring of 1969. We wanted revenge.

Both teams were quite young. The average age of our team was 32; Walsh's foursome averaged only 30.

Walsh himself was quite a character. He hasn't played bridge in America for a long time. He made millions in the commodities market in the late 1960s and moved to Switzerland. I haven't heard anything of him in years. Walsh was known in some circles as the Great White Whale. I don't know where the whale part came from – he was a large fellow but not at all fat – but it was easy to fathom the white part. Walsh was quite pale, very fair-skinned.

Walsh's partner, John Swanson, was another large fellow and one of the nicest guys you'll ever want to meet. A computer programmer, Swanson helped Walsh develop his system, which was quite famous at one time. It includes many of the gadgets you find in today's two-over-one game-forcing systems. In 1975, John and I were on the U.S. team that lost to Italy in the Bermuda Bowl when the infamous foot soldiers did their thing.

The other two members of Walsh's team were Paul Soloway and Gerald Hallee. Soloway, a bridge pro, had already made a name for himself by winning the 1968 McKenney Trophy, awarded to the player who earns the most masterpoints in a calendar year (he won again in 1969). Paul, who later joined the Aces, was well known as a fine player. Hallee, another computer genius, was a pretty good card player from the Seattle area.

On hand to watch the showdown were Oswald Jacoby – anointed by the ACBL as non-playing captain of whichever team won – and Edgar Kaplan, appointed coach of the winning team.

Despite – or perhaps because of – our intensity, we started slowly against Walsh and company. They led by 22 IMPs after the first segment and stretched it to 26 after two.

Incredibly, one night we had to contend with the noise of four big bands that were raising holy hell all around us at the Del Webb Town House – the hotel where we were playing. On another night, we were forced to listen to a political speech from next door – and the walls seemed as thin as paper. It was quite a distraction, but since we could do nothing about it, we pressed on.

In the third segment, we blew the match open, winning the set 54-7 and going from 26 IMPs down to a 75-54 lead. This is one of our gains (note that Eisenberg and Goldman seemed to have taken my admonition about bidding games to heart here):

Billy	*Bobby*
♠ A Q 7 5 2	♠ 10 9 4
♥ A 4	♥ K J 10 3
♦ 9 3	♦ A K 10 6
♣ J 9 5 2	♣ 10 3

WEST	NORTH	EAST	SOUTH
Billy		*Bobby*	
	1♣	Dbl	Pass
2♣	Pass	2♥	Pass
2♠	Pass	3♦	Pass
4♠	All Pass		

Eisenberg played the contract brilliantly, guessing that North held the ♠KJ doubleton while managing the side suits very well. The contract was a bit of a stretch, but they were vulnerable, so the risk was worth it. At the other table, Swanson and Walsh were in the more reasonable contract of 2♠, so we gained 10 IMPs.

We killed them on this deal, too.

Dlr: West	♠ J 8 6		
Vul: Both	♥ K 9 6 2		
	♦ J 7 3 2		
	♣ J 10		

♠ Q 5 2		♠ K 3
♥ A Q 10 7		♥ J 8 5 4
♦ 4		♦ 9 6 5
♣ A 9 4 3 2		♣ Q 8 7 6

	♠ A 10 9 7 4	
	♥ 3	
	♦ A K Q 10 8	
	♣ K 5	

WEST	NORTH	EAST	SOUTH
Goldman	*Swanson*	*Eisenberg*	*Walsh*
1♣	Pass	1♥	2♣
2♥	3♦	Pass	3NT
All Pass			

This screwy contract cost Walsh's team a huge swing. Goldman led the ♥A and continued with the 10. Walsh won the king and played the ♠6 to Goldman's queen. Bobby cashed the ♥Q and played a heart to Eisenberg's jack. A club came back and Walsh – by now despondent over the disaster which was taking place – desperately put up the king. The result was down five for minus 500.

At our table:

WEST	NORTH	EAST	SOUTH
Hallee	*Lawrence*	*Soloway*	*Me*
1♣	Pass	1♥	Dbl
3♥	Pass	Pass	3♠
Pass	4♠	All Pass	

Hallee led the ♣A and continued with a club. I led a heart at trick three and Hallee pounced on it with the ace. Another heart put me in dummy and I tried the ♠J. Soloway covered and it was all over. Plus 620 and a 15-IMP gain.

Once we took the lead, the match was child's play. They were outmanned from the beginning, plus they were playing four-handed. For a long, grueling match like this, they should have added a pair. Anyway, the final score was a slightly embarrassing 423-282 in our favor.

We had taken the next big step and had earned a trip to Stockholm in the spring of 1970. Could we bring home the Bermuda Bowl title? In the minds of the Aces, it was a done deal.

10

Ⓥindication

ON OUR WAY to a world championship in Stockholm in 1970, three members of the Aces took a detour to Rio de Janeiro.
It was bad.

I joined the Aces in January of 1969 with the understanding that I would be allowed to practice occasionally with Eddie Kantar so we could get ready to play in the Bermuda Bowl that May. Eddie and I had qualified in the Team Trials in Atlantic City the previous fall, as had Billy Eisenberg and Bobby Goldman. Sidney Lazard and George Rapée finished on top in the trials. The six of us made up the American team.

The Italians — Garozzo, Belladonna, Forquet and three stiffs — were heavily favored, but we entered the event with optimism. Don't forget, under Musumeci's direction Eisenberg and Goldman had become tough as nails as members of the Aces. Kantar and I had played well before I moved to Dallas, and Rapée and Lazard had considerable international experience. Rapée had played in the Bermuda Bowl five times — winning three — before the trip to Rio.

Rapée, an attorney and real estate investor back then, is truly an amazing guy. Not many people know that he was the developer of the convention known today as Stayman. It's called Stayman because Sam Stayman wrote up Rapée's convention.

Rapée is nearing 80, but I still see him at all the Nationals – and he's usually in contention in the team events. A short fellow who looks a lot like George Burns, Rapée may have the strongest constitution of any man who ever lived. He could party all night long and still play good bridge for an entire tournament. I've never seen anyone with so much energy.

The Bermuda Bowl format was similar to previous years. The five teams – us, the Italians, France, China and Brazil – would play a qualifying round-robin. We would play three 32-board matches against each of the other teams and convert the IMPs to Victory Points, with a maximum of 20 VPs for the winner of each round. Losers could actually get minus VPs (as many as five) if they were really thrashed. The top two finishers in the round-robin would play a 128-board match for the championship. Third and fourth would play off for the bronze medal.

We were playing at the Rio Country Club on Ipanema Beach, a really classy part of Rio de Janeiro. No hotel space for the tournament was available because the Bermuda Bowl had been awarded to Brazil pretty late in the game. There was nothing wrong with the playing site, however. What was wrong was the way our team played.

We started poorly and things got worse from there. We played Brazil in the first round and were trounced, 16-4. Italy, meanwhile, romped, winning 20 to minus 2 despite the fact that they were missing Forquet. His father had been killed in a domestic gas explosion the day he left for Brazil, so he turned right around and went home after landing in Rio.

We lost round two to China, 13-7, and then we were clobbered by France, 19-1. By the time we played Italy in the fifth round (we had a bye in round four), Forquet was back on the team. They manhandled us, 16-4. We were one-third of the way through the round-robin qualifying and we hadn't won a match. Dead last in the standings, we were not a happy group.

Our captain and coach was the venerable Oswald Jacoby, who had definite ideas about how the game is supposed to be played. It was hard to argue with his credentials. He had won dozens of North American championships, developed several bidding conventions (Jacoby transfers and 2NT as a forcing major-suit raise among them) and won the McKenney Trophy (for most masterpoints in a calendar year) four times.

If Jacoby wasn't a bona fide genius, I've never seen one. He and I would occasionally play chess in our heads. It's not as hard as it sounds, but it usually impressed bystanders to hear us calling off moves – "pawn to queen-four" – with no board or chessmen in sight. I played bridge with Ozzie a few times, and it was always a pleasure. We respected each other and were good friends.

Relations were somewhat strained during the Bermuda Bowl, however, partly because we were doing so poorly. During the tournament, it was customary for Ozzie to sit at the table to observe the happenings – and give us the benefit of his wisdom when necessary. Eddie and I were playing against China when this deal came up. Ozzie was sitting at my elbow.

```
Dlr: West        ♠ 4
Vul: N-S         ♥ 5 4
                 ♦ 8 6 5 4 2
                 ♣ K J 9 8 7
♠ J 6 3 2                        ♠ 10 9
♥ K 9 7 3                        ♥ Q J 10 6 2
♦ A J                            ♦ K 10 9 7
♣ A 5 2                          ♣ Q 6
                 ♠ A K Q 8 7 5
                 ♥ A 8
                 ♦ Q 3
                 ♣ 10 4 3
```

WEST	NORTH	EAST	SOUTH
Kantar		*Me*	
1♠	Pass	1NT	Dbl
Pass	2♣	2♥	Pass
3♥	Pass	4♥	All Pass

You might say I went to game on my good looks. Unfortunately, my play for the contract was no better than my bidding. I needed tricks – 10 of them – and I got only nine. South cashed the top two spades and shifted to a club. I ducked, North won the king and I finished down one for a 6-IMP loss since Eisenberg had played in 3♠ doubled, down one, with the South cards at the other table.

Anyway, Ozzie started to fidget when he saw the dummy – something was bothering him. Later, during a break, Ozzie called Kantar and me aside to discuss Eddie's opening bid of 1♠ (I did then and still do prefer four-card majors). Jacoby started off trying to be tactful.

"I may not play bridge as well as you fellows do any more, but I know better than to open one spade on four to the jack."

I wasn't in much of a mood to be preached to. "What do you mean, any more?" I snapped. Eddie gulped. Ozzie blanched.

"Well," he snarled, tact now sailing straight out the window, "I won't have anybody on my team opening one spade on four to the jack."

"It's a little late," I countered, "to teach us how to play bridge."

"Well," said our captain, "it's not too late to kick you bastards off the team." And he meant it.

A couple of days later, I picked up essentially the same hand – an opening bid with four spades to the jack. Clearly a 1♠ opener. As usual, Ozzie was sitting next to me. I started thinking, "Hamman, are you a man or a mouse? Are you going to open one spade on this hand as you should or knuckle under?"

I'll never know – Eddie opened the bidding and took me off the hook. I will admit to breathing a sigh of relief, and I'll tell you something about pressure: playing in the Bermuda Bowl, Italians or no Italians, was a piece of cake compared to Ozzie Jacoby's glare.

We finally won a match in our second meeting with Brazil, but all we could manage against the Chinese was a tie. France ate our lunch again. We ended up going backwards with a minus 2 VPs.

Although we gave the Italians their first loss of the tournament – 16-4 – it was too little too late. We still had a slim chance with five rounds to go, but Brazil beat us 17-3 in round eleven and that was it. We knocked off Italy again in our third meeting, but neither team was taking things seriously by then – we were out of it and they had first place in the round-robin sewed up. We finished a poor third and had to settle for playing off against France. Italy would play the surprising Chinese – second-place finishers – for the championship.

I give a lot of credit to Kathie Wei (now Wei-Sender), non-playing captain of the Chinese team. Without a lot of tournament experience herself, she instilled the Chinese team with confidence and managed her players adeptly. It was an impressive performance.

It was a cakewalk for the Blue Team. They won 429-182, while our team beat the French, 150-115, in the bronze-medal match. I got sick from either the results or the flu and played only one set. My heart wouldn't have been in it, anyway. I wanted to be playing for all the marbles – not for the consolation prize.

Right after the tournament, the Blue Team announced that they were retiring with 10 world championships to their credit. In a way, I was disappointed. Perhaps the exit of the Blue Team would clear the way for the Aces to win in 1970 if we could earn our way to Stockholm, but it wouldn't be the same. I wanted an Italian pelt to hang on the wall of my den.

I must admit that, a year later, no such thoughts entered my head as the Aces boarded the plane at Dallas for our trans-Atlantic flight. It was the summer of 1970 and we were headed for Stockholm to play in the Bermuda Bowl. To a man, we didn't care who was there or who wasn't. We couldn't do anything about the fact that the Blue Team had retired. Our aim was to bring back a world title, even if our stiffest competition was the Little Sisters of the Poor. We would rough them up, too, if necessary.

The year had been a series of ups and downs for the Aces. We had played the longest match that I am aware of – seven 120-board matches against Omar Sharif's Bridge Circus. Sharif's team consisted of three members of the Blue Team – Garozzo, Forquet and Belladonna – Claude Delmouly, a former world champion from France, the late Leon Yallouze and of course Sharif himself. Omar's team jumped off to an early lead which grew to more than 100 IMPs, but we took the lead in Dallas and eventually won by about 150 IMPs. The Aces finished strong by winning the final match handily in Philadelphia. We felt extremely upbeat about the result – even though it was an exhibition match, we had beaten a damn good team convincingly after a poor start.

On the other hand, the Aces lost a close match in the Vanderbilt final at the 1970 Spring NABC in Portland, Oregon. After our runaway victory in the Spingold the year before, we didn't consider the possibility that another team could get the better of us in a long knockout match. Ironically, two members of the team that beat us in Portland were our teammates in Rio de Janeiro – Rapée and Lazard.

Losing to that team – which also had Edgar Kaplan, Norman Kay, Sami Kehela and Eric Murray – was a bitter pill for me, especially after Kaplan's coverage of the 1969 Bermuda Bowl in *The Bridge World*. It rankled that his story was headlined, "Disaster in Rio."

The Aces had also lost a couple of the practice matches Corn was always setting up for us – definitely not what we expected of ourselves.

Still, the mood was upbeat and our confidence was unshaken as our plane wended its way from Dallas to New York, where we would take off for Sweden. We had climbed aboard all decked out in our matching blazers and with wives and girlfriends in tow. We had an amazing amount of luggage, mostly to carry all our "uniforms" for the Bermuda Bowl. Corn had bought blazers and tuxedos for the Aces from a fellow named Steve Greenberg, a good bridge player who was living in Oklahoma City at the time. Before we left for Stockholm, Moose gave us a list of what we were to wear every day – dark blazers some days, blue blazers other days. At night, it was either the black or gray tux. It was first-class all the way for the Aces.

Corn was in high spirits, as were our "seconds" – Ozzie was back as non-playing captain, Ira was deputy captain, Kaplan was the coach (anointed as such by the ACBL) and Moose was "deputy" coach.

We knew we would be the prohibitive favorites in the five-team field. We would be playing against Brazil (some of the same players from the Bermuda Bowl in Rio the previous year), China (ditto), Norway and a bad Italian team. It was kind of a joke that the Italians weren't even sending their *second* best team. Italy had won the European championship in 1969, and that team was eligible to play in the Bermuda Bowl in 1970.

But when the Italian Bridge Federation decided to have a pair trials – similar to what we used in the U.S. prior to 1969 – to pick a representative, the outraged winners of the European championship refused to take part. I don't blame them. Why should they have to qualify twice?

Anyway, no one outside Italy had ever heard of the characters that ultimately made up the Italian team – Barbarisi, Cesati, De Ritis, LaGalla, Morini and Tersch. It was quite strange, once play began, to discover that two of the Italians – Tersch and Cesati – were playing Standard American while Wolff and Jacoby trotted out their version of the Neapolitan Club, the system created by the Blue Team.

The plane landed in Stockholm in the dark, and when we arrived at the Hotel Foresta – a magnificent converted castle overlooking the Gota River – our rooms weren't ready. It was a good thing we arrived a few days early to make sure we shook off the jet lag. If we hadn't been preoccupied with the world championship, there might have been a riot in the lobby.

I didn't notice much about Stockholm except that it had a lot of modern buildings mixed in with the old structures you typically see in European cities. During my stay in Stockholm, I was vaguely aware of anti-American protests, probably associated with the United States involvement in Vietnam. Sweden welcomed Americans who, for whatever reasons, didn't want to serve in the U.S. Armed Forces during the Vietnam war. Our welcome by the Swedish bridge officials was certainly warm, however, as we overlooked global politics to concentrate on bridge.

We found out, however, that the bridge politicians weren't taking a holiday. Shortly after we arrived in Stockholm, we found that the conditions of contest – for the final, anyway – had changed!

In every other Bermuda Bowl prior to 1970 – and since then, for that matter – the final was played as one long match. Whoever scored more IMPs was the winner. In Stockholm in 1970, it was decreed that the final would be four short matches. The IMP score of each segment would be converted to Victory Points on the same scale as in the qualifying round-robin play.

In other words, no team could score more than 20 VPs per segment. Since the Aces were considered a lock to win the round-robin and play in the final, this was clearly an attempt to even up the contest against whatever team we faced for the championship.

It would have been laughable if it hadn't been a rather serious breach of fair play. What they were doing to the Aces was like telling the teams who show up to play in the Super Bowl that, "Oh, by the way, touchdowns and field goals won't count this year. We're giving one point to the winner of each quarter. Four touchdowns in one quarter to a field goal by the other team will still count as only one point." Can you imagine that happening? At the last minute?

There was no point in protesting. The WBF is not exactly a democratic organization, and we had already had a preview of how our opinions were regarded. At the captains meeting the day before the tournament started, Ozzie suggested that the competition be conducted using bidding boxes. That idea was shot down in short order.

All we could do was press on. Perhaps everybody was rooting against us – as is often the case when Americans play overseas – but we were the best team in the event by far and we weren't to be denied. We asserted ourselves on day one by knocking off Brazil – considered one of two teams, along with China, that had the best chance to make it to the final with us. The margin was not typical Aces – only 56-39 – but once we got our feet wet there was no holding us back. Italy performed as expected. They were drubbed, 78-55, by Norway.

On day two, we clobbered China, 71-39, and matters got worse for Italy. Both pairs in the Italians' match against Brazil appeared to have played well only to discover that they had both sat North-South during the first half of the match. A replay was necessary, of course, and Brazil mopped the floor with the dispirited Italians, 111-37.

We won all our matches but one by embarrassingly large margins (we lost to Norway, 72-51, after we had forged an insurmountable lead in the round-robin). In our three head-to-head matches with Italy, we won 97-54, 106-37 and 81-31. Our VP score against them was 60 to minus 1. What a joke. It wasn't much different with the other teams, and we ended up with 229 out of a possible 240 Victory Points. We had scored 95% against supposedly world-class competition.

This deal, from our second match against Brazil, was one of many huge swings that went our way.

Dlr: North   ♠ A J 7 3
Vul: None   ♥ J 10 8 7 6
               ♦ A
               ♣ 7 5 4

♠ —   ♠ 10 9 6 2
♥ A 3   ♥ —
♦ K 9 8 7 4 3 2   ♦ Q 10 5
♣ A Q J 8   ♣ K 10 9 6 3 2

               ♠ K Q 8 5 4
               ♥ K Q 9 5 4 2
               ♦ J 6
               ♣ —

WEST	NORTH	EAST	SOUTH
Ferreira	*Wolff*	*Barros*	*Jacoby*
	Pass	Pass	1♥
3♦	4♦	5♦	5♥
6♦	Pass	Pass	6♥
Dbl	All Pass		

There wasn't much to the play – West got his trump ace, but that was all – Jacoby and Wolff chalked up plus 1210. At the other table:

WEST	NORTH	EAST	SOUTH
Eisenberg	*Chagas*	*Goldman*	*Assumpção*
	Pass	Pass	1♠
2♦	2♥	4♦	4♥
4♠	Dbl	Pass	Pass
5♦	5♠	6♣	6♠
Dbl	All Pass		

Brazil was using a canapé system, in which the opening bidder starts with his shorter suit. Once North responded 2♥, there was no way Brazil could get to a slam that could make. If North played a heart slam, West could double for a spade lead. South realized this, so he tried 6♠. Assumpção was tapped at trick one when Eisenberg led the ♣A. Declarer couldn't afford to pull all the trumps before tackling hearts. When he led a heart, Eisenberg won the ace and gave Goldman a ruff. That was plus 100 and 16 IMPs to the Aces.

China finished second in the round-robin. We started the final against them on a Wednesday afternoon.

Surprisingly, the team from Taipei won the opening set, 57-46. We were flat, I suppose, partly because we knew that ultimately the Bermuda Bowl final would be no contest. Still, it was quite a shock to us and everyone else when we lost. No doubt the wizards who engineered the format change were congratulating themselves when the first segment ended with China leading in VPs, 13-7.

The elation didn't last long. We won the second match by 37 IMPs, which translated to an 18-2 win in VPs, so at the halfway point, we led 25-15. The second half of the final had barely started when we put a virtual end to China's hopes. This was board 4.

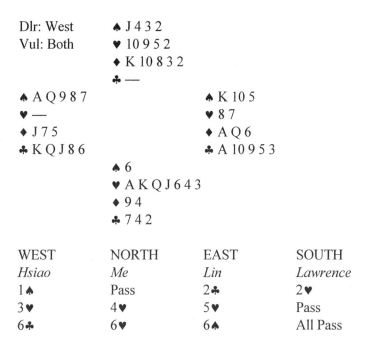

```
Dlr: West          ♠ J 4 3 2
Vul: Both          ♥ 10 9 5 2
                   ♦ K 10 8 3 2
                   ♣ —
♠ A Q 9 8 7                        ♠ K 10 5
♥ —                                ♥ 8 7
♦ J 7 5                            ♦ A Q 6
♣ K Q J 8 6                        ♣ A 10 9 5 3
                   ♠ 6
                   ♥ A K Q J 6 4 3
                   ♦ 9 4
                   ♣ 7 4 2
```

WEST	NORTH	EAST	SOUTH
Hsiao	*Me*	*Lin*	*Lawrence*
1♠	Pass	2♣	2♥
3♥	4♥	5♥	Pass
6♣	6♥	6♠	All Pass

I led the ♦3 – it pays to be aggressive on deals like this – and declarer went up with the ace, a reasonable play that just happened to be disastrous. As you can see, my lead was the only one that would let the slam make (assuming West didn't do anything double-dummy with the spade suit), but declarer could hardly be blamed for not putting all his eggs in one basket. After all, he was only in six – not seven. If spades split 3-2, as could be expected, he would make the slam even if I was leading a singleton diamond. But if he ducked and my lead was a stiff, he might go down in a cold contract. Anyway, West didn't guess how to play spades and he went down one. At the other table:

WEST	NORTH	EAST	SOUTH
Jacoby	*Tai*	*Wolff*	*Huang*
2♣	Pass	2♦	3♥
3♠	4♥	6♣	6♥
Pass	Pass	7♣	All Pass

Jacoby's 2♣ opening was natural and in keeping with their Neapolitan Club system. Note Jacoby's pass of 6♥. This guaranteed first-round control of hearts, so Wolff knew his gamble of 7♣ was reasonable. Jacoby might also have gone down with a diamond lead, but North led a heart and it was quickly over. When spades proved to be 4-1, Jacoby took the diamond finesse for plus 2140 – and a 19-IMP gain.

This deal put the last nail in the coffin for the Chinese:

```
Dlr: South        ♠ A 3
Vul: Both         ♥ K Q 10 8 7 5
                  ♦ A 9
                  ♣ 9 7 2
♠ J 9 7                         ♠ K Q 10 8 6
♥ 9 6                           ♥ J 2
♦ K 10 5 3 2                    ♦ J 7 4
♣ Q 10 6                        ♣ A J 4
                  ♠ 5 4 2
                  ♥ A 4 3
                  ♦ Q 8 6
                  ♣ K 8 5 3
```

WEST	NORTH	EAST	SOUTH
Hsiao	*Me*	*Lin*	*Lawrence*
			Pass
Pass	1♥	1♠	2♥
2♠	4♥	All Pass	

Didn't I say I believe in bidding game? Okay, it's somewhat of an overbid, but the proof is in the pudding, right?

East led the ♠K and I ducked. Lin continued with a spade and I won perforce. Next came the key play – the ♣7. I passed this to West's 10, and the defense was helpless. The defenders neither had the time nor the communications to set up a diamond trick. I could ruff the spade continuation in hand, play two rounds of trumps, leaving the ace in dummy as an entry even if trumps split 3-1, and play another club. If East rose with the ace, I would have the vital 10th trick in the ♣8. If East ducked, I would go up with the king and play a third round with the same result.

Desperately, West switched to a low diamond, hoping his partner had the ace or that I would chicken out and not play low, but I ducked it around to the queen. Plus 620 was good for a 10-IMP pickup since North-South were in 3♥ (making only three) at the other table.

We won the third segment by 67 IMPs, giving us 20 VPs and the Chinese minus 2. Our lead at that point was 45-13, so the final segment was meaningless. The Chinese could win by 1000 IMPs and we would still be the Bermuda Bowl champs. The attempt to "even things up" by changing the format had made a farce of the championship round.

It wasn't necessary to play the final set, but we did anyway, partly because the Swedish bridge organization was hard up for money and wanted to collect the $2 per head for the vugraph show. To spice things up, Belladonna – one of the vugraph commentators – challenged Wolff and Jacoby to play the Roman Club in the final set. They agreed to do so, and they actually functioned pretty well with the system. We won the last "match" by 48 IMPs and ended the final with a 64-14 margin.

Naturally we were ecstatic to be world champions, and Ira was so high we thought he might fly back to the U.S. without a plane. Ozzie had tears on his cheeks as he accepted the trophy at the victory banquet from Sweden's Princess Christina.

We were all so happy we weren't even too perturbed at the victory banquet when Count Carl Bonde, a Swedish fellow who was president of the World Bridge Federation at the time, made several remarks denigrating our win. "This was not," Bonde said, "a vintage world championship. We look forward to the time when one of our stronger teams plays in the world championship so that the Bermuda Bowl Trophy will be returned to its rightful place on this side of the Atlantic."

Ozzie was burning – smoke was curling from his ears. He gave 'em hell when it was his turn to speak. "We won and we won convincingly" he said through clenched teeth. "The way our team played we would have beaten any team in the world." There wasn't much of a reaction from the crowd, but he had made his point. Despite this irritating aspect of the trip, we all felt satisfaction in knowing that we had done what we set out to do – win a world championship. No one could take that from us.

Right after the Bermuda Bowl, the World Pair Olympiad began in Stockholm, and all the Aces except Goldman stayed around to play. We did only passably – Jacoby and Wolff were 14th out of 158 pairs, Mike and I were 16th – but we had a good time.

Ira and a few of his cronies including Dorothy Moore flew off to Paris to celebrate. Ira loved to eat – it wasn't an accident that he weighed 350 pounds. Dinner at Maxim's started at about 7 p.m. Along about midnight, the check came. Ira perused the bill for a minute before looking up at the waiter. "I understand you make good omelets here," said the Great One. "Oui, Monsieur" said the waiter. "Well," cried Ira, "whip me up one."

It was a happy time for the Aces. Not only had we won our first world championship, but we were guaranteed another shot at the title the following year. In those days, the defending champion was an automatic qualifier.

Next on the agenda was capitalizing on our championships commercially. That would prove to be much more difficult. There were changes ahead for the Aces, and not all of them were good.

11

Winds of change

ALTHOUGH THE Aces had easily won the Bermuda Bowl in Sweden and were looking forward to defending the title in Taipei in 1971, we all knew changes were in the offing when we returned home.

At the top of the list was a realignment of partnerships. Before we left for Stockholm, Goldman had told Corn and Musumeci he didn't want to play with Eisenberg any more. The two had been quite effective, but Eisenberg was driving Goldman crazy with his free-lancing style. Goldman liked to play with discipline and to have a rational, defensible reason for any action he took. Billy, on the other hand, often made a bid or play just because he "felt like it." He had good instincts and he wasn't afraid to back his hunches. As often as not, he was right.

But even when Eisenberg's off-the-wall stuff was working, it drove Goldman nuts. Goldman told Corn and Moose he was unhappy playing with Billy and he didn't see the situation improving. This was somewhat alarming to Corn, whose vision of the Aces was that of a well-oiled machine. Although Corn didn't like what he heard, he knew Goldman was serious – Bobby wouldn't ask for the change without a good reason.

Finally, a compromise was reached: Goldman and Eisenberg would continue to practice together and play in the Bermuda Bowl in Stockholm but would change partners after that. In the meantime they would discuss no hands and not socialize at all. Corn also got Bobby and Billy to agree to visit a psychiatrist to see if they could work out their differences.

Actually Corn didn't really have to twist any arms. Eisenberg and Goldman were both pleased to be able to see a shrink and have someone else pay for it. Once a week, Goldman and Eisenberg went together to see a fellow named Shelton – a so-called "industrial" psychiatrist whose specialty was counseling in business situations.

Although the psychiatrist didn't help enough to make Goldman want to continue the partnership, he and Billy at least worked out that their basic problem was communication. In effect, Bobby's receiver was tuned to one channel and Billy was sending on another. To their credit, Goldman and Eisenberg continued to take the business of playing bridge seriously – in fact, they had a tremendous tournament in the Bermuda Bowl. In the post-championship discussions back in Dallas, Goldman and Eisenberg had the fewest "charges" of all the Aces. When it was all over, they shook hands and didn't play together again for nearly 20 years – except at the Summer Nationals in Boston right after we got back from Stockholm.

Corn didn't know it right away, but Goldman and Eisenberg weren't the only ones having problems. Lawrence and I also had some rough spots. Mike was kind of temperamental back then, and I didn't handle him very well. You might say he didn't handle me very well, either.

Mike and I also functioned well in Stockholm and contributed as much as any other pair to the win, but neither of us was particularly happy in the partnership. We reached a low point while we were playing together in the World Pair Olympiad after the Bermuda Bowl.

I had a hand something like

♠A 7 ♥A 5 4 3 2 ♦A 9 ♣A Q 5 4.

I opened 1♥ and Mike bid 2NT, natural and forcing to game. I bid 3♣ and he bid 3♥. Now I wanted to make some slam invitation, but if Mike was going to reject the slam invitation, I didn't want to be higher than 3NT. Finally, I just decided to bid 3NT. Well, Mike bid 4♥, and laid down a dummy something like this:

♠K Q 10 ♥10 7 6 ♦K J 10 9 ♣K J 7.

A good hand, but it proved to be a grossly inferior spot when the trump suit broke 5-0. In fact, he had a play for 12 tricks in notrump but I had no play for 10 tricks in hearts. This development made my blood boil and I got up from the table to try to walk off my anger.

Out in the hall I ran into Kantar, who knew me well enough to see that something was bothering me. "Well, Bob," Eddie said, "you look like you're in an even better mood than usual."

I growled and said, "You wouldn't believe what the son of a bitch did to me." Just then I turned around and discovered that the SOB had been half a step behind me the whole time. Oh brother, I thought, now I've done it! Mike was a sensitive sort back then and I was afraid my inappropriate demeanor at the table and in the conversation with Kantar would make matters worse for our partnership. Mike didn't say anything, and as it turned out, he played well the rest of the event and we finished a respectable 16th in the field of international players.

Still, Lawrence and I had lost a step as a partnership and it clearly wasn't in the best interest of the Aces for us to stay together.

The new Aces lineup, therefore, was to be Lawrence and Goldman, Hamman and Eisenberg – and Wolff and Jacoby, who were having no problems of any kind. They were happy as pigs in slop.

The first thing Billy and I had to do was decide what system to play. He cut his teeth on Eastern Scientific, based on five-card majors with lots of bells and whistles, while I was a dyed-in-the-wool four-card majorite. There was no way I was playing five-card majors and we couldn't see Billy playing four-card majors, so we settled on a strong club system. Wolff's and Jacoby's system was called the Orange Club. Billy and I called our system the Black Club for no particular reason other than we decided our system would be a color, just like Wolff's and Jacoby's.

Although the partnership changes were somewhat unsettling, none of it changed Corn's enthusiasm or his excitement at realizing his dream of returning the world championship to America.

When the Aces experiment started, Corn had three basic goals: to put together a team that would win a world championship, take commercial advantage of having accomplished that – and to improve his game enough that he could be a part of it. It soon became clear that his third goal – being a player on the team – wasn't to be, and that was abandoned post haste. Once the Aces won the Bermuda Bowl, however, objective two came to the fore.

We already had a small taste of what commercial backing could do for us before we went to Stockholm. In our series of matches with the Sharif troupe, Cosco, a company which manufactured card tables, had paid for the Sharif players to come to the U.S. Another company, Stancraft, a division of Brown & Bigelow and a playing card manufacturer, also was a sponsor of the tour. They got exposure for their products while we gained fame as America's bridge heroes.

The Aces got highly favorable news media coverage before and after the championship. The idea of this eccentric millionaire footing the bill for a team to win a world title had caught the fancy of newspaper and magazine editors all over the country before we went to Sweden. After we won, we were practically celebrities. When we got back to the U.S., the Aces appeared on the *Today Show*. *Sports Illustrated* wrote glowingly of our triumph and the fulfillment of Corn's dream. Corn started planning more challenge matches, some of them against the Blue Team. We were going to prove we could beat them, even if it wasn't in the Bermuda Bowl.

Corn's dream of turning the Aces into a commercial property never really came close to being a reality. For one thing, what we needed most was a way to get bridge on television. But no one had figured out a way to get people to watch bridge on TV. Corn put together a one-hour special on the Aces and bought television time for the production, but it was a dismal failure in terms of viewers (it came on around dawn on a Sunday morning). Corn spent a lot of money developing the show and trying to get sponsors, but he couldn't interest enough advertisers to fill all the commercial slots.

All this was going on around the same time that professional tennis was being transformed from a country-club game, with virtually no popular following, to a sport with a regular tournament circuit and players who are major celebrities. Corn observed this phenomenon and had the idea that the same transformation could be accomplished for bridge.

Corn was a visionary and a man not easily denied. He succeeded in business and in life through his dogged pursuit of his goals. The Aces' winning the Bermuda Bowl is an example. As hard as Corn tried, however, his attempts to popularize bridge remained a dream unfulfilled.

Perhaps the closest the Aces ever came to a solid commercial spin-off of the world championship was a deal Corn had worked on with the Hallmark Company, the greeting card people. They were impressed with the showing the Aces made in Stockholm and were on the verge of starting a campaign featuring the Aces in all their stores throughout the country. They planned to sell playing cards and lots of other bridge paraphernalia in special Aces sections with displays of our smiling faces – Corn's too, I'm sure. Hallmark could brag that the world champion Aces endorsed their products.

A senior Hallmark officer was a bridge enthusiast and it seemed that the deal was done – until Ira went to a meeting of the Hallmark board of directors at their headquarters in Kansas City. Bobby Wolff was with him. Wolffie was working for Michigan General in addition to helping Ira with the bridge development projects.

At that point, Hallmark had already invested $132,000 in the Aces project and was looking forward to taking full advantage of the big win in Stockholm. Well, Corn strode into the Hallmark board meeting and queered the whole deal.

The chairman of the Hallmark board, with about 15 other directors on hand – at an average age of about 75 – told Corn and Wolff that Hallmark was looking forward to the association with the Aces. The initial plans, Corn was told, included a bridge scorepad featuring the team.

Corn spoke up quickly. "Thanks," he said, "but we'll call the bridge shots. You're familiar with greeting cards. We're familiar with bridge, so we know what to do."

An awkward silence fell over the group. Finally, the chairman said, "Thanks for coming. We'll be in touch."

About two weeks later, Corn got a letter from Hallmark saying they had decided to walk away from the whole venture. Despite their six-figure investment to that point, they were through dealing with Corn and the Aces. Corn misread the whole situation with Hallmark. He thought he had the upper hand. It was a major miscalculation by a man whose business judgment was normally impeccable.

Corn had some discussions with the 3M company after that, but they weren't willing to invest much money. The deal, if there ever was one, fell through.

Ira also had some trouble with the IRS over business tax deductions he was trying to take for expenses associated with the Aces. Corn's dream team and his vision of building a bridge dynasty weren't exactly unraveling at that point, but some frayed edges were beginning to show.

With the world championship under our belts, we went to the Summer Nationals in Boston full of confidence, although there was a slight feeling of discomfort because we hadn't made the partnership changes at that point. Eisenberg and Goldman were still together, as were Mike and I. Because of the World Pair Olympiad, we didn't even leave Sweden until the first week of July. Since the Boston tournament started only about a month later, there wasn't time to get the new partnerships tuned up. On top of that, Billy and I had agreed to play an entirely new, rather complicated system. To have any chance of success, we had to stick to the lineup we used in Stockholm.

Despite the lame-duck nature of two of the three Aces partnerships, the team played well and had an easy time getting to the Spingold final. However, we lost, just as we had done in the Vanderbilt – this time to a five-man squad calling themselves the Precision Team.

The young men – Steve Altman, Peter Weichsel, Joel Stuart, Tom Smith and Dave Strasberg – were all playing the system developed by C.C. Wei, the shipping magnate. It was the same system the Chinese team employed in the Bermuda Bowl in Rio and Stockholm. The Precision Team played in luck, but they also played well. They beat us pretty handily – by 59 IMPs. Another setback for the Aces, although not a critical one.

In the fall, at the Nationals in Houston, we were back on track, tying for first in the Reisinger. We had formed the new partnerships and things were clicking again – at least for the moment.

Another change for the Aces was our training routine. After Stockholm, we never returned to the rigid schedule we had followed before. I don't know whether it was a conscious decision on the part of

Moose or Ira to ease up a bit or just that it was natural since we weren't the unproven bunch that we were when we started. We still had the group discussions and practice matches, but things never were as intense as before.

In Atlanta at the Spring Nationals, the Aces won the Vanderbilt in a blowout. That was the time that we were absolutely on the ropes to George Rosenkranz's team in the quarterfinal, but Nail and Rosenkranz went for 500 on the last board of the match and we won by 3 IMPs. In the final, we played Ira Rubin, Chuck Burger, Eddie Kantar, Paul Soloway, Kyle Larsen and Ron Von der Porten. At the end of the first quarter, we went to compare scores with Wolff and Jacoby. Both of them were grinning, as were Billy and I. Both pairs had had monster sets. We won the first quarter 97-1. We argued briefly about how they got the 1, then got back to the business of smearing them. We won by 150 IMPs.

The Aces were top dogs again. It was a fine tune-up for the world championship in Taipei.

Two months after we won the Vanderbilt in Atlanta, the Aces boarded another airplane in Dallas headed for a foreign land. The full entourage was aboard – Ozzie was back as our non-playing captain – and we were decked out in our blazers again. The Dallas papers had been good to us, running several stories prior to our departure and hailing us as heroes. There was a sense among all of us, Corn included, that we were on a mission to prove that the Aces' victory in the 1970 Bermuda Bowl was not a fluke – that we didn't win just because the competition was weak.

We flew from Dallas to Taipei via Hawaii and Japan. The trip featured a stay in Japan. It seemed like it took years to get there. We stayed at the Mandarin Hotel, a modern building on a wide boulevard in downtown Taipei. Unlike Stockholm, there was no anti-American sentiment evident. The Taiwanese still viewed the government on mainland China as bitter enemies in those days and counted on Americans as allies against the Communists. To them, we were friends.

The 1971 Bermuda Bowl was the first one in history to have six teams in competition. We were back as the defending champions, and there was another American team, the winners of the team trials, who went to Taipei representing the United States.

This team consisted of Lew Mathe, my old pal and former partner, and Don Krauss, with whom I played in my first world championship; Edgar Kaplan and Norman Kay, one of the strongest and most enduring partnerships in history, and John Swanson and Dick Walsh. Swanson and Walsh were on the team that we had annihilated in Phoenix in the trials to get to the 1970 Bermuda Bowl. Swanson was to become one of my teammates in perhaps the most infamous Bermuda Bowl of all time – in 1975 – and again on our winning team in Manila in 1977.

Any team with Mathe on it was dangerous, even at that point when he was slipping somewhat. Mathe was such a dogged competitor that sometimes he could make up for in intensity what the team as a whole lacked in skill. Kaplan and Kay were also tough, but in a different way. They are great players and they have a tremendous partnership, but they win basically by outpointing the opponents in close matches. They aren't very good coming from behind. Jeff Meckstroth and Eric Rodwell, for example, are incredible at creating action and busting people up. Kaplan and Kay are not comfortable playing the kind of game where they have to go in and spill some blood and take chances. They don't like to risk looking foolish. Still, they have been remarkably durable and are hard to beat from the favorite's position.

The other teams in the Bermuda Bowl were Brazil, Australia, China and France. The Brazilians, with Gabriel Chagas in the anchor spot, kept showing up at these tournaments. We weren't about to underestimate them, even though they weren't expected to do much. China also fielded a team with experience in the Bermuda Bowl. Patrick Huang was their star. He was – and still is – a world-class player. Australia was also highly regarded, and the team had become a curiosity because two members were husband and wife – Jim and Norma Borin – a first for the Bermuda Bowl.

France was the team we feared most, and for a very distasteful reason. Just about everyone was convinced that their anchor pair, Pierre Jaïs and Roger Trézel, were cheaters. They were well known in bridge circles for their flawless opening leads – the opening leader could always find partner's ace if he had one. It wasn't clear how they relayed information to each other, but these were the days before screens. Besides worrying about being knocked off legitimately, we also had to be concerned about being jobbed out of a world championship.

Despite this, the Aces were overwhelming favorites again. And this time, the bridge politicians didn't tinker with the conditions of contest trying to even things out. Perhaps it was because the French team – who rated to make it to the final against us – was considerably stronger than any of our opponents in Stockholm had been.

We started off the round-robin playing our compatriots – Mathe and company. The result – we won by 48 IMPs – set the tone for both teams. Billy and I played against Mathe and Krauss. Don't think there wasn't some tension there. I know Lew wanted to beat me so bad he could taste it. Remember, after I walked away from the partnership with Mathe, I went on to become a world champion. Lew was not the kind of person to take such a development philosophically. On top of that, his game was not what it had once been, and I know he would have enjoyed beating me about as much as anything in his life at that point.

This was one of our good results.

```
Dlr: East        ♠ A 7 5 4
Vul: Both        ♥ 10 9 6 4 3
                 ♦ —
                 ♣ K 9 6 2
♠ K Q 9                          ♠ J 10 8 6 3 2
♥ K Q 8 2                        ♥ J 7
♦ J 2                            ♦ A 8 7
♣ A 8 7 3                        ♣ Q 5
                 ♠ —
                 ♥ A 5
                 ♦ K Q 10 9 6 5 4 3
                 ♣ J 10 4
```

WEST	NORTH	EAST	SOUTH
Eisenberg	*Mathe*	*Me*	*Krauss*
		Pass	1♦
Dbl	1♥	2♠	3♦
3♠	Pass	4♠	Pass
Pass	Dbl	All Pass	

Don probably should not have sat for the double with an eight-card suit, but as it turned out the contract could have been defeated. Krauss led the ♦K and Mathe thought for a long time before he discarded a heart. Mathe couldn't tell if Don was leading from the AK or KQ – the king would be led from either holding. If it was the AK and Mathe ruffed, he would be ruffing one of his side's winners. As you can see, the correct defense is for Mathe to ruff, put partner in with the ♥A and get another diamond ruff. The ♠A would be the setting trick.

Anyway, I won the ♦A and immediately played a heart to make sure I got a pitch for the losing club in my hand. Don went up with the ♥A and cashed the ♦Q. When he played another round, I ruffed with dummy's ♠Q and my good spade spots saw me home. Plus 790 for the Aces.

At the other table:

WEST	NORTH	EAST	SOUTH
Kaplan	*Jacoby*	*Kay*	*Wolff*
		Pass	1♦
Dbl	1♥	2♠	5♦
All Pass			

Wolffie's 5♦ bid blew them right out of the water. Kaplan and Kay would have been insane to bid on, but it wasn't clear to double, either. As it happened, after Kaplan led the ♠K, Wolff needed only a successful finesse for the ♣Q to make the 17-point game. The ♣Q was in the wrong hand so Wolff went minus 100, but we gained 12 IMPs.

Things didn't get any better for Mathe and his team after we manhandled them. In fact, they didn't win their first match until the seventh round – and they finished dead last in the round-robin. I didn't hold my breath waiting to see a "Disaster in Taipei" headline in *The*

Bridge World, but I can't really blame Edgar for not highlighting his disaster. I guess I wouldn't have handled it any differently in his place.

Meanwhile, we played France in the third round and were clobbered by 62 IMPs. It didn't feel good to lose by that much – and to lose to the team who rated to be our main competition – but it was early and we still considered ourselves the favorites. We proved that our status as the team to beat was justified. The Aces ended the round-robin in first place with 228 Victory Points. France was second with 182.

There was trouble, however. Although Eisenberg and I had played well enough since we started our partnership and the team had seemed at times to get a second wind from the changes, Billy and I weren't getting along the way a smooth partnership is supposed to. We had played a key role in winning the Vanderbilt in Atlanta that spring, but along the way to Taipei something happened.

My theory is that Billy made a decision sometime in 1971 that he wasn't going to be a part of the Aces much longer. In fact, not long after we got back from Taipei, Billy became an ex-Ace.

He had never liked Dallas much. The Broadway Billy nickname was truly indicative of his mindset. He longed for a city more cosmopolitan than Dallas – and the structured regimen of the Aces wasn't to his liking either.

Don't get me wrong. I'm not saying Eisenberg was completely at fault for our ineffectiveness as a partnership. Billy has always been an incredible competitor and an overachiever. If you were going to build a model bridge player from scratch, you would use a lot of Billy's characteristics. Billy also has many of what I call intangibles – table presence, intensity, mental toughness.

Still, once he made the decision to leave the Aces, there was a change in his commitment and his focus. It's easy to understand how that can happen. You've probably experienced something like it yourself if you've ever changed jobs. Once you give notice at your current job – or even if you've just decided you're definitely going to leave – your focus changes to your new position or situation. You just don't view the old job the same way. In his mind, Billy was headed for California – where he wanted to go – even though he was still playing for the Aces.

On paper, Billy and I rated to be outstanding. Unfortunately the tournament was not played on paper. We weren't getting the job done, and it was obvious we weren't getting along. Reluctantly, Ozzie benched us for all but one set of the final against France. I wouldn't necessarily categorize the difficulties as differences in style, unless you consider bad bridge a style. We were certainly engaging in plenty of that.

While Billy and I rode the pine, the other four were performing admirably. In fact, Wolffie and Jacoby were the stars of the show. Jacoby had a fine tournament – at that point he was playing the best bridge of his life.

Jim, the son of a legend, spent a lot of time in Ozzie's shadow. Jim – we often called him "Hero" because he could come up with some outstanding plays at really critical times – was unfairly denied respect as a player in many circles. In 1970 and 1971, he played outstanding bridge. Jim's performance was very much tied to his confidence level. When he was on a roll and thought he was King Kong, he was very tough for anyone to handle. But if something happened to dent his confidence, he often unraveled. In Taiwan, though, he was a tower of strength – and even the probable cheating by Jaïs and Trézel couldn't stop the Aces.

As long as I've been playing bridge, I've never been able to relate to cheating. If you do something dishonest to win – no matter what you're competing in or for – you haven't really won. I'm not trying to be a goody two-shoes or holier than thou. It's just that when I reflect on the wins I've had in my career, I can do so with a good feeling. I know that even though luck may have played more of a part in a victory than I would have liked, the trophies I took home were earned honestly by me and my partners and teammates – our best against their best.

For a variety of reasons, the laws of bridge are not set up to deal with cheaters. There is a seemingly infinite variety of ways people find to win illicitly. I'm not talking about practices commonly categorized as "coffeehousing" – hesitations, fumbles, etc. I'm talking about downright cheating: telling partner in an illegal way what you've got in your hand, or telling him with some sort of signal what to lead.

In one of the most famous cheating scandals, the venerable Terence Reese and Boris Schapiro of Great Britain were accused of giving signals with their fingers to show the number of hearts each held in his hand. This occurred during the 1965 world championship in Buenos Aires, Argentina. Two books, one accusatory and the other a defense, have been written about the scandal and the shock waves it sent through the bridge world.

In another famous case, two American players were kicked out of the ACBL after it was discovered that they gave signals to each other by the manner in which they placed their pencils on the tables. Others have been accused of relaying information illegally by coughing or by clicking cigarette lighters. The list is as endless as a player's imagination.

Dealing with cheats is a delicate matter. It is a serious offense to openly accuse another player of even a breech of the proprieties. You can get yourself suspended for making such an accusation. Usually such things are handled in private. In the serious cases that have come to some sort of conclusion, the bad guys are most often caught in the act after being observed over a long period of time by people who know or strongly suspect what is going on.

In the case of the guys with the pencils, it was observed that when the opening leader's partner had his pencil in a certain position, the opening leader always led the same suit. When the pencil was in another position, the lead was always another suit – but always the same one. What got the authorities interested were complaints by opponents about how uncanny these guys were with their opening leads. I mean, they were sensational.

In the Bermuda Bowl in Taipei, there was little doubt among those in the know that Jaïs and Trézel were using signals to suggest opening leads. It wasn't completely clear what they were doing – and they were never "caught" by the bridge authorities – but there were few doubters in the expert bridge community that the two were cheating. Jaïs, a physician, was an ordinary looking fellow with a slightly rumpled look when he wasn't in his tuxedo. He had short hair, almost a crew-cut. Trézel, a journalist, dressed like a wealthy businessman. He was a handsome fellow with a slightly superior air.

The fact that Jaïs and Trézel were former world champions was tainted by their reputation as cheats. This deal from the Bermuda Bowl final against the Aces caused a lot of talk – even while it was being played on vugraph.

```
Dlr: East        ♠ K Q 6 3
Vul: Both        ♥ 8 6 3
                 ♦ J 7 6
                 ♣ J 6 4
♠ J                          ♠ 9 8 7 5 4
♥ 9 4                        ♥ 7
♦ 9 8 5                      ♦ A 10 3 2
♣ A Q 10 9 8 3 2             ♣ K 7 5
                 ♠ A 10 2
                 ♥ A K Q J 10 5 2
                 ♦ K Q 4
                 ♣ —
```

WEST	NORTH	EAST	SOUTH
Trézel	*Jacoby*	*Jaïs*	*Wolff*
		Pass	1♣
3♣	Dbl	5♣	6♥
All Pass			

Wolff and Jacoby were playing the Orange Club system, so 1♣ was a strong, forcing opening. Jacoby's double showed 7 or 8 high-card points. When Wolff heard Jaïs bid 5♣, Wolff was convinced that Jacoby had few if any high cards in clubs, which meant the high cards he did have would fit well with Wolff's powerful hand.

While this deal was being played, it was shown on a screen in a big ballroom at the hotel, where an audience was encamped to watch the proceedings. As soon as the hands were flashed onto the screen, Pedro-Paulo Assumpção – a very savvy player and a member of the Brazilian team, which was out of the event – started taking bets.

"I'll give you five to one," Pedro-Paulo said, "that he (Trézel) leads a diamond."

Most of the people thought Assumpção was daffy. What do you think is the normal lead with the West hand? You can be 100% sure that declarer is void in clubs. When someone sails into slam the way Wolffie did, it's highly likely that he's void in some suit. Also, your partner has raised you, despite the vulnerability, to the five level, so there aren't many clubs left to go around.

On the other hand, declarer didn't seem interested in a grand slam, so your side may well have a cashing ace outside clubs. So what's your best chance to defeat this contract? Right! You lead your ♠J, hoping partner has the ace so he can win the first trick and give you a ruff.

Well, Trézel led the ♦5, a wildly anti-percentage action which was a stunning development given his holding. The vugraph audience and the commentators were struck dumb. Why did Trézel lead a diamond? What was going on?

It was simple. Trézel knew his partner had strength in diamonds. If Jaïs had no desire for a spade lead, only a diamond could succeed. He felt his only chance was to find Jaïs with sufficient strength in diamonds to defeat the contract. The choice of leads made it obvious that Trézel knew it was pointless to try for a spade ruff. He had to hope Jaïs had something else to go with the diamond strength.

Anyway, Jaïs won the opening lead with the ♦A and went into the tank for the longest time. I don't know if he knew something about Trézel's hand, but he did something very strange – he returned a club. Of all the possible returns, that is the least likely. His partner had bid clubs at the three level vulnerable, so it was highly unlikely he had fewer than seven of them, meaning Wolff was void. Furthermore, Wolff might easily have had a two-suited hand, including four spades. If so, Trézel would be void in spades and could ruff. And what about a two-suited hand which included five diamonds? If that was the case, a diamond return would scuttle the contract.

That was just one example of the fishy stuff that went on with this pair.

Near the end of the round-robin, Don Krauss and Lew Mathe sat down to play against Jaïs and Trézel. The French were a lock for the medal round and Don's team was hopelessly out of it, so the match meant nothing.

On that note, as Lew and Don sat down, Lew said to Jaïs: "It's Don's birthday today. Let's keep it clean." Nothing was said, but on the very first board, Jaïs held something like:

♠J 10 6 5 ♥A J 8 7 3 ♦8 ♣A K 5.

Mathe opened a weak 2♦ on his right and Jaïs passed! Well, guess what? Trézel's high-card holding consisted of a jack. Was it a lucky guess? If so, I'll eat the Astrodome. Of course, Don and Lew floundered around and got to 3NT – down three. So much for keeping it clean.

The whole thing gave me a rotten feeling. I don't like to play against sleazy types like that. What was unfortunate was that the other members of the French team – Henri Svarc, Jean-Michel Boulenger, Jean-Louis Stoppa and Jean-Marc Roudinesco – were very ethical, although, except for Svarc, a step below world-class level as players.

What was ironic was that although Jaïs and Trézel were cheating, many of their machinations didn't work out. They were signaling for leads, but frequently the lead that was asked for did not work as well as the normal lead.

Although the final score was relatively close – 243-182 – we took an early lead and maintained it throughout. We lost only two of the eight sets. We won the only one Billy and I played, 35-20.

This time, at the victory dinner, there were no snide remarks from the podium about how bad the field was or about "vintage" world championships. For the second year in a row, the Aces were Bermuda Bowl champions. We felt good to be on top, but there were more changes ahead. We hadn't been back in the U.S. very long before Billy packed his bags one day and bid us *adieu*.

We also heard that the Blue Team was coming out of retirement and would probably be playing in the World Team Olympiad in 1972. That event would mark a very definite change in the fortunes of the mighty Aces.

12

Nemesis

BOUT A YEAR before I joined the Aces – I guess it was 1968, while I was still living in California – I was playing bridge with Eddie Kantar in an exhibition match against two members of the great Italian Blue Team – Benito Garozzo and Giorgio Belladonna. They and some other experts from Europe were touring the U.S. and taking on the local yokels in various cities. Besides Kantar and me, our team had a mixed bag of players – Lew Mathe, Kelsey Petterson, Don Krauss and a couple of others. It was the usual lineup for this sort of thing. Selection of team rosters, after all, tended to become a political process.

Anyway, Garozzo, Belladonna, Eddie and I were playing in a small room at the Sportsman's Lodge, a hotel-restaurant complex in Studio City in the Los Angeles area. At the time, the lodge had *the* restaurant in the San Fernando Valley. The hotel was run by David Harlig, a bridge enthusiast, so it was a natural to have the show at his place.

Several hundred feet away from where we were playing, a large audience in a ballroom watched the play on vugraph. Eddie and I and the Italians were in the so-called "closed room," but all our bids and plays were relayed via telephone hookup to the ballroom where the big screen was set up. The audience could see everything.

At one point during the match, Garozzo and Belladonna – normally pretty sound bidders – became bogged down in an auction – it sounded as if they were headed for trouble. I don't recall the hands, but I do remember that when the cuebidding started I had a chance to double a club cuebid for a lead. I had something like KJx in clubs, which might make a double attractive, but I was afraid that if I doubled they might not bid slam, which they seemed determined to do. I decided they were going to bid slam anyway, and if they did, it would probably go down no matter what Eddie picked for his opening lead.

Well, they finally got to the six level – Garozzo was playing it – and damned if the only lead to beat it wasn't a club. Of course, I didn't know this at the time, but everyone watching the vugraph show could see it. While Eddie was pondering his opening lead, the commentators were probably discussing why I hadn't doubled the club bid when I had the chance.

Eddie took a long time to decide on his lead. At last, a club hit the table. A huge roar from the audience – which was naturally rooting for us, the home team – could be heard from the ballroom. Despite the distance, the cheering was so loud that our little room literally rocked.

Now Benito is normally a very serious fellow, not given to lighthearted banter at the bridge table, even in an exhibition match. But this time he looked up with a wry grin as he waited for the noise to die down. Then he said, "It doesn't look very good for me."

Sad to say, most of my experiences with the Blue Team did not have such a happy ending.

After we won the 1971 Bermuda Bowl, Corn was feeling his oats. He was ready to flex his bridge muscles, if only vicariously through the Aces. I guess it was inevitable: shortly after we got back from Taipei with our second straight world championship, Ira was on the phone to Italy. He dared the Blue Team to come out and fight.

To lure the Italians out of retirement, Corn set up a much-ballyhooed match at the Hilton Hotel in Las Vegas with a $25,000 winner-take-all pot. There would be lots of publicity with a lot at stake for both teams. If the Blue Team won, they would have bragging rights even though we were the world champions. If the Aces won, we would have vindication by proving we would have won back-to-back Bermuda Bowls even if the Blue Team had not retired. It turned out the Blue Team didn't need a boatload of incentives – they had already pretty much decided to come out of retirement. Sure, said Garozzo and friends, we'll be happy to meet you in Las Vegas.

Ira was almost feverish with excitement. It was time to start cashing in on the Aces' world titles – and what better way to promote the team than to thrash the legendary Italian *Squadra Azura*. Corn was also still feeling the sting of the comments by Count Bonde in Stockholm about the 1970 contest not being a "vintage" championship. If anyone still felt that our win was tainted by the fact that the mighty Blue Team was absent, the Las Vegas match would remove that stigma forever.

Before the match even got started – we played it in late December of 1971 – there was bad blood.

Sometime that year, Corn had arranged to publish a small paperback consisting mostly of newspaper columns published under the Aces' name. The syndicated column was one of the lasting spin-offs of the Aces' world championships. Wolff still writes it today in collaboration with Moose.

Anyway, at some point Corn got involved in designing the cover of this modest book. It was typical of Corn's style that the final result was a cover which read, *Here's the System that Beat the Famed Italian Blue Team*. Remember the book he was going to "write" about backgammon? Well, this book could have been its twin.

For one thing, the book had nothing to do with systems. Even more importantly, it was published before the match even took place. Corn's confidence and enthusiasm just could not be denied. At times, he was like a bull in a china shop.

Publication of this little "book" was greeted by howls of protest – and a lawsuit – by the Italians, who had their own financial aspirations in the United States by this time. The pot was boiling.

There was also a dispute over the disposition of the prize money in the challenge match. Before the match started, Corn wrote a letter to the Italians saying that he wanted the money split and paid to the winners of each segment of the match, as well as to the overall winner. Later on, the Italians denied receiving the letter.

I was beginning to worry that the main objective of the whole exercise – to play a tough match against a tough team – was being lost in all the controversy. Corn, meanwhile, plowed merrily ahead.

A couple of months before the big match with the Blue Team, the Aces had been involved in a serious contest – the trials to see who would represent the U.S. at the World Team Olympiad in Miami in June of 1972. We had gone to New Orleans in late October for a 160-board match against Lew Mathe, Don Krauss, Edgar Kaplan and Norman Kay.

With Eisenberg long gone, I felt like the fifth wheel that I was. It was not much fun for me at the time. Rightly or wrongly, I felt that I was the best player on the team, but I wasn't seeing much action. One of Corn's strongest convictions was that bridge is very much a partnership game. He was convinced that a good partnership of mediocre players had an advantage over an unfamiliar partnership of experts.

The Aces, Corn insisted, would stick with their best partnerships. Wolff and Jacoby were still perking along beautifully, while Lawrence and Goldman were functioning well, too. That left me holding the bag a lot of the time – and feeling uncomfortable.

Not that that had an impact on the match with Mathe and company – the Aces obliterated them by 171 IMPs. The other team was never in the match. We led by 36 IMPs after one session and kept pouring it on.

This deal pretty much sums up the different ways our two teams were headed.

```
        Dlr: South      ♠ 10 4 3 2
        Vul: E-W        ♥ 4
                        ♦ J 10 8 3
                        ♣ 10 9 6 5
    ♠ K 9 7 5                        ♠ A
    ♥ A K Q J 10 8 7                 ♥ —
    ♦ —                              ♦ A K Q 9 7 6 5 4
    ♣ K 7                            ♣ A J 8 4
                        ♠ Q J 8 6
                        ♥ 9 6 5 3 2
                        ♦ 2
                        ♣ Q 3 2
```

WEST	NORTH	EAST	SOUTH
Goldman	*Kay*	*Lawrence*	*Kaplan*
			Pass
1♥	Pass	3♦	Pass
3♥	Pass	3♠	Pass
4NT	Pass	7♦	Pass
7♥	Pass	7NT	All Pass

The grand slam in notrump probably would have gone down if the ♣K had been the ♣Q, but our guys were playing in luck. Look what happened at the other table:

WEST	NORTH	EAST	SOUTH
Krauss	*Wolff*	*Mathe*	*Jacoby*
			Pass
1♥	Pass	7♦	All Pass

It was typical of Lew not to involve partner in the auction, and he paid for his arrogance this time with down one when diamonds didn't break. We gained 20 IMPs on that one board alone. What was worse, he tried to blame Krauss for the bad result.

After Lew bid 7♦, Don took a little time before passing. Naturally, he was concerned about his void in partner's suit. When he tabled the dummy, Mathe said sarcastically, "Quite a show of confidence, partner." Jacoby looked at Krauss as if to say, "Is he crazy?"

After Mathe went down one, he said, "Well, I was afraid Don might have passed 3♦." What crap. 3♦ would have been a strong jump shift. Don had never played weak jump shifts in his life.

Right after the match was over, Lee Hazen, our non-playing captain, made my day by announcing that Paul Soloway was joining the Aces to replace Billy Eisenberg. Paul was going to play with me.

What great news! First of all, I knew Paul from way back. We had cut our bridge teeth in some of the same rubber bridge games in the Los Angeles area. When I was attending San Fernando Valley State University, Paul and I frequently played at the student center when we were supposed to be attending classes. Paul also became a fixture at the L.A. Bridge Club, where I practically lived for a time.

Paul started slowly as a player, particularly in the area of dummy play. People still tell the story that when Soloway became declarer at the L.A. Bridge Club, you'd often hear someone saying, "Long-distance phone call for Paul Soloway . . ." Anything to keep his hands off the dummy.

By the time he joined the Aces, no one joked about Soloway's play – in any phase of the game. He made himself into a great player – one of the best ever. By the time he became my partner, he was known as Win 'Em All Paul. I was delighted to have him on the team. I couldn't wait to start working on the partnership.

Soloway's tenure with the Aces was different from any other member – he didn't live in Dallas. He cut a deal with Ira that he could continue to live in California after joining the team. I never figured out how Paul got away with that. Maybe Corn felt Soloway's stature rated special consideration. Anyway, Paul and I had to try extra hard to get in our practice so we could hone the partnership to the level Corn demanded. We didn't play a hell of a lot of sessions together, but our system was simple enough that we didn't have a lot to remember.

At the Las Vegas Hilton, the atmosphere for the big match with the Blue Team was tense. For starters, we were disappointed with the spectator turnout. The press coverage was decent, but I guess the Blue Team – and the ersatz Gunfight at O.K. Corral that Ira had set up – loomed larger in *our* minds than in the general public's.

Also, we were nervous about how we would perform. Soloway and I were still feeling each other out. Having a new partnership in the works is the kind of change that can have an unsettling effect.

The Aces were confident, but we also were aware of the pressure. Even at the highest levels, bridge is a game of errors. I don't believe I've ever seen a flawless match. Most of the time, mistakes are made all around – at every table. The best players make mistakes, and in these big matches there is a lot of pressure. The experts know they are being watched and judged – by their peers and by regular players.

Of course, the Aces had been through all that and we felt we could handle the pressure. We wanted the Blue Team. We wanted to prove we could kick their butts.

It didn't happen.

Ironically, two of our pairs – Paul and I, Wolff and Jacoby – were using modified versions of the Blue Team Club system (Lawrence and Goldman played Eastern Scientific), while four of the Italians were playing American-type versions of Precision. C.C. Wei, the shipping billionaire who invented Precision, was paying the Italians to play it. That's not an uncommon practice for someone who wants to promote a system. George Rosenkranz once paid a group of professional players to use his Romex system, the idea being that when they won a lot he could brag that they owed it to his bidding schemes.

Anyway, we strode into the Hilton in our blue blazers – even Paul had been outfitted by then – and immediately stubbed our collective toe by falling behind early. Neither side played particularly well and the Italians had the better of the luck.

The one bright spot for me was that I was getting to play my fair share, a vast improvement over the Spingold and the Olympiad Team Trials.

This was one of the few triumphs for the Aces.

Me	Paul
♠ A 7	♠ K 6 5 2
♥ A K 10 8 6	♥ J 7 5
♦ A K J 7 5 3	♦ Q 10 9
♣ —	♣ K 4 3

Paul and I reached 7♦ on this auction (remember, we were playing a Blue Team Club variation):

Me	Paul
1♣	1♥
2♦	3♦
3♥	3♠
4♣	4♦
7♦	Pass

Paul's 1♥ bid showed at least six high-card points but fewer than three controls (Ace = 2; King = 1).

As you can see, the key to the hand is to figure out how to avoid a heart loser, assuming it was possible. Early in the play, I led the ♥J and Walter Avarelli, who didn't know I had a heart suit (remember, my 3♥ was a cuebid), declined to cover. Any good player would cover if he could in that situation, so I decided he didn't have the queen. My only chance, therefore, was to find the queen singleton or doubleton. I went up with the ace, drew trumps and banged down the king. When the queen fell, I claimed my grand slam. At the other table, the contract was 6♦, making only six (Pietro Forquet didn't guess hearts), so we picked up 11 IMPs.

Unfortunately, the Aces didn't have enough swings like that. We actually led in the match a couple of times, but we didn't seem to have the fire in our bellies we had shown so many times before. We lost by a rather substantial margin, 338-254.

What happened? How could the world champion Aces be drubbed this way? Well, we were beaten badly in the partscore trenches. The Italians' judgment in competitive bidding was superior almost the entire match.

If there ever was a time when the Aces' collective psyche was in need of an overhaul, it was after the Las Vegas fiasco. First, we lost to the Blue Team in the challenge match – a bitter pill to swallow, I assure you. But there was more. After the challenge match, there was a 22-team knockout match with the Aces and the Blue Team as part of the field. In between, we played a short exhibition match against Mathe's team.

We lost to Mathe and then lost in the knockout semifinal to Howard Schenken's team. On top of that, we lost again in the playoff for third place. You can guess which team won the knockout event. It was tough for us to sit by and watch the Italians grabbing the glory.

To a man, the Aces were disgusted by the performance in Las Vegas. Our only consolation – the matches were meaningless in every sense except that we had gone toe to toe with the team we most wanted to beat – and we had been beaten. Had the Aces lost something more important than a silly challenge match in Las Vegas? Time would tell. We would find out in Miami. We had six months to get ready for the World Team Olympiad. We knew the Blue Team would be there.

The 1972 Olympiad took place in Miami in June. We tuned up for the big event by losing in the semifinal of the Vanderbilt. Once again, the Aces lost to the Precision Team. It was another shot in the gut for the Aces. We were out to prove the disaster in Las Vegas was a fluke, but it was getting tougher and tougher to remain our old confident selves.

Thanks to Ira's upbeat posture, we had left all the negative feelings in Dallas as we headed for Miami in search of vindication.

The talk of the bridge world prior to the Olympiad was the possible rematch between the Aces and the Blue Team in the final. That buoyed our spirits and we were anxious to take on the world – literally.

It was strange to find myself back at the Americana Hotel, where Don Krauss and I had surprised everyone by winning the pair trials for the 1964 Olympiad. It had been nearly nine years since we took the trials field by storm, eight years since we had sat by and watched while our teammates at the Olympiad lost to the Italians. No matter what happened this time, I wasn't likely to be benched. Soloway and I had played well together since he joined the Aces. We were ready to get even for Las Vegas.

As in New York in 1964, Miami and the Americana had become one big melting pot. There were 39 teams in the Olympiad and they spanned the globe, from Finland to France, Canada to Chile. There were good teams – the Aces, the Blue Team, Great Britain, Canada – and bad teams.

Everyone had to play everyone in the round-robin – 20 boards against each other team. That amounted to 760 deals. The top four teams would compete in semifinal matches. The winners would play for the world championship.

Once again, we tripped right out of the starting gate. A team from Poland kicked our butts, 19-1 (all scoring was by IMPs converted to Victory Points; the maximum the winners could get was 20 VPs, while the losers could end up with minus 3). Italy, meanwhile, started with a 14-6 win over Morocco. On the second day, we were blown away by Italy, 20 to minus 3 – and then we lost to the Netherlands, 12-8.

We eventually regained our footing, however, and began to play well. Paul and I were quite effective as the round-robin wore on. No one panicked and we finally asserted ourselves. In fact, we lost only five matches out of 38 to finish a strong second in the round-robin. First, of course, was Italy.

As the winners of the marathon round-robin, the Blue Team had the choice of opponents in the semifinal. They could have chosen us, but the Italians had nothing if not flair. They preferred the drama of a confrontation with the Aces in the final. The Blue Team also knew we were dangerous. If they were going to lose to us, they wanted it to be in the final.

Well, if the Italians were looking for drama, they got it.

In the semifinals, we crushed Canada by 118 IMPs, while the Blue Team routed France by 90 IMPs. The showdown was set.

There's not much to say about our second match with the Italians except that they beat us. It wasn't much of a final. They jumped out to a 42-7 lead and we never caught up. It was 32-0 before we scored our first IMP. We closed to within 28 IMPs after the fourth 16-board segment (with two to go), but the Italians responded with a 33-8 fifth set to put the match out of reach. The final score was 203-138. Edgar Kaplan, writing about the match in *The Bridge World*, put us in our place with these words, ". . . any way you look at it, the better team won."

That about summed up the Aces at that point. We were no longer the kings of the hill. We were still Bermuda Bowl champs – they hadn't taken that away from us yet. But we knew the bridge world was watching when we were vanquished by the Blue Team. I've always hated to lose, but I've also recognized that it's part of the game. You play enough, you eventually lose. But I hated worse than anything to lose to the Italians.

There was more to my feelings of unease than a bitter loss, however. The fact is, the glue that had held the Aces together was coming unstuck. That elusive quality that made us formidable world champions was fading like a sunset. Things were changing for us – not necessarily for the good.

Shortly after the Olympiad loss, Soloway jumped ship. It didn't suit him to be tied down to the Aces, and it didn't suit Corn for Soloway to be part of the team and not live in Dallas, even though he had agreed to it in the beginning. Once again, I was partnerless and restless. Luckily, I had my insurance business in Dallas to fall back on if the Aces experiment collapsed completely. Oh, Corn was still our benefactor and the spiritual leader of the team, but the complexion had changed.

I didn't like the fact that Soloway quit the Aces, but it did open up a new opportunity for me. It was in 1972 that I started playing more or less steadily with Bobby Wolff, who remains my regular partner today. Wolff and I became a pair because Bobby's regular partner, Jacoby, had dropped out. Once Corn stopped paying us regularly, guys like Jimmy – who had families and mortgages – needed steady incomes. They couldn't be part of the team for nothing. So Jacoby went off to make money playing with paying clients. It was sad to see the Aces coming unraveled, but it turned out to be good for me because it was the beginning of my partnership with Wolff.

Wolffie, who helped Corn put the Aces together, is a great guy. He's a wonderful player and a great competitor. He also drives me crazy sometimes. He thinks any convention invented after 1958 is no good, so he won't let me tinker with our system. Wolffie is also a neurotic sort, especially when it comes to travel. If I had a plane to catch at 9 a.m. and he had one to catch at 10 a.m., you can bet he'd be leaving for the airport ahead of me.

Sometimes I like to joke that Wolff and I more or less just tolerate each other. We don't see eye to eye on many issues and we've been known to get into some pretty heated arguments. But there's a basic respect between us – deep down we do like each other. It would be pretty difficult to play together for so many years and with such success if we couldn't stand each other.

Besides being a great bridge player, Wolff has also been quite successful in the political arena. He's been a member of the ACBL Board of Directors and was president of the ACBL. As this book is being written, he is president of the World Bridge Federation. Wolff is unusual for a politician, even a bridge politician, in that he's a straight talker and a straight shooter. There is never any doubt where he's coming from. He doesn't mask his intentions or hide behind rhetoric. In some ways, he may be too open, but I admire his honesty.

I just wish he'd loosen up a little on the system stuff.

Although I can look back on 1972 as the year I formed my most lasting partnership, for the Aces the year was anything but memorable. Besides being drubbed in Miami, we won nothing that year. I'm sure we all try to blot it out of our memories.

The following year was an improvement – in a way. The Aces won the Vanderbilt, but with an unfamiliar lineup. Our team was Wolff and me, Lawrence, Goldman and a fellow named Mark Blumenthal. Jacoby wasn't on the team and Goldman had chosen Blumenthal to bring the Aces up to a five-man team. Basically, Wolff and I played together and Goldman, Lawrence and Blumenthal formed a threesome.

Mark, a dark-haired fellow who wore a goatee, was a nice enough fellow, but he wasn't really good enough to be a member of the Aces. In my mind, the selection of Blumenthal was the only time I ever saw Goldman lose objectivity. My theory: he got so sick of Eisenberg's undisciplined ways that he wanted someone who would say "yes sir" and "no sir" and toe the line. Blumenthal was a good player who had moderate success in tournaments, but he was a notch below the Aces standard in my opinion. Blumenthal is a sad case – he had a congenital heart condition and some years later he went into the hospital for surgery. He came out of the operation with the symptoms of someone who had suffered a severe stroke. He has never been the same since.

We won the Vanderbilt with Blumenthal, but Goldman and Lawrence were playing in the key situations. Blumenthal was more like a reserve than a regular player. I guess I shouldn't complain too much, since 1973 was the last time I won the Vanderbilt.

Although we were still the Aces in 1973, the luster was coming off the name. What happened to us in the Bermuda Bowl further tarnished the image.

A couple of months after we won the Vanderbilt, we flew to São Paulo, Brazil. From there we drove to the little city of Santos, about 45 miles away and near the Atlantic coast. We hopped a ferry to the island community of Guaruja. Its sandy beaches, palm trees and flowers made it a popular spot for tourists. The place looked like paradise, but it became a living hell for the Aces.

By this time, Jacoby had rejoined the team – Corn was paying again – and was playing in a threesome with Wolff and me. Goldman, Lawrence and Blumenthal made up the other threesome. Unlike the Bermuda Bowl of today, the field back then was made up of only five teams – the Aces, Italy, Brazil, Indonesia and a second team from North America. The rules have changed since, but in 1973 the defending Bermuda Bowl champion got an automatic invitation to the party.

The Blue Team was slightly different from the one we played in Las Vegas. The big three – Garozzo, Belladonna and Forquet – still anchored the team, but they had added some new names: Benito Bianchi, Giuseppe Garabello and Vito Pittala.

The other U.S. team – designated as "North America" to distinguish it from the Aces – had won a trials event to get there. Ironically, ex-Ace Paul Soloway was one of them. He was playing with John Swanson, a regular partner of Paul's for years. The rest of the team were the legendary B. Jay Becker, Jeff Rubens, Mike Becker (B. Jay's son) and Andy Bernstein. The last three were playing in their first world championship.

The handicappers predicted an Aces-Blue Team final and that's what they got. We won the round-robin by 1 Victory Point over Italy, setting up the rematch between the Olympiad finalists and giving the Italians the chance to regain the Bermuda Bowl championship. Only the weak team from Indonesia kept our pals from the U.S. out of last place.

Of course, when it was all over, we might just have well have finished where the North American team did.

We had shown some strength during the round-robin, and the final looked to be a good contest. It turned out to be the worst showing ever by an American team in the Bermuda Bowl.

Both teams fielded their strongest lineups. The Aces played Wolffie and me, Lawrence and Goldman against Belladonna-Garozzo and Forquet-Bianchi.

We played eight 16-board segments. After the first two, the Italians led 124-6. We couldn't believe it. Everything we did went wrong. When Wolff and I bid a vulnerable 6♠, Forquet cashed the ♥A and ♥K and gave his partner a ruff for down two. Garozzo and

Belladonna stopped in 4♠ at the other table. Lawrence and Goldman bid 3NT with the heart suit wide open and the Italians took the first five tricks in hearts. Forquet and Bianchi bid to 5♦, which was unbeatable, on the same cards.

It was like that hand after hand. Some of our disasters were self-inflicted, some the result of good judgment by the Italians. This was the kind of thing that was happening to us.

```
Dlr: South        ♠ 7 5
Vul: Both         ♥ 10 7
                  ♦ A Q 10 5
                  ♣ Q 9 8 6 3
♠ K Q 9                          ♠ J 8 6 4 2
♥ J 8                            ♥ K 6 4
♦ J 9 8 7 6 2                    ♦ 3
♣ A J                           ♣ 10 5 4 2
                  ♠ A 10 3
                  ♥ A Q 9 5 3 2
                  ♦ K 4
                  ♣ K 7
```

WEST	NORTH	EAST	SOUTH
Garozzo	*Lawrence*	*Belladonna*	*Goldman*
			1♥
Pass	1NT	Pass	3♥
Pass	4♥	All Pass	

Garozzo didn't fancy entering the auction at the two level with that ratty diamond suit, and his pass had a marked effect on Goldman's play. Garozzo led the ♠K and Goldman won. Instead of playing a spade back right away so he could ruff one in dummy, Goldman played on clubs. Garozzo won the ♣A and returned the jack. Goldman won in dummy and finessed the ♥Q. He cashed the ace and started playing diamonds, expecting to be able to discard at least one of his spades. But Belladonna ruffed the second round and the defense cashed two spades for down one.

At the other table, Bianchi opened a strong 1♣, giving Wolff room to overcall at the one level. Thus warned, Bianchi played the contract more carefully and took his 10 tricks.

There's no way to describe how we felt at being manhandled – humiliated – by the Italians. They had such a big lead that they put in the two stiffs – Garabello and Pittala – in the third quarter. We were so far out of it we let Blumenthal play. With subs doing mop-up duty on both sides, the Aces won the final segment 80-3, and we still lost, 333-205!

There was no way Ira could put a happy face on this loss, no way he could muster an upbeat speech. We simply had to sit and watch at the victory banquet as the Italians happily accepted the trophy as the re-crowned Bermuda Bowl champions. I could have bitten through a tenpenny nail that day.

In late 1973, the Aces changed again. By winning the Vanderbilt earlier that year, we had qualified for the team trials in Milwaukee to pick a team for the 1974 Bermuda Bowl in Venice, Italy. About the time the trials were rolling around, Corn, who had had some financial reverses, decided he couldn't afford to pay the Aces any more on a regular basis. He would foot the bill for expenses, but he didn't want us on his payroll any more.

That was fine with most of us – we were all earning money other ways – but Lawrence didn't like it. He was yearning to return to California anyway, so he told Corn that he couldn't stay in Dallas unless he was paid to do so. Corn bade him farewell.

So the Aces were Wolff and me, Goldman and Blumenthal. Corn decided to add the Canadian stars, Sami Kehela and Eric Murray. They were still in their prime so the addition was a good one for the team. We won the trials easily after falling behind early, and once again we were among the Bermuda Bowl favorites.

About two weeks before the Bermuda Bowl, we all traveled to the Canary Islands for the Fourth World Pair Olympiad. It was in that exotic spot that Wolffie and I had one of our greatest thrills playing together. We won the World Open Pairs, a rather unusual accomplishment for us. Nearly every major win we've ever had together has been in a team event. Nowadays when I go to the Nationals, I usually book pair games with other players and play in the teams with Wolff.

The tournament was played in Las Palmas, the capital of the Canary Islands, off the coast of Africa. It was quite different, pretty dry in most spots because of its proximity to the Sahara Desert.

Bobby and I made it through three days of qualifying sessions and then had a huge game in the second final session to win by nearly two boards. This was a fun hand in our final session:

```
Dlr: East        ♠ J 6
Vul: Both        ♥ A
                 ♦ A Q 9 8
                 ♣ A K Q 10 6 4
♠ 8 5                            ♠ A K 9 4
♥ K J 8 5 4                      ♥ 10 9 6
♦ K 4 2                          ♦ J 10 6 3
♣ 7 5 2                          ♣ J 8
                 ♠ Q 10 7 3 2
                 ♥ Q 7 3 2
                 ♦ 7 5
                 ♣ 9 3
```

WEST	NORTH	EAST	SOUTH
	Wolff		*Me*
		Pass	Pass
Pass	1♣	Pass	1♦
Pass	2♣	Pass	2♠
Pass	3♦	Pass	3NT
All Pass			

Remember, we were playing a system in which a 1♣ opener is an artificial bid showing a strong hand. My 1♦ bid showed a weak hand. The rest of the bidding was natural.

West led a heart which I won perforce in dummy. Even assuming clubs broke reasonably, I still had only eight tricks (I didn't have an entry to take the diamond finesse). I wasn't about to give up, however, so I ran clubs. East had to make four discards, and I noticed that he threw two spades and two hearts. It was starting to look like he was trying to guard diamonds.

After I ran the clubs, I got off dummy with a spade. East, really uncomfortable now, won the ace and cashed the king before playing a low diamond to West's king and dummy's ace. I now had nine tricks, but in a matchpoint game you're supposed to take risks for extra tricks. At trick 11, I played the ♦9 from dummy. East won with the 10, but he was left on lead with the J-6. Dummy had the Q-8. How sweet it was.

Bobby and I were ecstatic about the win. It was our first and only victory in a world pairs event.

A day or two after our triumph in the Canary Islands, Bobby and I left for Venice to play in the Bermuda Bowl. We were still high with the thrill of victory. Yet another loss to the Italians was to bring us back to earth with a thud.

Corn was with us on the trip to Venice and we were still calling ourselves the Aces, but things had been different ever since we got back from Taiwan and Eisenberg took off.

Again, the Bermuda Bowl field was small. There were six teams: us, Italy, Brazil, France, Indonesia and New Zealand. The Italians won the round-robin by 1 VP and we were second. Once again, we went head to head with our nemesis. Once again, we lost. It was closer this time – 195-166 – but the Blue Team still came out on top. As you can imagine, this was becoming a source of extreme frustration for me. I wasn't used to losing like this.

In 1974, I was truly innocent – I had no idea what real frustration was. I found out on the island of Bermuda the following year.

13

On the verge of scandal

IN JANUARY of 1975, the island of Bermuda was aflame with scandal. Two Italians playing in the Bermuda Bowl had been caught exchanging information by touching their feet together under the table while they were playing. The news swept the bridge world almost overnight. Suddenly newspapers everywhere were interested in the world championships.

Early in the tumult, a telegram arrived addressed to the World Bridge Federation. All the WBF bigshots, of course, were in Bermuda. The telegram was from my old friend Eric Murray, the Toronto attorney who still ranked as one of the top players in the world.

Eric had read about the foot tappers in a Toronto newspaper, and his telegram requested that the WBF convey a message to the Italians.

"I would like to play for the Italian team," Murray cabled. "I'm fairly well known as a bridge player, and above all, I wear a size 12 shoe."

If I had known about the telegram at the time, it might have given me a grin or two. As it was, there was absolutely nothing for me to smile about in Bermuda that winter.

By the time the Silver Anniversary of the Bermuda Bowl rolled around in 1975, there were scarcely any vestiges of the Aces. There certainly was no official Aces team.

In the team trials – held in Washington DC over the Labor Day weekend in 1974 – Ira Corn was non-playing captain of a team sponsored by Bud Reinhold. Bud was a ruddy-faced Miami businessman who had taken up bridge late in life. Although a virtual beginner, he was an enthusiastic player who could hold his own in certain settings. His team, after all, had won a major championship in 1973. Wolff was Bud's partner – and the reason Corn was NPC of the team. Don't forget, Wolff and Corn were the original conspirators on the Aces project.

I wasn't on any of the teams in the trials. The story of how I got to play in the Bermuda Bowl despite sitting out the trials – and how Wolff got to play in the Bermuda Bowl despite *losing* the trials – is worth telling.

It started with the winners of the 1974 Grand National Teams – a six-man squad from Los Angeles. There were Paul Soloway and John Swanson, Eddie Kantar and Billy Eisenberg, Richard Katz and Larry Cohen.

Katz and Cohen were doubly qualified for the trials, however, because they won the 1973 Reisinger playing with Reinhold, Peter Weichsel and Alan Sontag. Bud offered Katz and Cohen a bundle of cash to play with him in the trials, so they dropped off the Grand National Team even though it was the best in the field. The rules required six members on each trials team, and Wolffie was loose at the time, so he was recruited as the sixth to play with Reinhold.

With Katz and Cohen defecting, Soloway and his team needed a third pair, but they couldn't add just anyone. Their new pair had to be from their home district (Southern California). The Grand National Teams was supposedly a grass roots event that started at the club level and ultimately was contested among representatives from ACBL's 25 districts. The GNT augmentation rules were that the extra pair had to be from within the district.

Now, Soloway and his bunch were far and away the best team in the trials. They could have won with Mutt and Jeff as their fifth and sixth – especially if Mutt and Jeff didn't play. The reality was that Soloway had his eye on Wolffie and me right from the start.

Paul told me he planned to add a couple of warm bodies – eligible warm bodies, to be sure – for the trials. "They might get near the table if they happen to walk by," Paul said, "but when the trials are over we'll boot them off and add you guys for the Bermuda Bowl."

That sounded great to me. Of course, the whole plan was down the drain if Bud's team – with Wolff on it – happened to win the trials.

Soloway picked a couple of Los Angeles-area players – Ira Cohen and Larry Mandel – to make up his full complement for the Washington showdown. It would be easy to get the idea, from the way things developed, that Cohen and Mandel were just a couple of bums called in to keep our chairs warm. The truth is that they were an up-and-coming pair with some ability. Mandel has dropped out of the tournament scene, but Cohen has developed into a very good bridge player with a national championship to his credit.

The real issue at the time, of course, was experience. Wolff and I had been in the trenches at the top levels and had won – and there's no way to duplicate that except in world championships. Not that our joining the team was unanimously applauded – Billy Eisenberg, our erstwhile teammate, wasn't overjoyed with the selection. For one thing, his experience with the Aces wasn't altogether positive, and he didn't feel that he had received proper respect from the team. For another, Eisenberg preferred Alan Sontag and Peter Weichsel, a hot pair who had made their mark.

In our first encounter with Eisenberg after joining the Soloway team, Billy spoke up directly. "Remember," he told us, "you are invited guests. You're not taking over this thing."

Looking at the four teams in the big playoff in Washington, it was almost like an Aces reunion. Bud's team had Wolffie and Ira Corn as NPC. GNT had former Aces Soloway and Eisenberg, and the Vanderbilt team had Mike Lawrence and Bobby Goldman – more erstwhile Aces. I was there in spirit, of course, rooting like hell for GNT.

Four teams made up the trials field – GNT (Soloway *et al*), Reisinger (Reinhold, Wolff and company), the winners of the 1974 Vanderbilt and the winners of the 1974 Spingold.

In the opening round, GNT routed Spingold 316-227, while Reisinger flattened Vanderbilt 312-222. Soloway and his bunch would play their former GNT teammates – Katz and Cohen – for all the marbles.

There was another point of interest to the trials – screens and bidding boxes. The World Bridge Federation had approved the use of the devices throughout the 1975 Bermuda Bowl competition – the first time this had ever been done – and it was seen as a prudent move for Bermuda Bowl contenders to practice with the screens. The ACBL had already used screens and silent bidding in the late stages of the Vanderbilt and Spingold at the Nationals in Vancouver and New York in 1974.

We – American players and bridge officials, that is – had been lobbying for years to get the WBF to require screens and silent bidding at the world championships. Before 1975, all the arguments and agitation had been for naught. One big reason: violent opposition by the Italians.

It's difficult to explain why screens are so important without sounding paranoid about cheaters, but in 1975 (and in previous years) cheating was an important issue to many knowledgeable observers in the bridge world.

Proving that someone – almost always a pair rather than an individual – has cheated is difficult. The resulting scandal, usually accompanied by lawsuits, is distasteful. The whole process, frankly, is not in the best interests of bridge.

It is much better to prevent the shenanigans – as many as possible, anyway – on the front end. Then everyone feels better about the competition and you can devote more of your energy to playing your best game.

Truthfully, screens and bidding boxes take a lot of pressure off the players. They don't worry nearly so much about giving or receiving – or even appearing to give or receive – unauthorized information by a voice inflection or facial expression.

Also, when you're playing behind screens and it takes someone a long time to make a call – don't forget, the bidding boxes make all auctions silent – in many cases you can't tell whether it was your partner or his screenmate who had a problem. Once again, this removes the pressure of possibly giving or being the recipient of information you or your partner are not entitled to. I like it that way. There's enough pressure already without such extraneous issues.

At the Washington trials, the players were perfectly comfortable with the screens and bidding boxes, and the winners had that much more practice with a relatively new element of competition.

Screens and boxes aside, GNT won the trials, 293-271. The fill-in pair Soloway had recruited – Cohen and Mandel – played exactly 16 boards out of 128 in the final. The rules said they had to play 37.5% to be eligible to represent the U.S. in the Bermuda Bowl. Of course, the ACBL Board of Directors could have granted them a dispensation from this regulation, but no one seriously believed the board would even be asked.

Alfred Sheinwold, non-playing captain of the winning team, made it plain that he wanted to add Hamman and Wolff to the squad. Mandel and Cohen had already been given the heave-ho, and the team needed another pair. Finally, Sheinwold petitioned the ACBL Board to allow the team to add us.

Naturally, there were political reverberations and chest thumping by some ACBL board members. It was obvious that Soloway and his team had planned to make an end run around the ACBL rules right from the start, and that didn't sit right with some of the bridge politicians. My view: when you make dumb rules, people find ways to circumvent them.

There was talk of putting Katz and Cohen back on the team, but that notion was mercifully scrapped. Eventually we were approved as the new members of the North American team.

Thus did Wolffie become, to the best of my knowledge, the only player in history to lose the trials and still end up on the international team.

Before we played the first card in the 1975 Bermuda Bowl – indeed, before we even got to the island itself – there was tension. It permeated the world championship and loomed like a specter. What's more, the atmosphere had nothing to do with the intensity and the fierce competitive spirit you usually find at a high-level bridge tournament.

This was bad blood, pure and simple.

Our captain, Alfred Sheinwold, started the ball rolling by writing an article for *Popular Bridge* magazine in which he all but accused two members of the Italian team of cheating. The Italian Bridge Federation was incensed and proceeded to harass the European Bridge League into petitioning the ACBL to have Sheinwold removed as our captain.

As expected, the ACBL turned a deaf ear to the EBL's complaints – Sheinwold remained as our captain. So be it, said the Italians, but we will have no direct contact with Sheinwold in Bermuda. Writing in *Australian Bridge* in an article reprinted in the 1975 world championship book, Denis Howard noted that "Benito Garozzo is reported to have threatened direct contact of another sort."

Meanwhile, Sheinwold's article was the hottest item in the bridge world for months. Everyone was talking about it and writing about it. *The Bridge World* magazine took Sheinwold's and the ACBL's side – at least as far as the captaincy issue was concerned. "It is surely not the function of bridge organizations to discipline the bridge press – nor is it the job of a captain to be loved by his opponents . . . (Sheinwold) is an urbane, highly respected senior citizen of the bridge community."

On the other hand, there was this blast from England's *Bridge Magazine*: ". . . the villain of the piece is Sheinwold, a man hitherto regarded with respect and indeed affection, who wrote articles . . . in which he attacked the ethics and behavior of the Italians in a series of astounding innuendoes which have proved to be without foundation. Then – wait for it – the Americans actually selected this man as non-playing captain of the North American team . . .The wind was sown . . ."

I think Freddy would tell you that acting as our NPC turned out to be one of the toughest jobs he ever had.

Sheinwold is an interesting fellow. He is now in his eighties and is somewhat frail, but in 1975 during the Bermuda Bowl scandal he was a tower of strength in a situation that became more and more difficult as it progressed. The diminutive Englishman was and still is a man of integrity and courage. When it was time to stand up for the American team, Freddy was right there in the middle of the melee.

Sheinwold was born in London but moved to the U.S. at the age of 9. He worked for America's OSS – the predecessor of the CIA – during World War II as chief code and cipher expert. After the war, he established an outstanding reputation in the bridge world.

He earned respect as a player by winning the Spring National Men's Teams and the event now known as the Reisinger Board-a-Match Teams. Away from the tournament world, Freddy is known chiefly for his writing – he has a syndicated bridge column and several books – and as co-inventor of the Kaplan-Sheinwold bidding system.

Sheinwold also was chairman at one time of the ACBL Laws Commission and a member of the WBF Laws Commission, both very prestigious positions. He served as chairman of the Appeals Committee at many Nationals.

I knew Sheinwold from my days as a bridge player in the Los Angeles area. He didn't frequent the rubber bridge clubs, but I saw him occasionally at tournaments – and Sheinwold was a big name in bridge even when I started out. Freddy is a strong-willed man with a definite opinion on most issues and no fear of expressing himself.

One of my most vivid memories of Freddy revolves around his participation as director of a Calcutta game in Los Angeles that I played in with Eddie Kantar after I had moved to Dallas to join the Aces. The format was similar to an IMP pairs competition – you get your score on each board by comparing it to a datum (the average of all scores after the highest and lowest are removed).

Well, Kantar and I were playing against a one-time photographer named Larry Weiss, whose partner was Bill McWilliams, a fellow I knew from my beginning days in the bridge world of L.A.

Kantar and I had been out of touch somewhat since I left to join the Aces, so we took time before the Calcutta to discuss the old stuff we played when we were regular partners.

One of the discussions we had had at one point in our partnership concerned what to do with jump-shift hands. We played, for example, that if partner responded 2♠ to a 1♣ opener, that was a strong jump shift. On the other hand, 1♣ - Pass - 3♦ was weak. In our discussion we decided that if an opponent overcalled directly, it wouldn't affect whether the jump shift was strong or weak.

The trouble with these ruminations is that it was never clear with Eddie and me when something left the discussion stage and officially became part of the system.

As luck would have it, I was dealt this hand:

♠J 5 4 ♥10 5 ♦K Q 9 8 6 3 2 ♣6.

Eddie opened 1♣ and Weiss overcalled 1♥. I couldn't remember whether 3♦ was weak or strong, but this looked like a weak jump shift to me, so I bid 3♦. Kantar was asked to explain the bid. Well, Eddie didn't want to give me information by what he said, so I was chased away from the table. I found out later that Eddie told them that our agreement as he remembered it was that it was a weak bid, but he thought it was strong – that I had forgotten.

I came back to the table and Eddie bid 3NT on this hand:

♠10 8 7 6 2 ♥A Q 7 4 ♦ — ♣K J 8 7 4.

Weiss, whose hand was

♠A Q ♥K 9 6 3 2 ♦A 4 ♣A Q 9 2,

doubled with alacrity.

This came back to Kantar, who knew me as the sort of belligerent fellow who would redouble in a flash if I had the strong jump shift. So Eddie retreated to 4♣. Now Weiss chose to consider that we were in a forcing auction and tried to get the edge both ways by passing.

This once was a common tactic among some players when they thought the opponents had gone wrong in some way, such as failing to Alert. You pass and enjoy the expected disaster rather than risk a double that might wake somebody up to what's happening. If the opponents somehow land on their feet, you scream for the director. Weiss knew my jump shift was weak. He had 19 high-card points and Kantar had opened the bidding. If I had a strong jump shift, that would mean there were about 50 points in this deck.

Well, I passed and McWilliams, who naturally had a weak hand, also passed. Kantar went down four tricks vulnerable and Weiss started screaming for the cops. The cop in this case was Sheinwold, the sole arbiter of bridge law at this event.

Freddy trotted over to our table and the bullshit ensued. Weiss claimed he had been screwed because he was given a wrong explanation of my bid. I didn't like what I was hearing, so I started with the needle. "Suppose we bid Blackwood, Larry," I said, "and bid to 7NT and you were on lead with two aces. I assume you wouldn't double because we had shown them all. I guess you'd figure your eyes were bad, right?"

Naturally, that added fuel to the fire. Weiss was getting red in the face. "Besides," I continued, "if you double 4♣, we'll find our 5-3 spade fit."

It's often said that the first liar doesn't have a chance, and Weiss proved the point on this occasion. "Okay," he snorted, "if you bid spades I'll double and lead the ace and queen." That defense, not at all likely, would have resulted in down three.

Sheinwold, in his wisdom, ruled that the final contract was 4♠ doubled, down 800. I guess he was having a bad day.

We landed in Bermuda a couple of days before the tournament started and checked into the Southampton Princess Hotel. It was then and still is Bermuda's finest. Though not a tall structure, it is nonetheless a massive edifice and quite imposing. The management, harking back to Bermuda's British heritage, ran the hotel like one of the grandest in London. For dinner, we found, we were expected to dress formally.

I didn't see any member of the Blue Team when we arrived at the hotel, but there was a definite Italian presence. As might be expected, the 1975 Bermuda Bowl – considering all that had gone on leading up to it – was of special interest to Italians and many Europeans, who flocked to Bermuda. All of them hoped to see the haughty Americans get their comeuppance.

As for the Italian team, I could almost feel them there. From the moment we landed on the island, I couldn't shake the feeling that something, sooner or later, was going to hit the fan.

The team the Italians sent to the Bermuda Bowl was not completely familiar to all of us. The great Pietro Forquet, a fixture on the Blue Teams of old, did not play in 1975. But the Blue Team had Giorgio Belladonna and Benito Garozzo, who were enough by themselves to make the Blue Team formidable. Then there were Arturo Franco and Vito Pittala, respected as players but not in the class of Garozzo or Belladonna. Finally, the two men who would become the focal point of the whole miserable mess – Gianfranco Facchini and Sergio Zucchelli.

Although I had never played against them, I knew them by reputation. In the year previous to the Bermuda Bowl, these rather ordinary players had won three major pairs championships in Europe in top-flight competition – the prestigious *Sunday Times* Invitational and the two biggest money prizes on the circuit.

From what he had heard about them on the grapevine in Europe, Wolff knew Facchini and Zucchelli were weak players. His suspicions were confirmed when he kibitzed them in Monte Carlo about a year before the Bermuda Bowl. Bobby had been playing in a knockout event and was eliminated early, so he watched this famous Italian pair who were routinely racking up 70% games.

Wolff was astonished at one point to see what Facchini did defending 5♦ doubled. At trick 11, he was down to AQx in diamonds in front of declarer, who held KJx in trumps with none in dummy. Facchini could have guaranteed two more tricks by just leading a low diamond from his hand. If declarer won, he would have to play back into Facchini's A-Q. It doesn't take a genius to figure out what to do in this case. Well, Bobby noted that Facchini took a long time before finally playing the trump ace, the only play to let declarer escape with only one more loser.

When you see a gaffe like that, it's a very strong clue that something stinks. You don't make plays like that and still string together 70% games without creating suspicion among knowledgeable players. We wondered how the Italians could be leaving Forquet at home while allowing these bozos to play.

Meanwhile, our team had arrived in a somewhat somber mood, in part because Sheinwold had been a bit peevish because some members had brought girlfriends with them. Barbara and I were separated and I was going with Susie Kennedy (now Marshall). Eisenberg and Swanson also brought their girlfriends, and Sheinwold and his wife, Patricia, didn't like it. It was never clear whether the objection was that we might be distracted from our mission – or just that they thought it was immoral and distasteful. Anyway, the Sheinwolds' disapproval merely added to the tension.

The people of Bermuda, meanwhile, were more than excited about the tournament. It was the 25th anniversary of the Bermuda Bowl and of course, Bermuda was a natural to serve as host for the championship since the first Bermuda Bowl took place in Bermuda. The government provided money to help finance the tournament and even printed commemorative Bermuda Bowl postage stamps – in four different denominations – as a tribute. There was to be a big ACBL regional tournament right after the Bermuda Bowl.

Bermuda's support for the event made the bridge politicians even more nervous about the bad blood that had developed between the Americans and the Italians. What if fist fights broke out? How would the government react? Would they withdraw the money that was promised?

Naturally, there were many American bridge officials on hand, including Lew Mathe, who was president of the ACBL that year. Lew could be like a bull in a china shop, and he turned out to be one of the major players in the scandal that developed.

It was a great relief to me when we finally started play. I needed an outlet for some of the tension that had enveloped the island, and I'm sure others felt the same. One of the great things about bridge is that you can lose yourself and your cares in the cards and the competition – and that's just what I wanted to do.

Besides Italy, our rivals in the Bermuda Bowl were France, Indonesia and Brazil. We were the only team with a real chance to dethrone the Italians, who had captured two straight Bermuda Bowls after the Aces won in 1970 and 1971. I liked our chances. Soloway and Swanson were an excellent pair who were playing well. Kantar and Eisenberg were solid, too. Wolffie and I were ready to regain our rightful place as world champions. Once again, we were hungry. It seemed like 100 years since we had won a Bermuda Bowl.

The conditions of contest called for us to play two 32-board matches against the other four teams. Scoring was by IMPs converted to Victory Points. The most a team could win in one set was 20 VPs, but a team which lost badly might end up going minus by as much as 5 VPs. The top four teams after the round-robin would play in the semifinals, which led up to a 96-board championship round.

As it happened, we had to cool our heels in the opening round, which began on a Friday night, while everyone else was playing. With an odd number of teams in the event, there was always a team with a bye. Our team had it the first round.

Rather that setting up play in one huge ballroom, each match was contested in a small room at the hotel. We couldn't watch any tables in person, but we could keep track of what was happening via the vugraph and the big board where everyone's scores were posted.

So we were spectators as the Bermuda Bowl got under way. The Italians started off with France, beating them 62-26, which translated into a 16-4 win in Victory Points. When our team finally went to bat – in the first session Saturday – it was against Brazil. We had an easy time with a 73-38 win.

Our team was due to play the Italians on Sunday in the fifth round. The Blue Team had jumped out to an early lead in the round-robin and seemed destined to trample the rest of the field, so it would be up to us to stop them. There wasn't much discussion of the impending match among team members. What could we say? We knew we had to beat the Italians to win the event, and there was no need for us to remind ourselves of it.

Naturally, all of us were uncomfortable because of the swirl of controversy which imbued the United States presence with an Ugly American flavor. With the infamous Freddy as our captain, we were certainly the bad guys in the eyes of the European contingent. This was a matter of honor. We had insulted their comrades and were challenging the great Blue Team in a world championship. How dare we!

Making our way about the hotel, we would occasionally run into Garozzo or Belladonna or one of the other Blue Team members, but nothing ever came of it. I think they felt as we did that all the players were, in a sense, victims of the political by-play of the tournament. We and they were in Bermuda to play bridge. We recognized that there was a lot of extraneous noise about – noise we were hoping to be able to ignore while we did battle at the table.

Bobby and I were ready to play the Italians, but we knew that – at least at first – it would be somewhat awkward when we finally sat down against them. We had always enjoyed at least a respectful if not warm relationship with Belladonna and Garozzo. Now we were part of a team whose captain had challenged the integrity of *their* team. The first time we sat down against them, with the screens a symbolic reminder of our attitudes about their ethics, it was bound to be chilly. But what could we do? If we were going to win this world championship, which we had every intention of doing, we would have to get to the top over the bodies of the famous Blue Team.

The confrontation with the Italians loomed in our collective consciousness as we sat down to play against France Saturday night. The French beat us, 83-51. Were we preoccupied? Were we looking past the French to Italy? Perhaps. But there was nothing to do but go to bed and try to rest up for the following day. We were to play Indonesia in the afternoon and Italy that night.

As I made my way back to my room that night, I had an uneasy feeling. I was disappointed, of course, at our performance against France, but it was more than that. I think the same inner "antenna" that gives bridge players table feel must have been at work inside me – and I don't believe I was alone in these feelings. I had no conscious knowledge of what was to come, but the atmosphere at the Southampton Princess was still electric with tension.

We didn't play our match with Italy the next day – and the whole world quickly learned why.

14

Scandal

DURING THE 1975 Bermuda Bowl, most of the bridge players ate their meals at the restaurant in the Southampton Princess Hotel. In the dining room where the players congregated, there was a small orchestra. Most of the time, the music was of the dignified sort you would expect at a ritzy place like the Princess.

During the height of the scandal involving the Italian toe-tappers, a group of Americans had assembled for a meal in the dining room.

Sometime during the evening, the toe tappers – Gianfranco Facchini and Sergio Zucchelli – were spotted as they walked into the dining room.

Someone, I'm not sure who, surreptitiously visited the orchestra shortly after the Italians had been seated and slipped the band leader a few bills. Before long, the orchestra was playing *I Get a Kick Out of You*. The Americans who were familiar with the song thought it was a scream. The Italians, who probably didn't know the song, didn't get it.

If justice had been served, the WBF would have been doing the kicking, and Facchini and Zucchelli would have been on the receiving end – right out of the Bermuda Bowl.

The porridge actually hit the fan Sunday, but long before that, the biggest news ever to come out of the Bermuda Bowl spread like wildfire around the Southampton Princess Hotel. It may have been the worst-kept secret in the history of bridge.

The whole mess started with Bruce Keidan, a newspaper reporter from Philadelphia. Keidan was a bridge player who covered the game for the *Philadelphia Inquirer*. The newspaper didn't do a helluva lot beyond running a syndicated column each day, but when bridge news was published, Keidan was the writer.

Anyway, Keidan had wangled an assignment to cover the Bermuda Bowl from his editors. He had been in the bridge world long enough to know many of the name players, including Wolff and Sheinwold, and he convinced his bosses at the *Inquirer* that the Bermuda Bowl was a big deal. Getting to Bermuda from Philadelphia wasn't terribly expensive then, so Keidan was on his way.

Keidan and Wolffie ran into each other in the Baltimore airport and found that they were both heading to Bermuda. They sat together on the plane from Baltimore to the island. Naturally, their conversation revolved around bridge and the world championship, and when Wolff mentioned his view of the ethics of certain Italian players, Keidan was openly skeptical. Keidan said he thought Wolff was paranoid and that all the suspicions might have affected his bridge. That was about as far as the conversation went, but it was clear that Keidan, if anything, had a bias in favor of the Italians going into the event.

Once he landed in Bermuda, Keidan set about making sure the tournament officials would allow him to cover the event close up. In the process of arranging things, Keidan learned that there was a shortage of monitors for the various matches.

The function of a monitor was to record the bids and plays in the room to which he was assigned. The job is an important one, so when Keidan – who had been a monitor at a team trials in the U.S. – volunteered to help out, the offer was readily accepted. It was an ideal assignment for Keidan the reporter, incidentally, because being nearer the action would help him write a better story.

As it happened, Keidan was assigned to the room where Facchini and Zucchelli were playing against Henri Svarc and Jean-Michel Boulenger of France. The Frenchmen were North-South, Facchini was East and Zucchelli was West.

Keidan had to sit near the table he was monitoring to make sure he caught all the bids and plays. Keidan had the habit of slumping back in his chair when seated for long periods. On the evening of Friday, January 24, 1975, he had lowered himself, quite inadvertently, to the point where he could see underneath the table. Keidan – a short, pudgy man – was somewhat lower than anyone else in the room.

The screen dividing the table was positioned diagonally, and Keidan was on the same side as Facchini (East) and Boulenger (North). He could not see Zucchelli and Svarc.

He could, however, see the legs and feet of the players. What he noticed at first was that Facchini, a small wiry man, usually sat with his feet twined around the legs of his chair. On the other hand, Zucchelli was a large, robust man whose feet stayed planted on the floor.

Early on, Keidan noticed something very strange. He saw Facchini's foot go out and sort of kick his partner's foot. What caught Keidan's attention was Zucchelli's reaction – it wasn't the typical one. If your feet are under a table and someone's foot hits yours, your natural reaction is to move your feet. When Facchini's foot hit Zucchelli's, Zucchelli did not move his foot at all. Nothing.

Keidan watched intently. As he did, it became more and more apparent that something was going on. During the auction, Facchini unwrapped his legs from his chair and continually pressed his feet against Zucchelli's – right foot to right foot, right to left, left to right, almost like a skilled piano player manipulating the pedals of his instrument. When the auction was over, Zucchelli pulled his feet closer to his chair, as did Facchini.

Keidan's heart began to race. He couldn't believe what he was seeing. This was the Bermuda Bowl, for Pete's sake – and these guys were cheating! Wolff was right! Keidan looked around to see if anyone could tell he was nervous. The implications of what he had seen were mind-boggling. As any good reporter would, Keidan started thinking about the enormity of the story. It could be the biggest story he had ever covered.

It occurred to Keidan to start keeping track of the times that Facchini played foot music on Zucchelli's toes. He did so surreptitiously for the remainder of the 16-board set. By the time the evening was finished, the shell-shocked Keidan had recorded much more than the bids and plays. He had noted five instances of unusual foot movements by Facchini.

In his excitement at this monumental discovery, Keidan overlooked the step he should have taken right from the start – reporting his discovery to the Director-in-Charge. On this occasion, it was Maury Braunstein, a respected, veteran tournament director. Before the Bermuda Bowl ended, Maury's calm under fire would be severely tested.

Keidan acknowledged later that he should have gone directly to Braunstein. However, in his anxiety to see the Italian cheaters nailed, Keidan was fearful that reporting his discovery to Maury would let the cat out of the bag. The cheaters would be confronted, Keidan feared, immediately clean up their act, and justice would never be served. What Keidan didn't realize was that Braunstein would *not* have confronted Facchini and Zucchelli.

Although he didn't know the right thing to do, Keidan had to do something. He had to tell *someone* about what he had seen. Because of the conversation with Wolff between Baltimore and Bermuda, Keidan naturally thought of telling Wolffie first. When the match was over, Keidan – white as a sheet – found Bobby in the hotel bar and said, "I've got to talk to you." After Keidan related what he had seen, he and Bobby sought out Freddy Sheinwold and Edgar Kaplan to continue the meeting in Sheinwold's hotel room.

After Keidan told his story again to Kaplan and Sheinwold, Kaplan – a member of the appeals committee at the tournament – asked, "Who else knows about this?"

"No one," said the breathless Keidan.

Kaplan suggested that a plan of action was in order. It would take more than the word of an American journalist to nail these guys. "We need some other witnesses," Kaplan said. The group decided to do some recruiting. They asked a Bermudian, a tournament official named Tracy Denninger. It would be natural for him to want to observe a match or two and would arouse no suspicion if he sat through a set. Although Denninger was about 6-foot-6 and it was difficult for him to see under the table without appearing obvious about it, he, too, reported seeing the foot tapping by the Italians.

Kaplan and Sheinwold went to Julius Rosenblum, an American who was president of the WBF at the time. Rosenblum's first concern was the political fallout. The Bermuda government had pledged a $20,000 subsidy for the regional which was to follow the Bermuda Bowl, and Rosenblum was fearful that the money would be withdrawn if there was a scandal.

Rosenblum tried to talk Keidan into not writing about what he had seen and what was developing from it. Keidan said he would hold off writing the story while the investigation was going on, but nothing would keep him from filing the story after that.

The incredulous Rosenblum went to the room where Facchini and Zucchelli were playing and watched them play a few boards. He didn't want to believe it, but Rosenblum could see something funny going on, so he asked a couple of other people for help.

An Australian member of the WBF executive council, Jim O'Sullivan, was asked to observe the Italians. He reported 12 incidents of foot-tapping in 15 boards. Johannes J. J. Hammerich, a Venezuelan who was first vice president of the WBF, saw six incidents in nine boards.

In each case, Facchini was always the sender. Zucchelli was always the receiver. It wasn't clear exactly *what* information was being exchanged, but Facchini wasn't relaying the time and temperature to his partner.

It was clear that the creeps were cheating, but Rosenblum persuaded the group that one more step was needed. He wanted to recruit a couple of Europeans to observe the Italians Sunday night in their match against our team – they had a bye Sunday afternoon. If the Europeans also saw foot tapping and were honest enough to tell on the Italians, it would be strong evidence to take to the WBF Executive Council.

Ironically, the Italians played one of their matches that Saturday against Indonesia, whose team had a pair – the Manoppo brothers – who were also highly suspect in the ethics department. Perhaps fittingly, Facchini and Zucchelli were matched against the Manoppos. At one point during the match, Keidan saw Facchini's foot stretch out and accidentally hit the foot of one of the Manoppos. The Indonesian moved his foot. Nothing more came of the chance encounter.

Later on in the round-robin – after the scandal had erupted – when Facchini and Zucchelli were on vugraph against the Manoppos, Gabriel Chagas was in the audience. The little Brazilian is a proud, feisty man and a great player. When he saw the lineup, Chagas suggested sarcastically from the audience, "Let's take down the screens and see some *real* bridge."

Anyway, although Keidan's discovery was supposed to be a secret, word was spreading fast. Wolffie filled me in on Saturday, although he swore me to secrecy. Naturally, that was happening all over the hotel. Sheinwold commented mournfully later that he had learned in his security work during World War II that the only safe secret is one that is known by only one person, who happens to be dead.

Meanwhile, the main ones in the know – Kaplan, Sheinwold and Wolff – were still trying to figure out what to do. Wolff said that at one point someone hatched a plot for Bobby and me to catch the Italians in the act – "red-footed," if you will. The plan was for Wolffie and me to sit down at the table against the cheaters and, at some point, jump up and hoist the table high enough so that everyone would be able to see Facchini's feet on top of Zucchelli's. Perhaps we should have tried that. What actually happened didn't work at all.

As Saturday wore on, Sheinwold became more and more concerned about the fact that Lew Mathe, ACBL president, had not been told what was going on. Kaplan was dead set against that because he knew what a big mouth Lew had. It seemed very important not to blow the lid off the story until there was enough of the right kind of evidence against Facchini and Zucchelli to nail them but good. As soon as Lew was told, the last shred of secrecy would vanish.

Sheinwold could not be dissuaded, however. Freddy believed he was acting as ACBL's agent in his capacity as non-playing captain, and he felt protocol demanded that he inform Mathe of what had been happening.

At 3 a.m., Sheinwold called Mathe's hotel room. "Can you come up to my room?" Freddy asked. Mathe was there almost immediately. He knew what the meeting was about because of all the talk that had been going on around the hotel, but he allowed Freddy to run over the details anyway.

Predictably, Mathe was livid. Why wasn't he told? What the hell was going on? Who did Sheinwold think he was?

Freddy explained, as best he could, why Lew wasn't told right away – and he begged Mathe not to go public with the accusations. "I'll think about it," Mathe said, but Sheinwold had a sinking feeling anyway.

The next morning, Mathe was at a regular meeting of the WBF Executive Council. Rosenblum, who had been planning to have the Europeans watch Facchini and Zucchelli that night, didn't mention the accusations during the meeting.

As the meeting drew to a close, Mathe spoke up. He was there only as an observer, but no one was going to muzzle Lew at that point. "I know something," he said, loud enough for everyone to hear. Why, Lew asked, wasn't the WBF Council discussing the allegations against those "cheating bastards"? What, Lew wanted to know, is the WBF going to do about the Italians who are tapping toes under the table during the matches?

This episode was appropriately described in the ACBL *Bulletin* by Henry Francis, who wrote in his diary of the Bermuda Bowl, "This is the day the bomb exploded."

It was a blast heard around the world. Keidan, no longer feeling the restraint of the thin veil of secrecy, filed his story that day (for the Monday editions), as did Sheinwold, who was covering the Bermuda Bowl in his capacity as bridge columnist for *The Los Angeles Times*. Alan Truscott, Henry Francis and Albert Dormer filed their reports on the scandal with The Associated Press, The United Press and Reuters respectively. Word of the scandal went around the world in an instant. Walter Bingham, representing *Sports Illustrated*, was also there to record the miserable scene and all that ensued.

Naturally, everyone was upset by the charges, and the WBF convened a special Appeals Committee to deal with it. Rosenblum chaired the meeting and the scene was ludicrous. There was Garozzo, who spoke English, interpreting for the Italians' captain, Sandro Salvetti, as he denied, denied, denied. He kept spreading his hands and muttering, "IM-POSS-EE-BEE-LAY."

Keidan, of course, testified to what he had seen. Outside the meeting room after his testimony, Keidan was accosted by Mathe. You should have said this, you should have said that, Mathe harangued. "Lew," said Keidan, "if you knew what I should have said, perhaps you should have told me that *before* I went into the hearing – not after." Mathe was definitely a loose cannon at this point, and his antics didn't help a difficult situation. Keidan, meanwhile, returned home. His editors didn't like his reporting on the story after he became part of it.

Naturally, our match with Italy in the round-robin – the first of two scheduled matches against them – was postponed Sunday night while the committee deliberated.

While we sat around waiting, I contemplated the joy of seeing Facchini and Zucchelli getting their comeuppance. I couldn't wait for the WBF to throw the scoundrels out of the tournament and out of bridge. I didn't see what else they *could* do. Let cheaters go unpunished? It was unthinkable.

The unthinkable happened about 3:15 a.m. Monday. The WBF Appeals Committee "severely reprimanded" Facchini and Zucchelli for "improper conduct" relating to the foot movements. But they would not be tossed out of the tournament. They would be allowed to play.

Our team was stunned. Sheinwold told the WBF they could go on without us if Facchini and Zucchelli were allowed to play. "We will not play against that pair," Freddy said. "We will withdraw."

Freddy's statement alarmed the members of the ACBL Board of Directors who were at the tournament. Sheinwold was immediately accosted and told that the team was *under orders* to play. If any member of the team refused, they could forget about playing in any ACBL tournaments for a couple of years.

A player like Soloway – who earned his living as a bridge professional – could not afford a suspension of two years, and Kantar and Eisenberg were in the same boat. Sheinwold put the matter to a vote by the team, and we decided to play, although the team issued a statement saying we endorsed the committee's verdict of guilty against the cheaters and "deplore the failure of the World Bridge Federation to bar this pair from further international competition." They were empty words, of course, but there was little else we could do.

Italy's captain, Salvetti, announced that Facchini and Zucchelli would not play against us in the first of our two round-robin matches. Salvetti said his boys' nerves were "in thin pieces" because of the horrid accusations against them.

It was interesting to me that the WBF saw fit to put coffee tables under the card tables to prevent foot contact between players. If Facchini and Zucchelli were such innocent lambs, why was that necessary?

Our Sunday night match with Italy had been postponed to Monday afternoon while everything was sorted out. I wish I could say we crushed the Italian bridge machine when we finally sat down to play against them Monday afternoon. Unfortunately, it was the other way around – and not because anyone cheated. They just plain kicked our butts.

Luckily, that one disaster didn't ruin our chances for getting into the medal rounds of the Bermuda Bowl – plus, we would get another chance at the Italians later. Even after getting clobbered by Italy, we were still in second place in the round-robin. We would get to the semifinals as long as we didn't drop into last place.

On Tuesday afternoon, we bombed Brazil, 19-1, while Italy was beaten rather easily by Indonesia, 18-2. We were back to within shouting distance of first place. As the round-robin dragged on, our hold on second place became rather tenuous. In fact, when we lost the ninth round to Indonesia, we found ourselves tied for second with France with one round to go. Our final-round opponent: Italy.

Once again, Facchini and Zucchelli were held out of the action by Salvetti. Poor things. I guess their nerves were still in pieces from all the cruel demands that they play bridge without exchanging information illegally.

Anyway, I was proud of our team for sucking it up when we had to and beating the Italians, 108-65 (17-3 in Victory Points). We finished comfortably in second.

In the semifinals, Italy played Indonesia and we played France. The Italians made a joke of their match, winning 280-134. By contrast, our match against France was a tight, well-played battle. We prevailed, 159-147. We were in the final against our nemesis, the Italians.

After all the crap that had gone on, we wanted these guys in the worst way. A successful bridge player learns to take emotion out of his makeup when it's time to play. On this occasion, it was tough. We wanted to show Facchini and Zucchelli how bridge is played by honest people with integrity. It was hard not to start the match with the adrenal glands pumping.

It was game day at last. Considering all that had gone on so far at the tournament, it was no surprise that more controversy arose. Salvetti listed Facchini and Zucchelli as one of the starting pairs in the final. Sheinwold immediately protested, saying his team had no intention of sitting down against the pair who had been reprimanded by the WBF.

The Appeals Committee was assembled again and rejected Sheinwold's protest. So did the ACBL. Once again, we were ordered to play – or else. Later on, the ACBL issued a statement saying Sheinwold was not speaking for the organization in lodging the protest. It was not an official action of the ACBL.

The truth is, we were better off with those two in the lineup against us. With no chance to signal each other what to bid and play, they would be far less effective than they had been. The cheaters would have no way to cheat. Here's an example of the two screwing up against us.

Dlr: South	♠ A K 10 9 7 4		
Vul: E-W	♥ A 8 3		
	♦ K 4		
	♣ Q 2		
♠ Q J 2		♠ 6	
♥ Q J 10 6		♥ 9 7 4	
♦ J 9 7 3		♦ Q 6 5 2	
♣ K J		♣ A 10 9 5 3	
	♠ 8 5 3		
	♥ K 5 2		
	♦ A 10 8		
	♣ 8 7 6 4		

WEST	NORTH	EAST	SOUTH
Wolff	*Belladonna*	*Me*	*Garozzo*
			Pass
Pass	1♣	Pass	1♦
Pass	1♠	Pass	1NT
Pass	2♠	Pass	3♠
Pass	3NT	All Pass	

Bobby led the ♥Q and Garozzo won in dummy. He continued with the top two spades and another spade. I threw the ♦2 to show I had nothing in that suit and when Wolffie won the third round of spades he plopped the ♣K onto the table. Bobby continued with the ♣J, and down two was easy. Plus 100 for us. At the other table:

WEST	NORTH	EAST	SOUTH
Facchini	*Soloway*	*Zucchelli*	*Swanson*
			Pass
Pass	1♠	Pass	2♠
Pass	2NT	Pass	3NT
All Pass			

Zucchelli picked the right suit to lead – clubs – but without help from his partner via foot signals, he selected a very wrong spot card for his lead: the 10. Now the sorry club holding in dummy turned into a stopper. Facchini won the ♣K and returned the jack, taken by Zucchelli with the ace. He abandoned the suit and switched to hearts. Soloway won in hand with the ace and played three rounds of spades. West won and continued hearts, taken by Soloway in dummy. He got to his hand with the ♦K and ran spades. Zucchelli threw his ♥9, which set up a double squeeze for 10 tricks. 11 IMPs to our team.

It was a good start for us. The Italians had started the final with a 9-IMP carryover, but on the first three boards, we had outscored them 26-0. They rallied after that and we ended the first set with a 42-40 lead, including their carryover.

Facchini and Zucchelli were taken out for the second quarter, so we faced a stronger lineup. We won that set 57-13 and our lead grew to 99-53. We were gaining confidence. It looked like it was our turn to win. Although we were rolling, none of us mentioned winning. We had the Italians on the ropes, but I guess it was kind of like the players in a dugout not mentioning a no-hitter, fearful they'll jinx the pitcher and spoil the whole thing. More than that, we knew better than to count our chickens before they hatched. There was still a lot of bridge to be played.

The cheaters returned for Italy in the third set – the last they would ever play for Italy in international competition. We beat them, 39-12. Our lead had grown to 138-65 after 48 boards – the halfway point. Bobby and I had played every set so far and we were hungry for more. We were still in there for the fourth round, which we lost, 44-18. We didn't like it, but there was no panic. We still had a 47-IMP lead. Two sets to go – 32 deals. We might have been breathing a little hard, but we could make it across the finish line first. Or so we thought.

The final two sets were played on Saturday morning and early Saturday afternoon. The long tournament was drawing to a close. We were tired but determined. The Italians were just as determined to get back into the match, and they won the fifth set, 49-27, to cut our lead to 183-158 with 16 boards to go.

The whole match was shown on vugraph in an auditorium at the hotel. The place was packed beyond capacity as we got under way early Saturday afternoon, February 1. The crowd was heavily pro-Italian, but not entirely because of the big European contingent. Believe it or not, there were Americans in the audience rooting for Italy. Look at it this way: if you were a bridge player with reasonable expectations for success and another team beat you routinely, wouldn't it be natural for you to cheer for whoever that other team happened to be playing at the time? In Texas, lots of people say their favorite team is whoever is playing Oklahoma. It was that kind of mentality.

Anyway, Wolffie and I played against Franco and Pittala. Kantar and Eisenberg opposed Garozzo and Belladonna.

Italy started off with a 2-IMP pickup as Wolff went down two in 3NT while Garozzo went down only one. The Italians drew real blood on Board 82.

Dlr: East	♠ 10 8 7		
Vul: N-S	♥ 9 8 7 4		
	♦ 10 9		
	♣ 10 8 6 3		

♠ A 4 3 2		♠ Q J
♥ A 2		♥ Q 10 6 5
♦ A Q 5 2		♦ J 7 3
♣ K 9 2		♣ Q 7 5 4

	♠ K 9 6 5
	♥ K J 3
	♦ K 8 6 4
	♣ A J

At our table:

WEST	NORTH	EAST	SOUTH
Franco	*Me*	*Pittala*	*Wolff*
		Pass	1NT
Dbl	2♣	Dbl	Pass
Pass	Redbl	Pass	2♦
Dbl	Redbl	Pass	2♠
Dbl	All Pass		

Our 1NT openers showed 15-17 points, and Bobby's hand certainly qualified for it. There was little we could do after that, however, to avoid the penalty. We were simply outgunned. As it was, the Italians dropped a trick to let us off for minus 500. At the other table:

WEST	NORTH	EAST	SOUTH
Eisenberg	*Belladonna*	*Kantar*	*Garozzo*
		Pass	1♦
1NT	Pass	2NT	Pass
3NT	All Pass		

The values were there for game, but Eisenberg didn't have enough tricks after Belladonna led the ♥9. Billy finished down two. Italy had just shaved another 12 IMPs off our lead, which now stood at 11.

They gained another 6 IMPs when Belladonna and Garozzo bid a game that Bobby and I missed. If our two teams had been boxers in a prize-fighting ring, the announcers would have been describing us as rubber-legged. It didn't get any better for us.

We lost another 3 IMPs on Board 84 and our lead was at 2 IMPs. Board 85 was a push, but we lost 3 IMPs on Board 86 when Kantar went down two vulnerable in 4♥ while Pittala went down only one.

The Blue Team was in the lead. They had the momentum. Our big lead had shriveled up and disappeared, gone like so much vapor. Of course, we played all 16 boards of the final set straight through without comparing, so we weren't completely sure about the scores. All of us, however, had been around long enough to know that things were going badly and that North America was on the ropes. We needed a spark, something to put an end to the skid.

It didn't come.

Board 87 was a push. We lost 11 IMPs on Board 88 when Garozzo made two overtricks in 3NT while Wolffie went down one in the same contract.

```
        Dlr: West       ♠ K 8 5 4
        Vul: None       ♥ K 8 6 3 2
                        ♦ 8 5
                        ♣ Q 6
    ♠ Q J 9 2                           ♠ 10 3
    ♥ 10 7 4                            ♥ A Q 5
    ♦ J 7 4 3 2                         ♦ 10 9
    ♣ 10                               ♣ J 9 7 5 4 3
                        ♠ A 7 6
                        ♥ J 9
                        ♦ A K Q 6
                        ♣ A K 8 2
```

WEST	NORTH	EAST	SOUTH
Franco	*Me*	*Pittala*	*Wolff*
Pass	Pass	Pass	2NT
Pass	3♣	Pass	3♦
Pass	3♥	Pass	3NT
All Pass			

Franco led the ♠Q, ducked by Wolff. Franco continued with a low spade, taken by Wolff with dummy's king. Bobby now led a low heart away from dummy and Pittala smoothly ducked. Wolff put in the ♥9, losing to the 10, and he was finished. Franco got out with a diamond and, try as he might, Wolff could come to no more than eight tricks.

At the other table:

WEST	NORTH	EAST	SOUTH
Eisenberg	*Belladonna*	*Kantar*	*Garozzo*
Pass	Pass	Pass	1♣
Pass	1♥	Pass	1NT
Pass	2♣	Pass	2♦
Pass	2♠	Pass	3NT
All Pass			

Garozzo got a diamond lead from Eisenberg. Benito won in his hand and played the ♥J, riding it to East's queen. Kantar played a second diamond, won by South. Garozzo then played the ♥9, riding it when West did not cover. Kantar ducked, but Garozzo went to dummy with the ♣Q and played another heart, claiming when the ace fell.

We were now down by 12 IMPs with eight boards to go.

The next three boards were pushes. Five to go. Our friends and family in the vugraph audience knew the cumulative score – and they could see that we were running out of time. The next board has lived in infamy for American partisans and has been the subject of much scrutiny over the years.

```
Dlr: West        ♠ A K 10 9
Vul: N-S         ♥ —
                 ♦ A 9 7
                 ♣ J 9 8 6 3 2
♠ 4 3                            ♠ 7 6 5 2
♥ Q 10 8 7                       ♥ K 4 3 2
♦ Q 10 6 4                       ♦ J 5 3
♣ 7 5 4                          ♣ K 10
                 ♠ Q J 8
                 ♥ A J 9 6 5
                 ♦ K 8 2
                 ♣ A Q
```

At our table:

WEST	NORTH	EAST	SOUTH
Franco	*Me*	*Pittala*	*Wolff*
Pass	1♠	Pass	2♥
Pass	3♣	Pass	4NT
Pass	5♥	Pass	6NT
All Pass			

In our system, my bidding showed 12-16 points with longer clubs than spades. Bobby's 4NT was Roman Blackwood, and my response showed two aces but without extra values. Naturally, he signed off in a small slam – the reasonable spot.

At the other table, Garozzo and Belladonna conducted an auction that could be described only as bizarre.

WEST	NORTH	EAST	SOUTH
Eisenberg	*Belladonna*	*Kantar*	*Garozzo*
Pass	2♣	Pass	2♦
Pass	2♠	Pass	3♥
Pass	3NT	Pass	4♣
Pass	4♦	Pass	4NT
Pass	5♦	Pass	5♥
Dbl	Redbl	Pass	5♠
Dbl	5NT	Pass	7♣
All Pass			

Here is what the world championship book published by the ACBL said about Board 92:

When this deal was flashed on the vugraph screen it brought the audience to a fever of excitement. A flat board would probably clinch the match for Italy. . . . An inspired opening lead might win it for North America if Italy reached the same contract as Hamman and Wolff. No one anticipated that the world's top bridge pair would give a hostage to fortune by bidding a 13% grand slam.

Indeed, if the grand slam had failed, the Italians would have lost 17 IMPs and we would have been back in the lead.

Clearly, Belladonna and Garozzo each pictured the other with stronger clubs. They were much too experienced to take such an insane chance with the match going their way.

Throughout this tortured auction, Kantar had been sitting behind Belladonna with the precious ♣K burning a hole in his hand. Looking at what he thought was the setting trick, Eddie could think only, "God is not an Italian after all – I'm going to be a world champion!"

Imagine his shock when Garozzo put down the dummy with the ♣AQ. Imagine Belladonna's chagrin to find himself in a grand slam with the opponents holding five trumps to the king-ten between them.

Kantar led a heart and Belladonna ruffed. The next card he played was a low club toward dummy. Kantar followed with the 10 and Belladonna's face lit up – he saw a glimmer of hope. He finessed the queen. Then he played the ace. When Kantar played the king, Belladonna stared at it a moment, then triumphantly claimed 13 tricks.

The vugraph audience was in a frenzy. The Italians had gained another 12 IMPs and had a virtually insurmountable lead. They had snatched victory from the jaws of defeat. We were vanquished. Despite the cheaters on their team, we had them down and we let them up. We should have finished them off, but we didn't. It was a miserable feeling.

It has been suggested that Kantar might have saved the day by playing the ♣K when Belladonna played the low club from his hand at trick two. If Belladonna believed that Kantar's play was a true one, he might have played differently. Belladonna might have decided to play West for at least three spades (possibly four), at least a doubleton in each red suit and four clubs to the 10, a hand such as

♠4 3 2 ♥Q 10 8 7 ♦Q 10 ♣10 7 5 4.

Declarer would win the ♣A at trick two, discard a diamond on the ♥A and play three rounds of spades. Next would come the ♦A and ♦K, followed by a heart ruff. If West had the hand declarer hoped for, this would be the position:

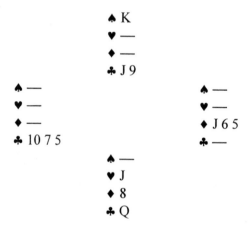

North could lead the ♠K, ruffing in dummy. West would have to underuff and then would be caught in a trump coup at trick 12. Of course, that plan would fail on the actual layout because West would ruff the third round of spades.

If Kantar had played the ♣K, would Belladonna have bitten? Or would he have smelled a rat? After all, Kantar was (and still is) a world-class player and a great analyst – more than capable of such a falsecard.

After the match was over, Belladonna was asked what would have happened if Kantar had played the ♣K at trick two. Belladonna replied: "The North Americans would be world champions today."

Wolffie and I actually got to see the grand slam played on vugraph. In the vugraph, the boards shown from the "open room" are boards that have already been played in the "closed room." That way, the commentators and audience know what has happened and the potential swing is known. It heightens the interest.

Bobby and I had finished playing in the closed room, and we knew we hadn't played well, but we still thought it was a toss-up as to who won.

We squeezed into the auditorium just as the 7♣ hand was being shown. Our hearts were in our throats. We knew it was doom for our team. And the room was cheering for Italy. *Americans* were cheering for Italy. Bobby started crying. He was sick to see our compatriots rooting for the cheaters. It was more than he could bear. I was momentarily, perhaps morbidly, enthralled by the scene and I forgot where I was. When I turned around, Bobby was gone.

The team assembled in Sheinwold's room after we had dressed for the victory banquet, and I tried to lend a little humor to the dark mood of the group. "This calls for a human sacrifice," I said. I don't know if Eddie thought I meant him, but it was the farthest thing from my mind. No one on the team blamed him for not playing the ♣K. We didn't lose the match on that board. We lost it on several boards. We were outplayed and out-lucked.

Sitting through the victory banquet – watching those cheaters claim a world championship – was one of the most difficult things I've ever done in bridge. I've lost a lot of championships through the years, but defeat was never so bitter for me as on that occasion.

We made our way to the victory banquet, all suited up in tuxedos but feeling anything but jaunty. We were bitter, but we were also determined to show class in the face of this outrage. We weren't going to be poor losers on top of everything else.

Freddy felt as much anguish as anyone, but when it was his turn to speak at the banquet, he tried to be conciliatory. He told a story of a group of Americans visiting Rome. When one of the Americans fell into a pit and was injured, Belladonna was called for help. He was on the scene in no time, Sheinwold recalled, organizing help and caring for his fellow bridge players. All turned out well, Sheinwold said, but if not for the help of their friends, there might have been tragedy. "We've had our ups and downs, but we are one big fraternity as bridge players," he said.

There was applause from many parts of the banquet hall that evening, but the Italians in the audience reacted with venom. Sheinwold was booed loudly, and many of the Italians cursed him and cried, "Buffone! Buffone! (Buffoon! Buffoon!)." As Freddy made his way back to his chair, several Italians rose from their chairs, shaking their fists and moving toward him.

Bobby and I immediately flanked Sheinwold and escorted him back to the table. The jeering continued after we sat back down. It got to the point where Swanson threatened to knock the crap out of an especially obnoxious Italian sitting at the next table. John is normally a pretty mild-mannered guy, but he's big enough to scare most people. The boor shut up pronto.

It was a miserable scene, and our team's mood matched it pretty well.

One of the great things about bridge is that there's always another day, and I'm as optimistic as they come when considering my chances of playing in big events.

As fate would have it, I was to be involved in a remarkable bridge event that same year – one that turned out quite differently from Bermuda.

15

Redemption

IN 1964, Don Krauss and I were playing in the Men's Board-a-Match Teams at the Nationals in Portland. Our teammates were Eddie Kantar and Lew Mathe. You may remember some of my experiences with Mathe, one of the most intense competitors ever to play the game.

With one 28-board session to go, we were in contention, standing second or third in the field.

A board-a-match movement looks like a pair game while it's in progress. East-West pairs move around the room while the North-South pairs stay at the same table. You don't compare until the very end. Don and I were East-West, so we left Eddie and Lew to start the final session.

Well, Don and I had the kind of game that not even a mother could love. I mean, it was really bad. I've probably had worse games in my life – mercifully, they're blotted out of my memory. We had just one awful result after another. I later learned that we had 8.5 out of 28 for the session. Horrible.

When the session was over, we headed back to the table where Eddie and Lew were sitting. As we approached, I could see that they were playing the last board. A gallery had formed around their table, and Lew – looking like a drill sergeant with a peptic ulcer – was sitting there with his jaws clenched and a cigar sticking out of his mouth. Lew was defending slowly, carefully and intensely. He was under the mistaken impression that his team was in contention to win the event.

Suddenly, I came to my senses.

"I'm too young to die," I told Don as I headed in the other direction. "You go compare with them."

There was another occasion like this involving my old friend Alex Tschekaloff, a very good player who lives in the Los Angeles area. Alex is still an active player.

He was playing in a Board-a-Match Teams event with Kelsey Petterson and Erik Paulsen, both good players. Kelsey, who died in 1983, was an amusing guy. A bald-headed, nondescript kind of fellow, you might mistake him for your high school principal or the minister from your church. In real life, he was an attorney.

Anyway, Kelsey and Erik – a distinguished-looking Scandinavian type – had the same kind of session Don and I had in Portland, but they handled things differently. They both trudged back to the table to break the news to their teammates. Alex, a wiry fellow with a sharp look about him, has been known to be emotional about his bridge at times. In his view, losing is very similar to dying except that losing is worse since you will probably have the pleasure on other occasions.

What I am trying to say is that under the best of circumstances he doesn't tolerate bad bridge very well and that these were not the best of circumstances. As Tschekaloff and his partner were comparing scores with Kelsey and Erik, Alex became more annoyed with each bad result that was reported. Finally, he exploded.

"How dare you come back with a card like this?" Tschekaloff demanded, glaring at his crestfallen teammates. "How *can* you come back with a card like this?" Without missing a beat Kelsey quipped, "It wasn't *my* idea to come back."

Fortunately, there are times when you can't wait to compare. One of the most remarkable of those occasions occurred in 1975 during the Grand National Teams.

The team I was playing on is not one you'll find in anyone's hall of fame, but we were a congenial group.

Besides Bobby and me, this was our cast of characters – all from Dallas. There was John Fisher, a Dallas physician and a truly fine player. At the time of the GNT, John had more masterpoints than all but four ACBL members. Ten years earlier, he was on the winning team in the Vanderbilt. John and Barry Crane often played together and were dynamite in regionals. John seldom attends tournaments these days, but he can still play.

Fisher's partner was Charley Gabriel, a former nuclear scientist who worked for Corn at Michigan General. Gabriel was quite talented and had modest success in tournaments, but he was a mad scientist at heart. He and Fisher were next-door neighbors in Dallas. They had played a lot in the 1950s before Gabriel dropped out of bridge to pursue various business opportunities.

Next came Jim Hooker, a fellow who made a mint in the oil business and then moved to Los Angeles. At the time, Hooker was chairman of the board of Gibson Distributing Co., a discount store in Midland and Odessa, Texas. He had been playing with Wolff as a client. It was Hooker's idea to put the GNT team together.

Then there was Charles Weed, another businessman who has since moved to Shreveport, Louisiana. In 1975, Weed was vice president in charge of corporate development for Michigan General in Dallas.

With the right players playing together, our team would have had an edge over the competition – at least at the district level. Remember, the Grand National Teams was a supposedly grass-roots event with teams qualifying from each of the 25 districts for a knockout event just before the Summer Nationals.

If we could have lined up with Wolff and me and Fisher-Gabriel as the anchors, we would have been prohibitive favorites. But that would have left Weed and Hooker playing together. A very volatile partnership, they could produce disastrous sessions that no one could cover. So the deal was that I would play with Weed and Bobby would play with Hooker.

The district final was in Houston and somehow we made it to the final against a team of pros led by Malcolm Brachman. With three boards to go, however, it didn't look like we were going to take the next step in the GNT – a zonal playoff to see who would get to go to the Summer Nationals in Miami. The main reason: we were down by 24 IMPs.

Bridge, however, is a lot like other competitive endeavors in that it ain't over 'til it's over. With the help of some skill, the opponents, blind luck and the gods, we proved that point – and then some – over the final three deals.

On the first deal, the opponents at our table stopped in 3♥, which was the limit of the hand. Of course, the hand had to be defended with care – it wasn't just a cashout situation. At the other table, Bobby bid the filthy game – his side was vulnerable – and the opponents forgot to beat it. We gained 10 IMPs.

Then Weed picked up this gem:

♠Q J 5 ♥K Q 8 ♦Q J 4 ♣K Q J 10.

Naturally, he opened 1NT. This was my hand:

♠K 7 ♥J 5 4 3 ♦ — ♣A 9 8 7 6 5 4.

I bid Stayman (2♣) and when Weed bid 2♦ (no four-card major), I bid 3♣, which was forcing. Now, 99% of the people in the world would bid 3NT with Weed's hand, which was, after all, as balanced as it could possibly be – and with stoppers in every suit. But no! Weed boosted me to 4♣. I bid 5♣, which was unbeatable. As you can see, with a diamond lead – which he was going to get – Weed would have been down like a dog in 3NT.

Well, you guessed it. At the other table, they bid 3NT and went down on the diamond lead. Another 10 IMPs to the forces of good!

On the last board, slam was in the air – in fact, there were three possible slams that might be bid, but only one of them makes legitimately. The opponents at our table stopped short of slam. At the other table, Bobby picked the wrong slam, but the opponents gave it to him with an unfortunate – for them – opening lead. 11 more IMPs came our way. No problem – we won by 7 IMPs.

One moment we were on the brink of elimination, the next we were in the playoffs for a trip to Miami. Back in those days, the number of teams in the GNT was reduced to eight before they went to the national level to play. This was accomplished by putting the different districts into zones and having zonal playoffs. We played against Districts 15 and 17. In our three-way playoff, each team won a match. We won out because of a funny little device called quotient, which is the result you get by dividing your plus IMPs by your minus

IMPs. The team with the largest sum takes the next step. That was us, the boys from Dallas.

Once again, I found myself in South Florida for an important event – not that I thought our District 16 team had much of a chance in the Grand Nationals. We were a reasonable team for the district level but mediocre at the national level – and there were some excellent teams in the field, including a really strong one from New York.

Since we were starting at the quarterfinal stage, we needed to win only three matches to claim the 1975 GNT title. Our first opponent was a team from Edmonton, Alberta, a pretty good draw for us, actually. Not that they were pushovers, but there were several much tougher teams in the field.

For instance, there was the New York City team of Peter Weichsel, Alan Sontag, Jimmy Cayne and Matt Granovetter. Then there were Billy Eisenberg and Eddie Kantar and their team from Los Angeles. Our bunch did not match up well with either of those.

Our luck held, however, and we rallied in the fourth quarter to beat the Edmonton squad. Our next draw: Kantar, Eisenberg and company. And things didn't get any easier after that, because on the first round, a bad team from Tennessee had beaten a stronger team from Pittsburgh and was then matched against Weichsel and Sontag. We didn't see how Tennessee could beat New York, which meant that even if we got past Eddie and his friends, we would still be big underdogs in the final against a formidable team.

If you don't think luck was on our side against Eddie and Billy, consider this. On one hand, our opponents did extremely well to stop in 4♠. Slam didn't make, but it was difficult to stay out of it. We were almost certainly going to lose IMPs on that board. But what do you know – somehow, the board was screwed up before the replay. The directors decided the board would be thrown out and a substitute hand played.

Unbelievably, the substitute deal was almost like the first one, only this time slam made. Again, our opponents stopped in game, but at the other table Bobby and Jim bid the slam and made it. It was that kind of tournament for us.

Weed and I played the last quarter against Kantar and Eisenberg. Miraculously, we had a 29-IMP lead with a quarter to go. Charlie and

I had the best of Kantar and Eisenberg at our table, but Wolff and Hooker had a game that should have been sent off to the pound. "It's okay," Bobby told me, "we won . . . by one IMP." Interestingly, one of those IMPs came when Eisenberg inadvertently showed Weed his hand, allowing Charlie to take a risky finesse for an overtrick. If that hadn't happened, we would have been tied. Brother, were we living on the edge.

Our victory over the California team was only one of the evening's significant developments, however. As Weed and I were finishing up against Kantar and Eisenberg, we heard a blood-curdling scream from the other room. It could mean only one thing: Tennessee had come from 32 IMPs down with a quarter to go and had beaten New York.

What the hell, I thought, maybe we can win this thing after all.

We had one more scare before the curtain rang down on this incredible series of events. Going into the fourth quarter, we had a 48-IMP lead on the District 10 squad. We had arranged the lineups so that it was necessary for Weed to play the final quarter. He *had* to play. The only problem was that we couldn't find him at game time.

A frantic search finally turned him up – asleep in his room, of all things. We dragged him down to the playing area and plopped him in a chair.

Things didn't go well. Our team bid to 6♦ when nine tricks were the limit. The Tennesseans stopped in 3♦. We went for 1100 in a voluntarily bid game for another 14-IMP loss. Somehow, however, we hung on and won by 11 IMPs.

That qualified us for the international team trials in Palo Alto in the fall of that year. By the time we got to California, our lucky leprechaun or rabbit's foot or guardian angel had deserted us and we were eliminated in the first round by a pretty good squad led by Grant Baze. The funny thing is, we actually led that team at the half by 10 IMPs. But we finally succumbed, 331-294.

It was a good run. Sometimes there's a lot in the old saying, "I'd rather be lucky than good." Our strange win in the Grand National Teams didn't make up for losing the Bermuda Bowl to the Italians, but a win is a win. It beats the hell out of second any way you look at it.

There's not much to say about 1976 except that it was bad. Bobby and I won the Pan American Invitational Pairs in Mexico City, but otherwise I won nothing, did nothing, accomplished nothing. I might as well not have showed up at tournaments.

Also, if you can believe it, the Italians were defeated in the Bermuda Bowl in Monaco, but I didn't have the pleasure of administering the beating myself. I was happy for the Americans – Paul Soloway, Ira Rubin, Billy Eisenberg, Erik Paulsen, Hugh Ross and Fred Hamilton – but annoyed that I wasn't on the squad that dethroned the mighty Blue Team.

The one bright spot of 1976 is that I was back playing with Wolff again fairly steadily – and that led to the strange events of 1977.

In 1976 in Salt Lake City, Soloway-Swanson and Eisenberg-Kantar won the Grand National Teams again, which qualified them to play in the team trials in 1977 for the Bermuda Bowl in Manila, Philippines, that same year. This time, however, Soloway and his friends played four-handed in the GNT, so there was a lot less of a problem adding the pair they wanted (Bobby and me) for the trials.

The trials were scheduled for early January in Houston. The five-day contest would be at the grand old Shamrock Hotel, which has since been torn down but was one of the city's landmarks at the time.

Our opponents – there were only three teams in the event – were strong. First there was the team put together by George Rosenkranz. He and Roger Bates, John Mohan, Larry Cohen and Richard Katz had a bye to the final since they had won two of the qualifying events the previous year – the Vanderbilt and the Spingold. That in itself is a remarkable achievement. The venerable John Gerber – inventor of the ace-asking convention that bears his name – was their non-playing captain.

That left us to do battle with Fred Hamilton, Erik Paulsen, Hugh Ross and Ira Rubin, the winners of the Reisinger, another of the qualifying events. Their fifth and sixth were Ron Von der Porten and Mike Passell.

In those days, the defending Bermuda Bowl champions got an automatic invitation to the next tournament, so Hamilton, Rubin, Paulsen and Ross were going to get to play in Manila no matter what happened in the trials. They still wanted to win the trials, of course, because, as the winners, their expenses to Manila would be paid by the ACBL. If they didn't win the trials, they would have to pay their own way.

It was interesting to have all six members of the defending Bermuda Bowl champions back in the trials – not on the same team, of course. Soloway and Eisenberg had been added to the Reisinger team that won the 1976 trials and subsequently the Bermuda Bowl, but they weren't available in 1977 because they had won a qualifying event – the GNT – themselves.

So Soloway added Bobby and me. The defending world champions added Ron Von der Porten and Mike Passell. Interestingly, the two new players didn't play together – Von der Porten played with Rubin, Passell with Hamilton.

Meanwhile, if we could win the trials, the exact same team that had gone to Bermuda in 1975 would have a chance to fight again for a world title, presumably without foot-tapping cheaters.

It wasn't what I would call an easy fight, but the final score of our match against Rubin was fairly comfortable – 296-235. That put us in the final against the five-man team that had been resting for two days while we played 128 boards.

The Gerber team was definitely dangerous. Their anchor pair was Katz and Cohen, one of the hottest twosomes in North America at the time. They had won three major team events with Rosenkranz and they already had three major victories before that. Both of them lived in Los Angeles. Cohen was a pharmacist, Katz a physician. They played an unusual system they called Breakthrough – a kind of strong club system with lots of bells and whistles.

Bates and Mohan, both bridge professionals, were also a strong pair. They still play together today. In 1992, they surprised the bridge world by winning the Vanderbilt with a relatively inexperienced player on the team as a sponsor. Bates and Mohan were then, and are today, formidable opponents.

The two of them were switching around as Rosenkranz's partner. George doesn't play as much nowadays as he used to, but you can't argue with his record in big events. He's won more than a dozen North

American championships and he's nobody's fool. George can play bridge when he puts his mind to it.

There was a huge crowd at the Shamrock for the trials because the organizers had scheduled a sectional tournament to run concurrent with our event. There was also a vugraph show, and the sectional events were timed so that people who played in the tournament could watch the trials competition.

We were playing with screens and bidding boxes, and security was tight.

It's hard to know where to begin describing this match and its outrageous outcome. I could start at Board 4, the point at which Rosenkranz's team took a lead they never relinquished. Or I could start with Board 97, which we never got to play. As it happened, the bridge play became incidental. If that sounds strange, here's the explanation.

Going in, we had considered ourselves pretty sound favorites, but things had not gone our way. They led us 155-108 at the halfway point and after we had played 96 boards, they still had a 43-IMP margin, 233-190, with 32 boards to go. Obviously, 43 IMPs is not an insurmountable lead with that much bridge to be played, but I'd much rather be up 43 than down by that score. The other team seemed to be playing well, too, so if any betting was going on, the Gerber team was probably the favorite.

There was a vague air of tension, not unlike what we experienced in Bermuda in 1975, as members of our team sat around the players' lounge, Saturday night contemplating the next day's play.

Sunday morning we gathered in the lounge to have coffee and a light breakfast while we waited for play to start. It wasn't long before our captain, Roger Stern, walked in with a smile on his face.

"Congratulations on being the ACBL representatives in Manila," Stern said. "Your opponents have withdrawn."

"What happened?" someone asked. "What's going on?"

What happened was that Katz and Cohen had abruptly withdrawn from the match – and, we learned later, from the ACBL. That left the Gerber team with three members – not enough to continue – so they had to forfeit.

We were like a prize fighter lifted off the canvas and declared the winner.

Naturally, the whole city – and pretty soon, the whole bridge world – was abuzz with speculation about what had happened. There were front-page stories from San Francisco to New York. The ACBL was silent, saying only that Katz and Cohen had withdrawn from the match and the organization. ACBL officials, still feeling the sting of the scandal in Bermuda, were hoping to keep this little tempest from turning into a hurricane.

That might have been possible if my old buddy Lew Mathe, who was still on the ACBL Board of Directors, hadn't been there.

Lew was shooting off his mouth right from the beginning – just as he did in Bermuda – and other ACBL officials were red-faced with embarrassment as Mathe spoke out of turn at the drop of a hat. In reporting on the Houston incident, *The Bridge World* had this footnote on Lew's contributions to the mess:

A high League official was quoted as remarking, irritably, "The whole thing might have died – then that goddam Mathe had to open his mouth." A member of the ACBL Board apologized to Freddy Sheinwold for having criticized team-captain Sheinwold's failure, in the Bermuda scandal of '75, to notify Mathe, then League President, immediately after hearing about the Italian pair. "You were 100% correct not to tell him," the Board member said ruefully.

Much later, the ACBL's public position on what was ultimately dubbed "The Houston Affair" was influenced to a large degree by a $44 million lawsuit filed by Katz and Cohen after their resignation from the trials. When you're in the hot seat for that kind of money, you follow your lawyers' advice – which is usually to say nothing.

It was years before the matter was laid to rest. This is what Jim Zimmerman, then ACBL President, wrote about the resolution of the lawsuit in the ACBL *Bulletin* in 1982.

This case was unique in that Katz-Cohen resigned from membership in the ACBL rather than face charges of improper communication and certain ejection from the ACBL should these charges be sustained. No matter how one may feel as to whether there was or was not improper communication, the fact remains that because of their resignations no evidentiary presentation of this charge was ever made.

Those who were of the opinion that Katz and Cohen were guilty of exchanging information improperly have retained that opinion. I doubt that a resolution by a trial would have changed it, especially since that question would not have been the most relevant issue in the trial. Those who were on the other side were also vehement on behalf of Katz and Cohen – it is equally likely that their opinion would not have been changed by a trial.

This matter has been before the ACBL Board of Directors for five years. Management has been continually required to furnish information to all lawyers. Katz and Cohen, by their resignations, have not been members of the ACBL nor have they played in ACBL-sanctioned events for five years.

Estimates were that the trial would take five to eight weeks. A judge in Los Angeles County, therefore, made a most strenuous effort to dispose of this case without a trial.

The basic position of the ACBL, through all negotiations, was that Katz and Cohen should not play together as a pair. Katz and Cohen would not accept this restriction. When there was movement by Katz and Cohen toward acceptance of restriction, this basic concession made it possible to find a ground whereby they could be considered for readmission. On February 23, 1982, Katz and Cohen were re-admitted, but they agreed not to play together.

The Katz-Cohen lawsuit alleged a number of causes of action, all of which were terminated by this settlement. Payment of the plaintiffs' legal fees was made by the insurance company alone, a result of negotiations between the insurance company and the plaintiffs. No payments to the plaintiffs were made by the ACBL.

Is this settlement a precedent-setting case for any future lawsuits? Absolutely not! Each case will be dealt with individually.

It's been more than a decade since the incident and the settlement of the lawsuit and I don't want to revive allegations that never got a hearing. Katz and Cohen were the targets of an investigation by the ACBL – an investigation that came to a head during the trials. The two were never formally accused of anything, so there was no hearing on whether they did anything improper. Like other such incidents, The Houston Affair did nothing positive for bridge.

Once our team had gotten over the initial shock of the Katz-Cohen resignations, it sunk in that we were headed for a world championship again. The fact that we might not have been going if the entire match had been played mattered not a whit. My mind, and those of my teammates, was turned to the task at hand – winning the Bermuda Bowl. We had a date with the rest of the world in the Philippines.

A word about Ira Corn is in order here. Although we were no longer officially The Aces – mostly because Corn wasn't supporting the team with money on a regular basis any more – we were the "sort-of" Aces by the simple fact that Bobby and I were on the team. Also, Corn was contributing enough that he could call the shots now and then – and he was acting as our non-playing captain occasionally.

In Pasadena in the spring of 1977, the "sort-of Aces" were Bobby and me, Eric Murray and Sami Kehela. In the early rounds, we lost to a team we should have beaten. It was a team led by a guy from Little Rock, Al Childs. In fact, Childs and his team went on to post several more upsets before they lost.

For some reason, Ira blamed Murray and Kehela for the loss to the Childs team. I couldn't see that they were any more to blame than anyone else on the team. In fact, I liked them both and they were damned good teammates. Never one to be confused by the facts, however, Corn more or less booted Murray and Kehela off the team. It probably rankled Ira that the winning Vanderbilt team had two former Aces – Mike Lawrence and Mark Blumenthal.

Anyway, we played the Spingold in the summer of '77 with Edgar Kaplan, Norman Kay, Bill Root and Richard Pavlicek, with not much more success than with the Canadians – this time, we lost in the round of 16. At this point, I was somewhat put out with Corn. I didn't like the way he treated Murray and Kehela. In truth, there was kind of a general rot setting in with the team, although Wolffie and I did manage to win the Grand National Teams again, this time playing together. Actually, Wolff was added to our team – me, Eddie Wold, an old riverboat gambler-type named Curtis Smith and Dan Morse – after we won the district championship. We beat a team from Washington DC by 1 IMP in the final.

That aside, Corn's on-again, off-again support for the "Aces" left us more or less fending for ourselves. Corn had little or nothing to do with the 1977 Bermuda Bowl team. Ira could still swing a big stick, but he wasn't doing so in our neighborhood in late 1977.

Manila is a long way from Dallas. Despite the distance our team brought a large rooting section. I made the trip with Susie Kennedy, my girlfriend at the time, and my mother, who was still living in the Los Angeles area. My mother wasn't really into bridge, but I thought she might enjoy the trip, so I convinced her to go along. It seemed like we never stopped flying. We went from Dallas to San Francisco to Honolulu and – finally – to Manila. I thought I had been on long plane rides before, but this beat them all. It must have been close to a full day before we got there.

We were exhausted by the time we landed. Once we got to the hotel, we collapsed. If the opponents had seen us coming they would have licked their chops for hours.

The only fresh member of the team was Swanson. He and his wife Nina had flown in a week ahead of us. Nina worked at the Fox studios in Southern California, and one of her co-workers was a Filipino woman who suggested the Swansons stay with her parents in Manila. John told me when we got there that he and Nina had been treated like royalty from the moment they arrived.

In many ways, the Philippines in the 1970s was like Mexico today – most of the people were dirt poor and kept at bay by the small upper class of the very wealthy. In 1977, Ferdinand and Imelda Marcos ruled the Philippines with an iron hand.

We played the Bermuda Bowl in October of 1977, but it was warm when we arrived. The country, made up of about 7,000 islands in the western Pacific, has a tropical climate. There weren't many sights to see, so Susie and my mother didn't plan any excursions. Manila, teeming with people, seemed dirty and forbidding.

On the other hand, the tournament venue – the Manila Peninsula Hotel – was magnificent. It was a clean, modern facility with every amenity, which was fortunate since the women didn't fancy going out too often. We did have dinner at the home of one of the tournament officials, however. The people were very friendly and the hospitality was outstanding.

We could see one of the effects of our Bermuda adventure in the tournament equipment. Every table had screens that bisected the tables and went all the way to the floor. No pattycake with the feet at *this* Bermuda Bowl – and we heard no complaints about the security.

The field was somewhat uneven. For one thing, the famous Blue Team was missing. In 1970 and 1971, they were absent because they were in retirement. This time, however, they were on the sidelines because they lost to Sweden in the European championships.

The Swedes, in fact, were the only team given any chance to keep the two American teams from meeting in the final (the World Bridge Federation has since set things up so that no two teams from the same zone can meet in the final). The Swedes were dangerous, to be sure. One member of the team, Per Olof Sundelin – known to most of us these days simply as P.O. – is still a world-class player. His teammates – Anders Brunzell, Sven-Olof Flodquist, Hans Göthe, Jorgen Lindquist and Anders Morath – were also excellent. We wouldn't be taking them for granted any more than we would the Blue Team.

The other teams – Chinese Taipei, Argentina and Australia – were not considered contenders, but since I could remember losing to the Netherlands Antilles in the Olympiad in New York in 1964, you could bet I wasn't taking any team lightly.

Our captain was Roger Stern, a New York attorney; our coach was Steve Altman, another New Yorker. Steve was one of the original members of the Precision Team that C.C. Wei put together to promote his system. Altman was also coach of the 1973 Bermuda Bowl team, but I will always remember him as absolutely the *slowest player I have ever seen in my life*. It used to drive me insane waiting for him to make a bid or play. Altman didn't know how to play a quick card. It still escapes me how he managed to keep from being brained by an opponent – I'm sure they were all tempted. Mercifully, he doesn't play bridge in tournaments any more.

To say we started off slowly would be a masterpiece of understatement. As we expected, the two American teams were matched up right from the start in the round-robin. It makes sense, as I'm sure you realize, to get matches like that out of the way early so that no one could accuse either team later in the event of tanking to help their countrymen. We were to play two matches against each of the other teams, with IMPs converted to Victory Points.

Anyway, we lost the opening-round match to Rubin and his friends, 101 IMPs to 32, which translated into 20 Victory Points for them and minus 1 VP for us. We were more or less favored to win the whole thing, so it was embarrassing to get shellacked that way.

Of course, the round-robin was to last six days, so there was plenty of time to recover, but our head-to-head matches with the defending champions had a lot riding on them. The top two teams after the round-robin would play for the championship – and there would be a carryover from the head-to-head matches between those two teams. If the first-place team had the better of the round-robin matches, the carryover would be one-half of the IMP difference. If the second-place team won IMPs in the head-to-heads with the first-place team, the carryover for the second-place team would be one-third of the IMP difference.

We weren't the only contender to take it on the chin in the first round. Sweden was bounced by Argentina, 77-45 (16-4 in Victory Points). I found it ironic that in the posting of the scores for the round-robin, our "sort-of Aces" team was called the "North American Challengers." Rubin's team was dubbed the "Defending Champions."

We clobbered Argentina in the second round, 19-1, and after creaming Chinese Taipei in the third round, we moved into second place. We stayed there pretty much the rest of the way – never seriously threatened by the other teams but not really very close to Rubin and his team either. We ended up 27 Victory Points out of first.

Our second meeting with the defending champs was better than the first, but we won by only 8 IMPs. That meant that in the two matches with us, the defenders were 61 IMPs better – so they got to split the sum as their carryover for the final. They entered the 96-board showdown with what amounted to a 31-IMP lead.

We definitely had our work cut out for us.

The matches were played in hotel rooms where the beds and most of the other furniture had been disassembled and taken away. Each table had a screen and a little box on the side containing stopwatches that would be used to time the players during their bids and plays. If there were any problems with players taking too long, there would be no disputes about who the culprits were.

Things didn't start exactly swimmingly for our side. We were lucky to get out of one deal with a 2-IMP loss when Eisenberg doubled a 2♦ bid that got redoubled and passed out. Hamilton made it on the nose for plus 510 (old scoring). On another deal, Rubin made what would commonly be called an eccentric 3♣ preempt – with a void and an outside ace – got doubled and made it. We actually won the first set, but with the carryover we were still behind after the first 16 boards, 65.5-43.

The second set was a nightmare. Wolffie and I played against Hamilton and Passell while Von der Porten and Rubin were playing against Kantar and Eisenberg. They beat us 47-3. They were up 112.5-46.

Of course we had all been down before, so no one panicked. At least at this tournament we didn't have to worry about who was exchanging information illegally under the table. We could just play bridge.

We managed to hold within striking distance while we waited for momentum to swing our way. It was beginning to look like that wasn't going to happen – until the next-to-last set.

It was Thursday night and we had played 64 boards only to be trailing, 179.5-136 with 32 deals to go. If we were going to make a move, we had better get with it. Things didn't look great for us, but Paul was tough. "It's going to be a lot closer before this is over," he said.

Our lineups for Friday were Bobby and I against Hamilton and Passell, Swanson and Soloway against Paulsen and Ross.

The first board was a nothing 6NT. We bid and made it at both tables. Then came three hands that changed the course of the Bermuda Bowl.

```
Dlr: East          ♠ Q 4
Vul: N-S           ♥ Q J 9 6 4
                   ♦ K J 8 5
                   ♣ A 3
♠ J 8 6 5                              ♠ A 3 2
♥ A K 3                                ♥ 8 5
♦ 6                                    ♦ A 9 4 3
♣ Q J 10 6 5                           ♣ 8 7 4 2
                   ♠ K 10 9 7
                   ♥ 10 7 2
                   ♦ Q 10 7 2
                   ♣ K 9
```

WEST	NORTH	EAST	SOUTH
Ross	*Soloway*	*Paulsen*	*Swanson*
		Pass	Pass
1♠	2♥	2♠	3♥
All Pass			

Paul went down one trick when Ross got a diamond ruff. There was nothing so quiet going on at our table, however.

WEST	NORTH	EAST	SOUTH
Wolff	*Passell*	*Me*	*Hamilton*
		Pass	Pass
1♠	Pass	2♠	Pass
Pass	Dbl	Pass	2NT
Dbl	All Pass		

Bobby and I go out of our way to open our four-card majors. If his double of 2NT seems a bit unusual – after all, he opened pretty light in third seat – remember that he had a secret weapon: his five-card club suit. I had just what the doctor ordered on this deal – two aces – and Hamilton finished down two for minus 500. It was a 9-IMP gain for our side. Next:

Dlr: South   ♠ K Q 8 5 2
Vul: E-W   ♥ K 9 5
                ♦ A Q 4 3
                ♣ J

♠ A J 3   ♠ 9
♥ J 6 3   ♥ A 8 4
♦ K 10 8 6   ♦ 7 5 2
♣ 10 8 5   ♣ K Q 9 6 4 3

                ♠ 10 7 6 4
                ♥ Q 10 7 2
                ♦ J 9
                ♣ A 7 2

WEST	NORTH	EAST	SOUTH
Wolff	*Passell*	*Me*	*Hamilton*
			Pass
Pass	1♠	2♣	2♠
3♣	3♦	Pass	4♠
All Pass			

I led the ♣K, won by Mike with the ace. He played a diamond to
the queen and followed with the ♠Q. Bobby won the ace and played
another club, ruffed. Next came the ♠K, the ♦A, a diamond ruff, a
club ruff, a diamond ruff. He then misguessed hearts by playing low to
the king in his hand.

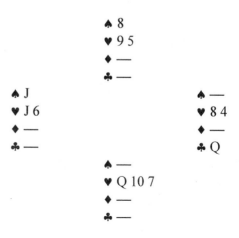

                ♠ 8
                ♥ 9 5
                ♦ —
                ♣ —

♠ J   ♠ —
♥ J 6   ♥ 8 4
♦ —   ♦ —
♣ —   ♣ Q

                ♠ —
                ♥ Q 10 7
                ♦ —
                ♣ —

I won the ♥A, and stopped to think about my next play. If I had Mike's hand counted correctly, he had only one trump left. If Bobby didn't have the ♠J, there was no way to defeat this contract. At the same time, if I made the lazy return of a club, Passell would be able to score his little trump *en passant* and make his contract.

I returned a heart, and Passell was finished. If he ducked, Bobby would win the jack and pick up Mike's last trump. If Passell went up with the queen, Bobby would win the next round of hearts and do the same thing.

At the other table, Soloway guessed everything in sight and made an overtrick. Another 11 IMPs for us. Then came:

```
Dlr: West        ♠ Q 10 9 8 7 3
Vul: Both        ♥ 7 5
                 ♦ K 9 3 2
                 ♣ 2
  ♠ K 6 2                       ♠ A J 4
  ♥ A 10 8                      ♥ K J 3 2
  ♦ A 8 7 5 4                   ♦ —
  ♣ A 9                         ♣ J 10 8 5 4 3
                 ♠ 5
                 ♥ Q 9 6 4
                 ♦ Q J 10 6
                 ♣ K Q 7 6
```

At the other table, Paulsen and Ross (East-West) languished in 3♣. In our room:

WEST	NORTH	EAST	SOUTH
Wolff	*Passell*	*Me*	*Hamilton*
1NT	Pass	2♦ (1)	Pass
2NT	Pass	3♣	Pass
3NT	Pass	4♣	Pass
4♦	Pass	5♣	All Pass

(1) Forcing Stayman.

South led the ♦Q, which I ruffed in hand. I played a club toward dummy and inserted the 9 when Fred didn't split his honors. I cashed the ♣A and ruffed another diamond. I played the ♠A and a spade to dummy's king. Then I cashed the ♦A, pitching my spade, and ruffed the fourth round of diamonds. Hamilton could have overruffed at this point (he threw a diamond on the second spade), but he discarded a heart.

I was determined not to take any major-suit finesses, so my next play was a heart to dummy's ace and the spade, which I ruffed. Fred overruffed at that point, but I claimed, since he had to lead into my heart tenace after cashing the other club. Another 10 IMPs for us.

Rubin and his boys were gasping for air. We had them on the ropes.

If there's one thing Bobby and I have been good at over the years, it's putting the opponents away when we have them at the point where their legs are rubbery. We also have staying power. There was a stretch from January of 1979 to May of 1991 in which we never lost a match of 100 boards or more.

In Manila, our team smelled blood at this point and we poured it on. One board after I made 5♣, Soloway was doubled by Paulsen in 2♥ and they couldn't beat it. Plus 470 to our side and another 9 IMPs our way. I went down one in 4♠ at the other table.

They made a small gain on the next board, but the roof continued to cave in for them. After a push board, Swanson made a heart game that was defeated at our table – 10 more IMPs. Soloway and Passell both played 2♦ – Paul made it, Mike didn't. 5 more IMPs. That board tied the score at 188 each.

We had overcome a deficit of more than 80 IMPs to pull even. Three boards later, we were ahead by 25!

First Soloway made 1NT but Passell went down – 4 IMPs for us. Then Wolff and I took a good save at 5♦ against their vulnerable heart game and went down only one (doubled) for minus 100. At the other table, Soloway pushed on to 5♥ and made it. 11 more IMPs. This deal was the crusher:

```
Dlr: North          ♠ A 10 5 3
Vul: Both           ♥ 6 3
                    ♦ K Q 9 3
                    ♣ A J 8
  ♠ K 9 6 2                           ♠ J
  ♥ A K Q J                           ♥ 7 4 2
  ♦ J 5                               ♦ A 10 7 4
  ♣ Q 10 9                            ♣ K 6 5 3 2
                    ♠ Q 8 7 4
                    ♥ 10 9 8 5
                    ♦ 8 6 2
                    ♣ 7 4
```

Paulsen and Ross, holding the East-West cards, had stopped at 2♣, making three. At our table:

WEST	NORTH	EAST	SOUTH
Wolff	*Passell*	*Me*	*Hamilton*
	1♦	Pass	Pass
Dbl	Pass	2♣	Pass
2♦	Pass	2NT	Pass
3♣	Pass	3♦	Pass
3NT	All Pass		

Hamilton led a heart and I immediately played the ♣Q. Passell won the ace and fired back the ♦K. I ducked, unblocking the jack from dummy. Passell continued with a low diamond. I won with the 10 in my hand and played a low club, maintaining communication with my hand. Passell had to take the jack or he wouldn't get it, and there was nothing he could do. If Fred could have gotten in somehow, he probably would have worked out the shift to the ♠Q, which would have beaten the contract. As it was, they were helpless and another 10 IMPs got away from the Rubin team.

When the dust had settled, we had won the next-to-last 16-board segment, 80-20, and we led 216-199.5 with 16 boards to go.

Stern had planned to put Eisenberg and Kantar in for the final segment, but Bobby and I and Paul and John had played so well that Stern was afraid to tamper with the lineup. I must say that over those last 32 boards, Bobby and I had two of the strongest sets we have ever had. In the final 16 boards we started with a couple of minor setbacks, but then we sucked it up and started throwing aspirin tablets. There wasn't an IMP available to Rubin and Von der Porten. We bid every filthy game in sight and guessed every jack that needed guessing. It was a performance of which we still have fond memories. There were not many swings and we won a rather quiet set, 31-18, for a wonderful comeback win – always the most satisfying way to mark paid to the opponents' ticket.

We were jubilant. Don't forget, this was the exact same team that had blown the huge lead to the Italians in Bermuda. This time, we got it right. *We* were the ones who came from behind. *We* were the team that would not be denied. *We* were the team that refused to fold after falling far behind. We could hold our heads up.

We had beaten a proud, strong team. They showed their class by coming to congratulate us, and I felt for each of them. No one likes losing, and they hadn't played badly. The worst you could accuse them of was being a little conservative in trying to sit on their lead. The fact is that our team got hot at just the right time.

You might say the Bermuda Bowl was the rubber match for our two teams. We had beaten them in the semifinal of the trials in Houston and they had thrashed us in the round-robin in Manila.

It's interesting that my memories of the victory banquets at the Bermuda Bowls in 1975 and 1977 are both so vivid I can almost reach out and touch them. Some memories are bittersweet . . . some are just sweet.

16

Valleys

ON MAY 7, 1994, I was watching the National Basketball Association playoffs. Seattle, the team with the best record in the regular season, was playing against Denver, the underdogs who somehow got to a fifth game against the top-seeded team in their bracket.

There was no way Seattle, playing on its home court, was going to lose this deciding game. Never in the history of the NBA had a top-seeded team lost in the first round of the playoffs.

It happened. Denver won in overtime, and the image still in my mind is that of Denver's center, Dikembe Mutombo, lying on the floor at the end of the game, clutching the basketball and crying. He was overcome by joy and disbelief. No one thought his team could win, but it did.

The other team – the heavily favored, can't-lose Seattle Super-sonics – was disconsolate. Stunned. Blown away.

These are the highs and lows of sports. They embody the cliché phrase about the thrill of victory and the agony of defeat, and you're mistaken if you think they don't apply to bridge. I've experienced both – the agony more than the thrills, unfortunately – and I've learned to take each in stride.

One of my most painful lessons in that aspect of competition occurred in Valkenburg, the Netherlands, in 1980.

Our 1977 world championship team – Bobby, me, Paul Soloway, John Swanson, Billy Eisenberg and Eddie Kantar – returned home from Manila, and the pairs immediately went their separate ways. That might strike some people as odd – like breaking up the Yankees right after they win the World Series – but that's the way it is with professional bridge players. They can't afford to stick together just for old times' sake. They've got to go where they find the paying customers – sponsors, if you will.

Bobby and I ended up playing with Cliff Russell. In the parlance of professional bridge, Cliff was a sponsor. That doesn't mean he was a bad player, although many sponsors are. Cliff, a brash Miami home builder and real estate developer, has won many national championships and is an extremely aggressive and tough competitor.

Cliff's main problem at the bridge table is that he is hot-headed and impetuous. Still, Russell and Dicky Freeman, his partner, were quite effective on their good days.

Freeman is a little guy who looks like he should be peering through a microscope in a laboratory instead of beating people at the bridge table. But he is a terrific player. In 1993, I had the pleasure of playing on two teams with Freeman that won the Spingold and Reisinger – both quite convincingly.

Freeman was an original Quiz Kid on radio in the 1940s. He was admitted to the University of Chicago at age 15, and if he doesn't qualify as a genius there ain't a cow in Texas. At one time, he was ACBL's youngest Life Master. He also worked some as a tournament director and had a reputation – in the days before computers, when pair games were posted and scored by hand – of being the fastest director with a sheet in all of the ACBL. He's still as fast as lightning in analyzing bridge plays. He's a good teammate and a fun guy to be around.

The Russell team was Bobby and me, Freeman and Cliff with Curtis Smith and Eddie Wold, two excellent players. Smith, a tall, good-looking Texan with curly hair and lots of bad habits, reminds me of a riverboat gambler. But in his prime he could play the spots off the cards. Wold is one of the top professional players in this part of the world.

We didn't do much in the fall of 1977 – and we lost in the Vanderbilt in Houston in the spring of 1978. It was yet another loss for me in that event, which I've won four times – but not since 1973. It's starting to get annoying, but that's another story.

The Russell team did venture to the world championships in New Orleans that year to play in a new event, the Rosenblum Cup. Freeman had been replaced on the team by Dan Morse, who played with Wold, while Smith played with Russell. Ironically, we were still identified as the Aces even though Corn had little or nothing to do with the team. Any team with Bobby and me on it was the Aces.

We lost to Brazil in the semifinals of the Rosenblum Cup, but we finished higher than any other American team. We stuck together for one more tournament – the Summer Nationals in Toronto – but that was it.

By the time we headed for the 1978 Fall Nationals in Denver, Ira was back as our bankroller and captain. Ira's interest in the team and the concept of the Aces never really waned – even when he was almost totally uninvolved – but he wasn't always willing to make the financial commitment. He went through some tough times economically and just couldn't come up with the money the way he did in the beginning.

Anyway, our new lineup was Bobby and me and a couple of sharks named Ira Rubin and Fred Hamilton. Hamilton and Rubin didn't invent intensity at the bridge table but they sure knew how to practice it. Playing against them was about as relaxing as shaving with a circular saw. Both of them played bridge with the same kind of suave gentility that Dick Butkus and Gene "Big Daddy" Lipscomb played football. They would do the intellectual equivalent of grabbing a pile of opponents, peel them off, one by one, until they found the guy with the ball, and then they would eat him. But don't get me wrong about me calling these guys sharks – if sharks were as tough as they were, you wouldn't be safe in your bathtub. I mean it in a complimentary way – as in they'll rip you to pieces, perfectly legally and ethically, if you give them the chance.

Rubin was a remarkable player. An East Coast, Yankee type, you'd often see him wandering about the hotel in sandals and looking like an absent-minded professor. He had perfected the art of writing all the knowledge worth having, namely his bridge system, on the head of a pin. If he had written *War and Peace*, the word count would have doubled and you could carry the entire manuscript in your wallet. Talk about having to read the fine print. Woe betide the partner who would forget either the system as it was written, or the logical (to Rubin) extensions to it. Beneath this oddball demeanor lurked an incredibly tough competitor. Ira had the ability to bear down on every hand, session after session. Playing against him was about as relaxing as being in a laboratory where they are testing chalk on blackboards.

Hamilton, the quintessential gambler and one helluva card player, was equally ferocious. Fred figured that he was at least 85% to guess a queen with absolutely no information about the hand.

In other words, these guys were good to have as teammates. One of the prime benefits was that you didn't have to play against them. The priorities of most of the beasts of the card table are really quite simple. First you destroy the opponents. If your teammates were less than perfect in your eyes, they're next. After that, partner must be hammered. Rubin always figured that since partner would inevitably be guilty of some infraction, it was both sensible and efficient to get started with his punishment at the time (or before) he either blundered, Rubin thought he blundered, or Rubin thought that he was thinking of blundering.

At least 90% of executioners are more forgiving than Ira Rubin. Rubin and Hamilton had a love-hate relationship without the love. The only reason that they played together was for the pleasure of grinding up some hapless opponents while they anticipated the joy of taking the wood to each other. To compound the problem, Ira has some really goofy ideas about bridge and it irked him that Fred didn't buy all of them. Since Ira has about as much use for dissent as your average religious fanatic . . . oh well, you get the picture. Ira can be mildly critical of partners.

On more than one occasion, Fred and Ira were on a team that won a qualifying event, but when it came time to play in the trials, they played with different partners. Also, they were teammates when they beat Italy in the Bermuda Bowl in 1976 – but they played with different partners, Rubin with Soloway and Hamilton with Eisenberg.

Hamilton and Rubin were cooking in the Reisinger in Denver that fall, however, and we won by the practically unheard-of margin of five boards.

Our win in the 1977 Grand National with Morse, Wold and Smith got us into the Bermuda Bowl trials in Cherry Hill NJ in January of 1979. We added Cliff Russell as our sixth man and the unheard of happened – the Aces lost. It was the first time – not counting the basket-case Grand National Team – that we had lost in the trials as a team where we had any kind of chance. At least we were beaten by a good team. The winners were Malcolm Brachman, another sponsor who has had considerable success; Mike Passell, Eddie Kantar, Billy Eisenberg, Bobby Goldman and Paul Soloway. Notice there were three former Aces.

They went on to win the Bermuda Bowl in 1979. The key session of that event was in the final when, with Brachman in the lineup, they beat the Italians 71-3 to take a lead that they didn't relinquish. Once again, the dreaded Italian Blue Team was knocked off, and I wasn't part of it. And it was Garozzo, Belladonna, Franco, etc. When was I going to have another shot at those guys?

The "Aces" road show – our four-man team of Rubin, Hamilton, Bobby and me – was impressive in the summer and fall of 1979. In Las Vegas at the Nationals, we won the Spingold. That fall, with Ira Corn as our non-playing captain, we tied for first in the Reisinger.

That tournament, in Cincinnati, ended with a spectacular scene in the playing area at the Netherlands Hilton in the wee hours of the morning.

Our team had tied for first with Bud Reinhold, Russ Arnold, Bobby Levin, Jeff Meckstroth and Eric Rodwell. Because the Reisinger was a qualifying event for the Olympiad trials in Memphis about a week later, we had to determine which team would earn the trials berth. So we sat down, ringed by at least 200 spectators, for a 12-board playoff as soon as the event was officially declared a tie.

The very first deal was a doozy. Wolffie, North, passed, and so did Levin. I opened a strong 1♣ with this collection:

♠A K Q 9 8 ♥A K 4 2 ♦J 8 7 ♣10.

Reinhold passed on my left and Wolff bid 1♥ (negative). Levin now sailed in with 2♠. I doubled for penalty – to my regret. This was the entire deal:

```
Dlr: North        ♠ 5
Vul: None         ♥ Q J 10 6 5
                  ♦ 5 4 2
                  ♣ J 8 7 5
♠ 7                               ♠ J 10 6 4 3 2
♥ 9 8 7 3                         ♥ —
♦ A Q 9                           ♦ K 10 6 3
♣ K 9 6 3 2                       ♣ A Q 4
                  ♠ A K Q 9 8
                  ♥ A K 4 2
                  ♦ J 8 7
                  ♣ 10
```

WEST	NORTH	EAST	SOUTH
Reinhold	*Wolff*	*Levin*	*Me*
	Pass	Pass	1♣
Pass	1♥	2♠	Dbl
All Pass			

I took five trump tricks and that was all. Plus 470 to their side.
Their teammates were minus 50 in 3♥ at the other table. Fortunately
for us, the playoff format retained the board-a-match scoring. Each
deal was a separate match and you could lose no more than one point
on each deal, no matter how big a number you went for.

Our results on the remaining 11 hands were up and down, but Ira
and Fred had us covered, so we won the playoff 6½ to 5½ despite the
loss on the first board. That gave us two qualifications for the
Olympiad trials, which meant an automatic bye to the trials final. Not
having to play a semifinal match can be a tremendous advantage in
terms of rest and freshness. If your team gets caught in a grueling
semifinal match, you can enter the final with nothing left. We liked
the idea of being able to take it easy while the other two teams slugged
it out.

At this point, Ira Corn was front and center as our non-playing
captain. Ira, a member of the ACBL Board of Directors, had been
elected ACBL President for 1980, and there was no doubt he was
going to maintain a high profile during that year. What better way to
do it than to resume his position as NPC of the powerful Aces.

And powerful we were. We added Mike Passell to play with Hamilton and Paul Soloway to play with Rubin. After all, we had won only three of the last four events we had played, so how could Rubin and Hamilton possibly continue to tolerate each other? We prevailed in the final of the trials in Memphis by 168 IMPs, one of the most lopsided margins in the history of the trials.

The team had journeyed to Memphis right after the Nationals in Cincinnati – and kicked up our heels while the other two teams duked it out. With Corn back as captain, Joe Musumeci was back as the coach. He didn't have the same disciplinarian role as he did previously, but he was just as effective. It was always good to have Moose around.

In the final of the trials, we played Eddie Wold, Mark Lair, Lou Bluhm, Tommy Sanders, Cliff Russell and Dicky Freeman. They had survived a very close match with a team from Chicago, winning 249-228. They had no chance against us. We jumped out in front right away and poured it on throughout. At the victory celebration, their NPC, Edgar Kaplan, graciously poured champagne for Corn. We didn't need anything to drink to be flying high.

The Olympiad was months away – we had finished the trials December 9, 1979, and the big tournament didn't start until the following September – but already we were being hailed as the mean machine of bridge. Alan Truscott wrote in *The New York Times* that the Aces had "no equal in North America and probably no equal in the world." We thought we were King Kong. Considering what happened to the big ape, that was an apt analogy.

We did nothing in the Vanderbilt and nothing in the Spingold in 1980, but we were still the team to beat when we got to Valkenburg in the Netherlands.

Valkenburg. The name itself has a romantic air to it. You almost expect to see Vikings or some such characters walking around. It's a small town nestled in a corner of the Netherlands between Belgium and Germany. It's not easy to get to. Susie and I flew into Germany and rode a train to the site of the world championship. As a rule, I don't notice much about where I am when I play in these tournaments, but at the time Valkenburg seemed like a smaller version of Stockholm to me.

Susie was more comfortable in Valkenburg than she had been in Manila, although there was some unpleasantness. At the opening ceremonies, there were Dutch protesters who objected to the participation by South Africa, which even then had a black eye because of its apartheid policy.

When the event started, Egypt and Surinam – on orders from their governments – refused to play their matches against South Africa. Before the Olympiad began, the contestants had all agreed to play anyone they were matched up against, so the WBF suspended Egypt and Surinam from world events for three years. Curiously, Egypt did sit down and play against Israel when that match came up.

The opening ceremony was an event to remember. Valkenburg has a system of caves beneath the city and they're outfitted for all kinds of events, including a big shindig like the Olympiad kickoff party. We were like a bunch of sardines packed into the tiny space underground, and it was cold – I was glad when it was over – but it was great to be at another world championship.

Just getting to the championship round of the Olympiad was complicated, to say the least. There were 58 teams in the field, divided into two groups of 29 teams each. A complete round-robin was played within each group, with IMPs converted to Victory Points. If you finished in the top four in either group, you got to play on. Two more round-robins were set up for 32-board matches. The competitors were the first- and fourth-place teams from one bracket and the second- and third-place teams from the other bracket. The winners of those round-robins would play 80 boards for the world championship.

We were clearly the best team in the event, but we started off slowly. Incredibly – or perhaps not so incredibly – we were blitzed by a team from Pakistan that was making its first appearance in the Olympiad. I bet you can guess who was on the team. Right! My friend Zia Mahmood, the dashing playboy. A year later, he would make a huge impression at the world championships in Rye, New York.

But the Aces didn't win world championships by panicking when something went wrong, and we came on strong at the end to finish in third place in our bracket, behind France and Indonesia. That put us in the semifinal round-robin with Indonesia, Denmark and the Netherlands.

We mopped the floor with Indonesia (93-43) and Denmark (119-42) and edged the Netherlands (64-62). In the other bracket, France lost to Chinese Taipei, 54-47, but they massacred Brazil and beat Norway by 17. Norway and Chinese Taipei also won two matches each, so the round-robin winner was determined by Victory Points, and France won out.

It was exciting to be in another world championship. Although we were the favorites, we didn't take the French team lightly. One of their members, Paul Chemla, is a great player and one of the all-time characters of the bridge world. Chemla believes that anything worth doing is worth doing to excess. While his gastronomic feats were not quite up to Corn's standards, he wields a mean fork and is a sommelier of the old school. A large man, he has dreamy eyes and a hang-dog look, as though he knows the world is against him but he's resigned to it. With a somewhat volatile temperament, Chemla once was known as "l'enfant terrible of bridge." Bottom line, Paul is a likable character with a wry sense of humor.

Once, in a world championship in Miami, Chemla emerged from a match in which France had been drubbed – again. It was a dreadful match in a series of dreadful matches. Someone made a comment to him about his ill fortune. "Bah!" he said. "Every match, it's seven against one. I can still win, but I need luck."

The other French players were all excellent. Some of them, including Chemla, are still around today. In 1980, the French team was Chemla and Christian Mari, Michel Lebel and Michel Perron (who plays with Chemla these days), and Henri Svarc and Phillipe Soulet.

Rumor had it that France's team unity – partly because of Chemla's cranky nature – was low. In fact, the team captain had brought along a couple of spare sets of system notes – for Chemla-Lebel and Mari-Perron – just in case.

Our players were using somewhat complicated bidding systems, although Bobby and I are pretty straightforward in our approach once you get past the forcing 1♣ opening. Rubin-Soloway and Hamilton-

Passell had quite a bit of razzmatazz up their sleeves. For example, all their two-level openings had multiple meanings.

Our opponents, meanwhile, were pretty much natural bidders, a style I would encounter in the French team 12 years later in another Olympiad.

In the opening set of the final, the French raced out to a 32-0 lead, but we still won the 16-board segment 45-39. That gave us strength, as though we had taken their best shot and were still rolling. We increased our lead with a 24-9 second set. They came back in the third segment, winning 22-8. Notice how low-scoring those two quarters were. This is usually indicative of strong play by both sides. Both teams knew they were in a dogfight and we were all grimly determined.

The closeness of the match added to the tension. Bobby and I barely exchanged pleasantries with Chemla and Mari when we sat down for the start of the fourth set. I won't say we were at a point where we hated each other, but it was all business.

Ira and Moose had rested Bobby and me in the third set, although I spent most of my time itching to get back into the fray. I was confident our team would win. After all, we were the Aces – the best team in the field and the favorites to win it all. But the French were like the prize fighter who is too "dumb" to realize he doesn't have a chance. The French were hanging in there, refusing to be put away. Whenever I encounter such a competitive drive, I admire and respect the other guy even if he beats me. It's the way bridge at this level should be played. Also, it feels better to win against opponents who are tough than against people who don't put up a fight.

A 3-IMP slow-play penalty had been assessed against our team in the third set, cutting our lead from 77-70 to 74-70. We were getting reports that the vugraph room was packed. Naturally, most of them were rooting for France. In Europe, we were always the Ugly Americans.

We opened the fourth set with a 1-IMP gain on an overtrick, followed by two push boards. This was the 52nd deal of the match:

```
Dlr: West        ♠ 10
Vul: Both        ♥ K Q 9
                 ♦ A 10 9 8 3 2
                 ♣ K 9 8
♠ Q 9 5 3 2                        ♠ A K J 8 7 6
♥ J 8 5 4                          ♥ A 10 7 6 3 2
♦ Q 6 4                            ♦ —
♣ 7                                ♣ 2
                 ♠ 4
                 ♥ —
                 ♦ K J 7 5
                 ♣ A Q J 10 6 5 4 3
```

WEST	NORTH	EAST	SOUTH
Perron	*Rubin*	*Lebel*	*Soloway*
Pass	1♦	1♠	2♣
4♠	Pass	5♣	6♣
Pass	Pass	6♠	Dbl
All Pass			

Even experts have trouble with wild deals like this – in a sense it's a crap shoot when everyone is bidding in leaps and bounds. All the conventions in the world are not worth the judgment gained from experience in the trenches, but with some deals you still have to guess what's right.

Note the bluff that Lebel put up – his 5♣ cuebid without first-round control. He was going to bid 6♠ all along with that freak hand after his partner leaped to 4♠, and Lebel wanted to inhibit a club lead.

Looking at all the cards, it's easy to see that Soloway could have defeated the slam by two tricks if he led a low club to Rubin's king, allowing Rubin to return the ♥K. Soloway would then have ruffed out the ♥A and Rubin would still have a heart trick coming. Soloway wasn't likely to lead a club after the cuebid, however, and after the diamond lead the slam could not be defeated by more than one trick.

Note that Lebel might have chosen to double 6♣. That might have been a bonanza if his partner had construed the double as a Lightner Slam Double. Such a double tells partner not to lead "our suit" – spades in this case – but to make an unusual lead, frequently dummy's first-bid suit. With a diamond lead, ruffed by Lebel, the slam could have been defeated if Lebel had then been able to figure out which major-suit ace to cash.

Perhaps Lebel could perceive that even if he got a diamond lead, he would still have to guess what to do after that, which is what persuaded him to take the push to 6♠. The other consideration, of course, was that 6♠ might be cold. Anyway, Soloway and Rubin ended up plus 200 on a deal that was easy to spot as loaded with potential disaster for either side.

Disaster was indeed in the offing on this deal. At our table, the bidding was even wilder.

WEST	NORTH	EAST	SOUTH
Wolff	*Mari*	*Me*	*Chemla*
Pass	1♦	2♦ (1)	2♥ (2)
4♠	4NT	5♠	6♣
Pass	6♦	6♠	7♦
Pass	Pass	Dbl	All Pass

(1) Michaels cuebid: both majors.
(2) Good diamond support and at least a limit raise.

My 5♠ bid – I, too, intended all along to bid 6♠ – was an attempt to lull the opponents into thinking that when I bid the slam I had been "pushed" into it. If they believed that, they would be more likely to double than to bid on – and I certainly thought Bobby had chances to make 6♠. I didn't ask, so I'll probably never know why Chemla bid on to 7♦ rather than doubling my 6♠ bid. Maybe he thought my slam was cold. Maybe he didn't want to have to choose an opening lead. Maybe he never sells out when he has an eight-card suit.

The upshot of his bid, of course, was that I was left on lead against this diabolical grand slam *sacrifice* (I hoped). I took a long time to decide on my lead, and I finally – fatally – chose the ♥A. We couldn't hear anything from the vugraph room, but I was told later the pro-French crowd went berserk. For an instant, I was the most popular player in Europe.

The sight of dummy's heart void was sickening, of course – and it didn't take Mari long to claim 13 tricks. He had to play diamonds just right, but after my bid showing the majors there wasn't much mystery to the hand.

Plus 2330 to France. A 19-IMP loss for our team – and a 28-IMP swing (we would have gained 9 IMPs if I had led the ♠A and defeated the contract one trick). All of a sudden, our 75-70 lead had become an 89-75 deficit. We never regained the lead after that. The final score was 131-111.

You can never say for sure what might have happened, but we probably would have won the championship in a breeze if I had led the ♠A.

Naturally, I felt bad about the mistake. I think I should have worked out the right lead. For starters, Chemla cuebid 2♥ – he could just as easily have cuebid spades – one clue that he might have control of hearts – even a void. The other clue was that Mari (North) bid Blackwood. Good players don't bid Blackwood with voids. Mari was marked with a singleton spade (he probably wouldn't have bid Blackwood with a doubleton, either). If Chemla, on my left, was void in spades, that meant Bobby had a six-card spade suit. He had bid strongly, but not like a man with a six-card suit.

I didn't like the result of my lead of the ♥A, but I didn't dwell on it. I'm not bragging here, but I think this is a really important point. At this point in my career, I was what I could characterize as extremely mentally tough. The bad opening lead was an error that turned into a disaster, but I didn't allow myself to think about it. I couldn't. I had another board to play – the next one.

I once got a birthday card that said, "Forget about the past – you can't change it. Forget about the present – I didn't buy you one." It's true that you can't change the past, but you can learn from it. In my mind, that's the only reason to review your own performance after the fact. You have to look at what you did with a very dispassionate eye, tell yourself honestly what you really think of what happened, add up the evidence and draw a conclusion. If you can be objective in this scenario you have an excellent chance of improving.

In these situations, many players fall into one of two categories. The first is the player who looks for rationalizations as to how he couldn't have known what to do. The second is the player who rushes to confess his sin so as to seek emotional support. It doesn't matter whether you should or shouldn't have got it right. The fact is you got it wrong. In most cases, there is no chance the hand will come up again that session. Dwelling on it is a distraction, which is just another way to lose.

Flogging yourself will do nothing but land you on the shrink's couch. It's a losing practice. Smart players – successful players – learn to avoid these losing habits.

It hurt to lose the world championship when we were the best team there, but we weren't through being disappointed in 1980.

The closing ceremonies of the Olympiad were on October 11. On October 30, our team had to play in the team trials in Memphis to choose the North American representative to the Bermuda Bowl in Rye NY. With the time it took to get home from Europe and to catch up with business after the long trip, we hardly had time to catch our breath before we had to gear up for another major battle.

Our team was still reeling from the unexpected loss in the Netherlands. We were not psychologically ready for this trials event. Plus, we started off with a huge problem: Soloway couldn't play.

We had qualified for the trials with a four-man team – Bobby and me and Rubin and Hamilton. So even though Soloway and Passell had played with us in Valkenburg, we would still have had to add them for the trials. Passell was eligible to be added, but Paul wasn't. The rules for international teams at that time were so convoluted and – I might as well say it – ridiculous, that Paul wasn't eligible to be added to our trials team because he hadn't won or placed high enough in the Vanderbilt or Spingold in the two previous years. Never mind that he had won three world championships in the previous five years, and had been second once. The ACBL Board of Directors in their infinite wisdom had approved rules restricting augmentation that had excluded the most successful player in world competition over the previous five years.

Well, we started casting about for someone to play with Rubin. He suggested Ron Andersen or Matt Granovetter. Corn nixed Andersen immediately. Ira was a man of strong emotions, and he had a grudge against Andersen that he wasn't about to forget.

A few years earlier, Corn was poised to play in the Grand National Teams at the national level with a squad from Texas that he was bankrolling. Somehow, Andersen found out that Corn had not played on the team when it won the district final. Ira had started with the team, but had gotten sick.

Corn, therefore, wasn't eligible to play at the national level and so was also ineligible to play in the zonal playoff. It was true that Corn's eligibility was doubtful at best, but the opponents were aware of the situation and had made no protest prior to the playoffs. If a protest had been upheld, they would have had to deal with a four-man team of Goldman, Blumenthal, Wolff and myself. When Andersen's second-place team protested Corn's presence after we had won the zonal playoff, the protest was upheld and we were disqualified. Corn never forgave Ron for that, so there was no way Andersen was going to be added to the Aces team.

That left Granovetter, a very good player and a nice guy – maybe too nice – but not the right player to be Rubin's partner. The partnership didn't work at all and we failed to make it out of the opening round-robin at the trials. There were five teams with four to advance to semifinals, and the Aces – runners-up in the world champ-ionship two weeks earlier – were bounced out of the trials. On paper, we were the best team in the field. In fact, we lost three out of four matches and finished last. The Aces, operating with a new partnership that failed to click, were flat and ineffective.

In 1981, Corn started tinkering again, adding Alan Sontag and Peter Weichsel. Soloway and Passell had been more or less a replacement pair who went their own ways after the Olympiad. Sontag and Weichsel were free, so Corn invited them to join the Aces. These two were a decidedly dynamic pair. They had developed a bidding system they called Power Precision, and they had made their mark in high-level competition, winning the *Sunday Times* Invitational in London and the Cavendish in New York, two of the toughest and most prestigious events in bridge. They won the Cavendish two years running (1976 and 1977), a remarkable achievement.

Both were extremely tough players, and it was Corn's and the team's good fortune they were available at the time. Sontag is a nervous, high-strung guy who talks and jokes a lot at the table unless someone tells him to shut up. He has lots of North American championships. His book *The Bridge Bum* is an all-time classic.

While Sontag is kind of dumpy in appearance, Weichsel looks like he just left the weight room. Trim and fit, his standard bridge outfit is a pair of tight-fitting jeans and a short-sleeved shirt with the sleeves rolled up. He wears his hair short these days, but in the 1970s and 1980s it was long. Sontag noted in his book that Weichsel often took pleasure in flouting convention with his long hair and upsetting the stuffy opponents. As for his bridge play, he's superb. He also has lots of national championships, and he and Juanita Chambers won the World Mixed Pairs in Geneva, Switzerland, in 1990.

With Weichsel and Sontag joining Bobby and me and Rubin and Hamilton, we came in second in the Vanderbilt in the spring of 1981. By summer, Corn had again decided that the expense of his bridge habit was too painful when we weren't winning, so he scrapped the team. We played in the Spingold with Jim Jacoby and a fellow from Tulsa named Jim Chew. We weren't destined to do much and we didn't.

In the fall, another dynamic pair, Ron Rubin and Mike Becker, were the new Aces, joining me and Wolffie and Weichsel and Sontag.

Rubin and Becker. After so many years, the names just go together. They have one of the most enduring partnerships in bridge.

Both are options traders who split their time these days between New York and Florida. Rubin, at one time one of the youngest tournament directors in the ACBL, is dark and handsome with an almost Latin appearance. When he hasn't shaved for a couple of days – and you see him like that occasionally at tournaments – he looks more like a gypsy than a bridge player.

Becker, on the other hand, looks like a college professor – bespectacled, very studious and serious. Together, Rubin and Becker play perhaps the most complicated bidding system in the world – their version of Relay Precision. Their system notes take up hundreds of pages. Often, when they get through with one of their convoluted auctions, one of them knows the other's hand down to each jack. It's impressive, but that kind of thing taxes the memory more than most players can stand. Their record, however, proves that their system serves them very well.

Anyway, the new lineup for the Aces represented a solid team. Corn was delighted with the potential. We finished 11th in the Reisinger that fall, not great but not a bad start. The team stayed together for the 1982 Vanderbilt in Niagara Falls. In the quarterfinal, we lost a close match to Richard Pavlicek, Bill Root, Edgar Kaplan and Norman Kay.

As usual, Corn was great in defeat. He had great expectations for the team and he wanted to win very badly, but he congratulated the other team and complimented everyone.

It all came together for us in the Spingold in Albuquerque that year. The win was our ticket to the trials that eventually led us to one of the most exciting world championships in the history of the game.

We dedicated them both to Ira Corn.

17

Peaks

BOBBY WOLFF used to talk about how it always seemed to be raining when we were losing world championships. It happened in Venice, Valkenburg, Miami and Seattle. To hear Bobby tell it, rain was usually the harbinger of something bad – namely a loss by our team.

It rained the day Ira Corn died.

It was April 28 – Wednesday. A warm spring day in Dallas. It was late morning. The receptionist announced, "Charley Gabriel on line one for Bob." I picked up the phone and heard Gabriel say, "Ira's dead."

The first warning had come a week earlier when Dorothy Moore had picked Ira up at the airport. He had been on a long business trip and had stayed the night at his brother's house in Little Rock. He told Dorothy he had had the strange sensation of feeling weird and not being able to make himself understood to people he was talking to at his brother's house. Ira didn't look good at the airport, but when Dorothy suggested that he visit his physician, Don Brown, Ira said, "I just need some rest and I'll be all right."

On Friday, April 23, we had flown to Austin to play in the Grand National Teams. Our foursome was Wolffie and me, Ira and Bud Creed, a pretty good old player who lived in Garland, near Dallas. Dorothy came along with Ira. We didn't win (George Rosenkranz did), but we didn't really expect to. We flew back to Dallas Sunday night.

On Monday, Ira flew to New Orleans. The next day, Dorothy picked him up at the airport again and they went out to dinner. Ira seemed to be in fine fettle.

The following day – Wednesday – Ira had driven downtown to the Southland Center to attend a meeting of the board of directors of the Tyler Corporation, which he had helped found. The meeting was to begin at 8 a.m. When Dorothy arrived at the Michigan General offices – in the Federal Building in the Preston Center – the receptionist told her Ira had called. Dorothy was to have Ira's assistant, George, drive her car over to the Southland Center and pick up Ira.

Dorothy decided she was going with George, so she went to the elevator to head for the parking garage. While Dorothy was waiting for the elevator, a secretary ran up and told her the Tyler people had called and suggested that she come, too. It didn't sound good.

On her way out of the building with George, Dorothy made a stop at one of the restrooms. She grabbed a white towel, which she hung out of one of the windows of her car as she and George sped over to the Southland Center, about six miles away. In Texas at the time, hanging something white out the window indicated an emergency.

The Tyler offices were on the 21st floor of the Southland Center. By the time Dorothy and George arrived at the center, everyone was in action. The parking garage attendants had Ira's car ready, the fire department medics had been summoned and a nurse was on the way to the Tyler offices with a wheelchair.

When Dorothy got off the elevator on the 21st floor, she found Ira lying on a sofa in the reception area. She had known before she got there that Ira was in trouble, but she wasn't prepared for what she saw. She told us later he looked "like death warmed over," with a pasty gray coloring that was more than alarming.

"Please," Ira said when he saw Dorothy, "get me out of here."

The nurse came with the wheelchair – Dorothy and George had beaten the fire department to the scene – and they went downstairs. The garage attendants helped Dorothy get Ira into the back of his Cadillac and she transferred the white towel from her car to Ira's.

Dorothy left the Southland Center like a bat out of hell. She was speeding and running red lights, heading for the Baylor Medical Center, which was about two miles away, as fast as she could go.

Corn was desperately sick but he didn't stop talking. He could tell Dorothy was breaking all the speed laws in Dallas. "Why are you driving so fast?" he asked.

"Because you're having a heart attack," Dorothy snapped.

"I'm all right," Corn said. "I think I just got something bad to eat last night. Slow down."

Dorothy went faster.

Corn told Dorothy that he had driven to the Southland Center that morning and on the way had felt a terrible pain, like a monstrous case of indigestion, and had been forced to pull off to the side of the freeway. The attack had passed, however, and he thought everything was all right.

Dorothy went faster still.

She was confident everything would be all right. Baylor Medical Center has one of the best trauma and emergency centers in the world. Also, his doctor, Don Brown, had an office right across the street. When Dorothy and Ira pulled up to the emergency entrance and Dorothy told the staff what was going on, they had him out of the car in a flash and rushed him in.

As Corn was wheeled into the emergency room, he was still talking to Dorothy. "Could you get my briefcase out of the car?" he asked. Ira was planning on doing some work in the hospital. She went out, grabbed the case and gave some fellow a $10 bill to park the car.

By the time she got back into the hospital, Ira was nowhere to be seen. She was comforted to know he was probably getting the care he needed right that minute. A member of the emergency room staff came up to her and said, "Mrs. Corn, come with me." Dorothy was led to a fancy sitting room. "You'll be more comfortable here," the woman told her. Dorothy didn't let on that she wasn't Mrs. Corn because she wanted to be sure she could be nearby if Ira needed her.

A minister came into the sitting room in a few minutes and told Dorothy that Ira had had a massive heart attack and that she had better notify his children. He had a son in Dallas and two other children in California. She found a pay phone to make the calls.

Just as she finished, Corn's doctor walked up. "He's gone," Brown said.

"What do you mean?" Dorothy pleaded. "You just don't die of your first heart attack. You get back in there and do something."

"Dorothy," Brown said with finality, "he's gone."

It was too much for Dorothy to believe. Corn was a mammoth man and terribly overweight, but he didn't have high blood pressure or elevated cholesterol, as you might expect. He appeared to be sound physically. The warning signs had come too late.

All the Aces or former Aces who were still in Dallas gathered at Ira's home. As we sat in the living room of the home we jokingly called "Chateau Corn," we all felt a deep sense of loss. Corn was stubborn, willful and headstrong. But his single-minded pursuit of his dream – bringing a world championship to the U.S. – inspired us.

The gathering was an unofficial wake, and Dorothy reminisced about Corn. She had met him through his ex-wife. Dorothy's mother knew Corn's ex-mother-in-law. Dorothy had met Ira while he was putting together deals as a professor at Southern Methodist. Ira asked Dorothy to teach him how to play bridge and later persuaded her to work for him. She was his Girl Friday, vice president of his company, his confidant, his companion. They never married but it didn't seem to matter to either of them.

"He was wonderful to work for," Dorothy often says. "He was lots of fun, but sometimes he would make me so mad I would want to kill him. Then again, he never bored me, and he was a winner."

The wake included Jim Jacoby, Wolffie, Bobby Goldman, Moose and, of course, Dorothy. Right at that moment it was hard to think of anything upbeat – just that we had lost a friend – but a lot of good came out of Ira Corn and his experiment with the Aces. A lot of good came out of knowing him.

Ira could be infuriating at times, but he was a great man to work for. He always got the best out of people. In fact, he was brilliant in that regard. All of the Aces will tell you that joining the team helped make them successful.

Ira was incredibly enthusiastic. At the Bermuda Bowl in Stockholm in 1970, he had the entire victory banquet videotaped. When the *Star Spangled Banner* was played for our team after we had won, Ira shed tears of pride in his country, tears of joy for his team. It was a great moment.

Someone commented on Ira sending for his briefcase from the hospital emergency room. "That's Ira – always giving orders."

A rainstorm had blown up while we were talking and commiserating. All of a sudden, a huge clap of thunder crashed outside. For a second, we were stunned into silence.

When someone finally spoke, it was me: "That's Ira and God, deciding who's going to be boss."

After Corn's death, we decided to keep the team together and try to win something – as the Aces – for Ira. We managed it in the Spingold in Albuquerque in the summer of 1982. We beat a team of Canadians in the final – Mark Molson, Eric Kokish, Peter Nagy and Billy Cohen. We didn't kill anyone the way the Aces of old used to do when we were clearly dominant, but we won most of our matches comfortably.

The Spingold win qualified us for the International Team Trials that fall right before the Nationals in Minneapolis. The winning team would receive the first Ira G. Corn, Jr. International Trophy. It didn't seem that it would be appropriate for Big Ira's last team to do anything short of winning the first presentation of his trophy. Fittingly, we would be fighting for a chance to play in the 1983 Bermuda Bowl in Stockholm, where the Aces won their first world championship in 1970.

Bobby and I talked to the ACBL *Bulletin* editors after the Spingold and reminded them what it was all about. "Ira would have loved this so much," Wolff said. "I remember when we lost to Kaplan in the Vanderbilt in Detroit. It was heartbreaking. But Ira always dealt with defeat magnificently. He never dwelled on what might have been or engaged in recriminations. His focus was always on how we would 'get the SOBs the next time.' He would have loved this. This was his team. The same six people. That's why we played together."

I added: "Just put in there that we won one for Big Ira."

Before the Nationals in Minneapolis – and the team trials that would precede the tournament – we flew off to Biarritz, France, to play in the World Bridge Championships. Bobby and I were 11th in the Open Pairs. Our team of Jim Jacoby, Jim Chew, Mark Lair, Mike Passell, Wolffie and I made it to the semifinals of the Rosenblum, but I certainly didn't consider that event a success.

Just getting to the Minneapolis trials wasn't enough, of course. We had to win something to get to Stockholm from there. Actually, we didn't have to win the whole thing. For the 1983 Bermuda Bowl, two teams from North America would be going, so all we had to do was get into the final. Naturally, I planned to win, but I would grudgingly accept second if I had to.

Once again, the format was unusual. There were five teams in the trials and we would play a complete round-robin – 24 boards against each of the other teams. Our IMP scores from the round-robin matches would be converted to Victory Points for the purposes of determining round-robin standings (the fifth-place team was eliminated). The four surviving teams would play semifinal matches.

What was interesting was that our round-robin scores carried over to our semifinal matches and, for the semifinal winners, to the final. That gave the round-robin phase of this competition added significance.

Our opponents' rosters were littered with former Aces. Grand National had Jim Jacoby (playing on George Rosenkranz's team), while San Francisco had Bobby Goldman and Paul Soloway. The other two teams were true dark horses, a group of unknowns from Canada and a team headed by Luella Slaner, a nice lady from New York.

Luella and Marty Bergen and assorted other pros had finished second in the Vanderbilt but got a berth in the trials when the Rosenkranz entourage earned a second qualification by winning the Grand National Teams. Luella was the sentimental darling of a couple of Nationals when her teams beat much more highly talented squads. It was remarkable for Luella and her friends to even come in second in a contest like the Vanderbilt. My hat was off to her. She did better than I did in the event that year. Still, Slaner and company weren't given much of a chance.

We took full advantage of the conditions of contest. We bombed
Canada by 47 IMPs and handled Grand National by 29. Unbelievably,
we beat Slaner by only 16 IMPs. Not so unbelievably, we lost to San
Francisco by 4. Even so, we won the round-robin by 3 VPs over Grand
National.

As the winners, we could choose our semifinal opponents. We
took Canada, giving us a 47-IMP head start. By the time the bloodbath
was over, we had won by nearly 200 IMPs. We were in the Bermuda
Bowl, no matter what. Grand National, meanwhile, beat San Francisco
by 55 IMPs.

Since we had beaten Rosenkranz's team by 29 IMPs in the round-
robin, we carried that over to our 96-board final. It turned out that we
needed it. Rosenkranz's teammates were Eddie Wold, Jim Jacoby,
Mike Passell – and Jeff Meckstroth and Eric Rodwell. These two have
the ability to carry a team. Their style is so active and imaginative that
they create swings better than just about anyone I've ever seen. Some
of the swings, of course, go against them, but they're just the right pair
for getting back into a match.

In fact, on the first board they bid to 6♠ on these cards:

♠ A 8 6 5 3	♠ K 10 9 4
♥ 9	♥ A Q J 8 7 3
♦ 10 3	♦ K 9
♣ A K 10 6 4	♣ 3

Everything was right (trumps 2-2, the ♦A in front of the king) and
they gained 11 IMPs, cutting our lead immediately and serving notice
that there was going to be a lot of bidding in this match.

Not to be outdone, Bobby and I came back a few boards later and
bid game on this sad collection.

♠ A	♠ 7 6 5 3
♥ Q 8 7 6 4 2	♥ J 9 5
♦ K 6 5	♦ A J 9
♣ 10 9 3	♣ A Q 4

We not only got to 4♥, Bobby made it by guessing everything in
sight and squeezing Rodwell in the end game. Bobby and I take a back

seat to no one when it comes to bidding filthy games – and making them.

Our team never lost the lead, but things did get kind of hairy near the end. Our lead had shrunk to 6 IMPs with nine boards to go and we were feeling the heat. People who had arrived early for the Fall Nationals had filled the vugraph room. They were delighted to see a close match. This deal put it away for us.

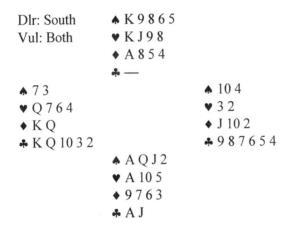

```
Dlr: South      ♠ K 9 8 6 5
Vul: Both       ♥ K J 9 8
                ♦ A 8 5 4
                ♣ —
   ♠ 7 3                        ♠ 10 4
   ♥ Q 7 6 4                    ♥ 3 2
   ♦ K Q                        ♦ J 10 2
   ♣ K Q 10 3 2                 ♣ 9 8 7 6 5 4
                ♠ A Q J 2
                ♥ A 10 5
                ♦ 9 7 6 3
                ♣ A J
```

This was the auction at our table.

WEST	NORTH	EAST	SOUTH
Wolff	*Passell*	*Me*	*Jacoby*
			1NT
Pass	2♣	Pass	2♠
Pass	3♥	Pass	4♣
Pass	4♠	All Pass	

At the other table:

WEST	NORTH	EAST	SOUTH
Meckstroth	*Weichsel*	*Rodwell*	*Sontag*
			1NT
Pass	2♣ (1)	Pass	2♠
Pass	4♣ (2)	Pass	4♦ (3)
Pass	4♥ (4)	Pass	4♠ (5)
Pass	5♣ (6)	Pass	5♥ (7)
Pass	6♠ (8)	All Pass	

(1) Forcing Stayman.
(2) An unbalanced spade raise with shortness in a minor.
(3) Which minor?
(4) Clubs.
(5) Signoff because of the wasted club values.
(6) A slight overbid – still interested in slam, showing a club void.
(7) Cuebid, since you insist.
(8) Serious overbid.

Passell's 3♥ was a slam try. When Jacoby cuebid clubs, Passell rated that as wasted values, so he signed off at 4♠, which seemed to be the right thing to do. Wolffie led a club and Jacoby drew trumps, eliminated clubs and played the ♦A and a diamond. Wolff got out with a heart and Jacoby lost another diamond later for plus 650.

After Meckstroth led a trump, Sontag didn't have the luxury of a diamond endplay in order to guess hearts. He had to find the queen himself and manufacture an endplay in diamonds to eliminate the extra loser in that suit.

Moose was sitting in the vugraph audience, watching in horror as Sontag and Weichsel overbid. He could see that the contract could be made, and he made a prediction. "He's going to make it," Musumeci said. He had better. Our lead had been slipping away, and Sontag knew Passell and Jacoby wouldn't be in this contract at the other table. We couldn't stand a major swing like this.

Alan drew trumps and then guessed right in hearts. He was influenced by the fact that Meckstroth, a very aggressive player, had led a passive trump. Sontag cashed the ♦A to discourage an unblock – it might be more obvious later in the hand – eliminated hearts and clubs and put a second diamond on the table.

Lucky for Sontag (and us), Meckstroth won the ♦K and had only clubs to play. The ruff-sluff took care of the last diamond loser and Sontag chalked up plus 1430 – 13 IMPs to the Aces. Our lead had grown to 19 IMPs.

I was happy that I hadn't had to watch the bidding on this deal, although I admit that it would have been a pleasure to see Alan play the contract. After that heart-stopper, the rest of the deals were pretty dull. We held on to win 231-207. That means we actually lost the final by 5 IMPs. We won because of the unusual conditions of contest which allowed us to carry over our entire round-robin margin against this team.

It was almost like backing into the championship, but I didn't care. All I could think about was getting to Stockholm.

I ended up going to Sweden a day or two before the start of the Bermuda Bowl, although we weren't there for the start of play because we had a bye to the semifinals. For this tournament, I was taking no chances – I brought my own rooting section. My fans were my son Chris, who was 16, Susie Kennedy, and her kids, Bill and Kathy.

When we got to Stockholm, I noticed that the city hadn't changed much since 1970, the first time I had visited Sweden to play in a world championship. Stockholm is clean, modern, cosmopolitan and very laid back. The Swedes are well known for their even temperament and calm demeanors. Stockholm reflected those traits. Somehow, the hustle and bustle of the big city didn't have the frantic air that you find in New York or London.

Although Musumeci was NPC of the team this time, he had a different role from the early days of the Aces. He wasn't our drill sergeant and curfew enforcer. This time, he was hoping to mold this squad of different personalities into a winner. He still wasn't going to take any crap from anyone, though. During a coin toss to determine seating, Moose made a decision which was questioned by Weichsel. Musumeci's response was quick and direct: "You play bridge. I'll take care of the other things."

For the first time, all three American pairs would be playing some variation of a forcing 1♣ system. Bobby and I had our Orange Club system, our version of the Blue Team Club. Weichsel and Sontag played what they called Power Precision, with five-card majors and strong 1NT openers. Becker and Rubin trotted out the Ultimate Club, a relay system with a four-card major base.

We felt that we were the favorites because we had three solid pairs, we would be well rested, we had brought our fan club and last but not least this team was the last stand for the Aces. All three partnerships were of long duration with lots of practice, although Weichsel and Sontag had decided to go their separate ways after this tournament. There was no animosity, however, and their partnership was as strong as ever.

Our trials victory in Minneapolis had given us a bye to the semifinals along with France, winners of the European championship. The other eight teams would play a round-robin. The winners and runners-up would be the other two semifinalists. The WBF had made rules for the Bermuda Bowl in 1983 that precluded two teams from the same zone meeting in the final – as had happened in Manila in 1977. That meant that if the other American team finished first or second in the round-robin, they would be automatically matched with us in the semifinal.

Europe actually had three teams in the championship. France and Italy had been 1-2 in the European trials. Sweden, as the host country, had an entry as well. Things really would have become complicated if Italy and Sweden finished first and second in the round-robin because of the zone rule for the final – a three-way round-robin with France, Italy and Sweden vying for one final spot while we played the third-place team from the round-robin for the other final spot.

We were really interested in two teams – USA 2 and Italy. USA 2 was Rosenkranz, Meckstroth, Rodwell, Jacoby, Wold and Passell – the team we had narrowly defeated in the trials in Minneapolis. We knew they relished another shot at us in the semis.

Then, of course, there was Italy. My mouth watered at the chance to go head to head with Garozzo, Belladonna and their buddies. The pain of the 1975 Bermuda Bowl with the foot-tapping cheaters, Facchini and Zucchelli, was still fresh in my mind – as was the fact that the Aces had let a huge lead slip away. Bobby and I had not been on the 1976 team that finally had beaten the Italians and we wanted their scalps dangling from our belts.

Of course, the Italians had a similar agenda. They had lost to America in 1979 and were also seeking redemption. Benito and Giorgio were playing with Soldano de Falco, Arturo Franco, Lorenzo Lauria and Carlo Mosca. The latter two had yet to make a name for themselves at the world level, but Garozzo-Belladonna, and de Falco-Franco were formidable opponents.

The Italians no longer seemed invincible – they had finished second to France in the European championships, after all – but no one was willing to dismiss the effects of their old magic. I was certain of one thing – I wanted to play them in the final if it could be arranged.

The other teams duking it out with USA 2 and Italy in the round-robin – two 32-board matches against each of the other teams – would be Brazil, Central America-Caribbean, Indonesia, New Zealand, Pakistan and Sweden.

This was going to be a long tournament. After the round-robin, there would be 160 boards to play in the semifinals and 176 boards in the final. Any team getting to the final from the round-robin would be brain dead before the Bermuda Bowl was over.

We arrived in Stockholm several days after the Bermuda Bowl started. We used the time to review our methods and to relax, overcome our jet lag and get ourselves psyched up for the semifinal. It made me nervous waiting around to play. In a way, I was wishing we had waited until the last minute to get there. I was ready to play.

While we cooled our heels, Rosenkranz and his hired guns stormed through the round-robin, crushing the other teams and finishing 75 Victory Points ahead of Italy, the runners-up. While USA 2 had run away from the field, Italy struggled to make the cut. Their total of 214 VPs was just barely above average, and they finished only 2 VPs ahead of New Zealand, 2.5 VPs ahead of Sweden.

Nevertheless, I was thinking "so far, so good." If the Aces could handle USA 2 and Italy could take care of France, Bobby and I would get our chance for revenge.

It was good to finally sit down at the table.

Bobby and I started against Eric and Jeff. It was a bit tense at first because relations between our teams were somewhat strained. First of all, when you lose a tough match the way they did in Minneapolis, it makes you grit your teeth and hunker down the next time you play against the team that beat you. There was more, though. While Meckstroth and Rodwell are exemplary in their deportment at the table nowadays, they had a wild and woolly side in their youth. That sort of thing doesn't bother me, but the more sensitive among us can make rough stuff an issue that causes hard feelings. Some of the talk may have come from our camp, making for a little more tension.

Eric and Jeff are now and were then good enough that they didn't need any extraneous factors to win. They had proven themselves in 1981 by winning the Bermuda Bowl in Rye NY. I've said it before – bridge at high levels isn't a tea party. Anyone who expects the Marquis of Queensbury rules will be sorely disappointed.

Both semifinal matches were expected to be donnybrooks. There was speculation that the rest we had during the round-robin was a minus rather than a plus. There's a certain validity to the theory that getting in there and slugging it out gets you "match ready" and that sitting around loafing can leave you sluggish. The Rosenkranz team had annihilated the round-robin field and seemed to be on a roll. We were coming off a period of inactivity. Which way, if at all, would that affect us?

Once again it was proven that theories and pre-game analysis don't mean diddly. It's the play on the field or at the table that counts – and we were right on the money in our match against USA 2.

We jumped out to a 43-19 lead after 16 boards, let them get to within 18 after two segments and then poured it on from there. We were up 118-56 after 48 boards and had them down by 118 at the halfway point. It was no contest. We won 440-338.

What happened? It's hard to say. The Rosenkranz team had the worst of the luck early on, and their wild attempts to get back into the match backfired for the most part. But the Aces were solid and our judgment was better than theirs in many situations.

Here, however, is a hand where the Aces were lucky – spectacularly so – rather than good:

```
Dlr: North      ♠ J 6 2
Vul: N-S        ♥ K 9 7 6 5 4
                ♦ —
                ♣ K J 4 3
♠ K 9                          ♠ 8 5 4
♥ A 10                         ♥ 3
♦ 9 8 6 5 4 2                  ♦ J 10 7 3
♣ A 8 6                        ♣ Q 10 7 5 2
                ♠ A Q 10 7 3
                ♥ Q J 8 2
                ♦ A K Q
                ♣ 9
```

The hand was played four times (the same boards were being played in both semifinal matches). The first three times, North played in 4♥, making five. At the fourth table:

WEST	NORTH	EAST	SOUTH
Meckstroth	*Weichsel*	*Rodwell*	*Sontag*
	2♦ (1)	Pass	2NT (2)
Pass	3♦ (3)	Pass	6♥
Dbl	All Pass		

(1) A weak two-bid in hearts or a strong hand with 4-4-4-1 distribution (any singleton).

(2) Asking for clarification.

(3) Supposedly showing a *balanced* weak two-bid with maximum values.

Weichsel apparently forgot the responses to 2NT. Who was it that said the more conventions you play the greater the chance of fouling up? A natural question in this case was why Alan didn't ask for key cards. Had he done so, he would have known his side was off two keys – two aces or an ace and the trump king. As for Meckstroth's double, it is worth noting that unless he hoped to defeat the contract more than one trick, the double wasn't going to gain. Plus 750 (6♥ down one undoubled against 650 at the other table) and plus 850 convert to the same 13 IMPs.

Anyway, Meckstroth led the ♥A to get a look at dummy, which must have been a surprise. Obviously, Jeff could have cashed the ♣A for down one, but he figured Sontag might well be void on the auction. So at trick two, Meckstroth continued with a trump. That was all Sontag needed. He won in dummy, played the ♠J, putting up the ace when Rodwell didn't cover. Sontag then played two rounds of diamonds, pitching spades, and played the ♠10, ruffing when Meckstroth covered perforce. Now a trump back to hand and Sontag threw away all of dummy's clubs on three good spades and a high diamond. Plus 1660 to our side. Instead of losing 13, we had gained 14.

Our win wasn't all luck, however. There was one deal where Rubin and Becker used their fancy relay system to get to an absolutely double-dummy 6NT contract where the rest of the pairs were bidding heart slams and going down because of a 5-0 trump split.

While we were pounding our compatriots, the Italians and French were going toe to toe in a pitched battle that wasn't settled until the final few boards. It was 25-all after one set, and Italy held slim leads after the second, third and fourth sets. France surged into the lead halfway through the last set, however, and led by 3 IMPs – 311-308 – going into the final 16 boards.

As usual, Italy rallied, using superior judgment in the competitive situations to win the seesaw final set. Benito and friends nipped France by 11 IMPs – 346-335. We had the opponents we wanted in the final.

Wolffie and I sat down against Garozzo and Belladonna Tuesday morning, October 4. I don't know about Bobby, but I felt a little bit like the Lakers going into Boston Garden for an NBA final. I knew we had the better team but, like Celtics' opponents in bygone days, you never know whether the old team's magic – or just confounded luck – would do us in.

I couldn't tell whether the seemingly endless round-robin, followed by the grueling match against France, had taken anything out of the old Italian warriors. Belladonna and Garozzo wouldn't show a strain even if they felt it. Players like those two never give away a psychological advantage by looking or acting feeble – unless they're trying to lull you to sleep. They were ready to fight, just as Bobby and I would have been in the same situation.

We were booked to play 176 boards against each other and there would be no letting up by either team. Both sides had seen world championships slip away by small margins. We would be fighting for every trick, every IMP.

My screenmate was Belladonna, the dashing, sophisticated man of the world. He was quite a charming fellow and a great bridge player. We were very business-like as we sat down to play. The last time we had played them – in Bermuda – you could have cut the tension with a knife. Time had apparently healed some of the wounds by 1983, however, and we weren't thinking about the past.

Play was going on in four rooms – France and Rosenkranz's team were battling it out for third place – and we weren't far from where the vugraph show was going on. It was a long ballroom, filled with chairs for spectators and a long table for the commentators. There were television cameras in the playing rooms so that spectators could see some of the bids and all of the facial expressions of the players.

As for the audience, my son Chris, Susie Kennedy, her two kids and Joe Musumeci would be among the very few who were rooting for the Aces. Virtually all the other people on hand were nearly rabid in their support for Italy – and they were quite vocal.

Bobby and I started the festivities by bidding 3NT on rather thin values and going down. At the other table, where Lauria and Mosca were playing against Rubin and Becker, the Italians played a partial. Italy had scored first. They racked up another 17 IMPs with a slam swing on Board 2. Still, it was close after the first 16 boards. Italy led, 49-41.

We lost the second set by a small margin before winning the third set, 35-33. When Edgar Kaplan wrote about this deal from the third set in *The Bridge World*, he called me "America's designated declarer for hair-raising 4-3 fits." It certainly was an adventure.

```
Dlr: East        ♠ A 8
Vul: N-S         ♥ A 9 2
                 ♦ K 8 5 3
                 ♣ A J 8 3
♠ J 10 7 4                        ♠ Q 6 5 3 2
♥ 10 7                           ♥ Q J 4 3
♦ 10 9 7 4 2                     ♦ A Q J
♣ Q 4                            ♣ K
                 ♠ K 9
                 ♥ K 8 6 5
                 ♦ 6
                 ♣ 10 9 7 6 5 2
```

Ron and Mike played it against de Falco and Franco.

WEST	NORTH	EAST	SOUTH
Rubin	*de Falco*	*Becker*	*Franco*
		1♠	Pass
2♠	Dbl	Pass	2NT
3♠	3NT	Pass	4♣
Pass	5♣	All Pass	

Franco played it very well. He won the ♠J lead in his hand and immediately led a diamond, ducking. Becker won the jack and returned a spade to dummy's ace. Franco ruffed a diamond, played a low club to the ace and ruffed a third diamond, felling the ace. Then he played the ♥K and a heart to the ace, cashed the ♦K (pitching a heart) and got out with a club. Rubin was in and had to give Franco and ruff and a sluff to let the heart loser go away. Plus 600 to Italy.

The auction took quite a different turn at our table.

WEST	NORTH	EAST	SOUTH
Garozzo	*Wolff*	*Belladonna*	*Me*
		1♠	Pass
2♠	Dbl	3♠	4♥
All Pass			

I won the spade lead in hand and played a heart to the 9. Belladonna falsecarded with the queen and played a second spade. Now I played a heart to the ace and another heart. I could have finessed the 8 to pick up the suit, but that wouldn't have helped me. With all the trumps gone and a club to lose, I would have gone down big time.

I went up with the king and Garozzo showed out. Crap! Now if I played the ♣10 to Belladonna's king, he would pull my last trump with his jack and they would take the rest of the tricks. Down six! If I played a club to the ace and another club, Belladonna could get in with a diamond and do the same thing for down five. This was not a happy contract.

There was nothing to do but press on and hope for some luck.

I led the ♣10 and Garozzo covered with the queen! I asked for luck, didn't I? I went up with the ace, felling the king, and suddenly my clubs were all good. Now I was in control. I simply ran clubs. Belladonna could ruff in, but I had a trump to keep them from running spades or diamonds. Plus 620 and a 1-IMP gain that only moments before had looked like a 15-IMP loss. Italy's lead had shrunk from 2 IMPs to 1.

The two teams continued slugging it out for a couple more sets before we finally broke through big in the sixth. We won that set 45-17 and were leading 224-210 with 80 boards to play. Bobby and I had played the first two sets, sat out the third and went back in for the fourth, fifth and sixth.

Bobby and I were out again in the seventh set, which the Aces won, 38-32, and the eighth, which Italy won by 2 IMPs. With 32 boards to go, we led by 18 IMPs, 344-326.

In the next-to-last set, things went sour. Garozzo and Belladonna bid a vulnerable grand slam against Bobby and me while Becker and Rubin stopped in six. 13 IMPs to Italy. Then on the next board, we let Belladonna and Garozzo play 5♥ while Lauria and Mosca pushed Becker and Rubin to six and doubled for plus 300. Another 13 IMPs to Italy, who had surged into the lead.

More bad things happened and we lost the set by 27. It would have been worse except that Bobby and I bid a vulnerable slam that was missed at the other table for a 13-IMP pickup.

The dreaded Italians were ahead 385-376 with 16 boards to go. Were the Aces hearing footsteps? Was that old Blue Team magic working? The crowd in the vugraph room certainly thought it was. The place was alive, crawling with people, nearly all of them rooting for Italy. There was the kind of electric tension you feel at heavyweight championship fights or at the Super Bowl.

With 16 boards to go, I couldn't allow myself to be distracted by superstition or figurative glances over the shoulder. If Italy was going to win this Bermuda Bowl, they would have to do it against the best effort we could put forth – all of it focused on bridge play.

Moose decided Bobby and I would play in the Closed Room against Lauria and Mosca while Sontag and Weichsel faced Belladonna and Garozzo in the Open Room, the one that would finish play last. One room is always ahead of the other so the commentators have something to compare with and a way to determine the score of the match.

We nearly didn't get started at all. The directors insisted that Moose post his lineup cards on their bulletin board one flight up from where play was going on. But the place was so crowded with people trying to get a look at the vugraph show that Moose couldn't get on an elevator to go upstairs. Finally, he got the lineups posted and we sat down to play.

Mosca, a dark, bearded young man, was grim-faced as he sat down to play. He was playing in the Bermuda Bowl for the first time and the tension was showing. He and his partner, Lauria, had played well in helping Italy eke out their second-place finish in the round-robin and he wanted to carry it through to a win.

Naturally, we didn't know how any of the boards turned out until later, but we started off the final set with a bang. After a push on the first board, we gained 1 IMP on an overtrick, then surged back into the lead on this deal:

Dlr: South	♠ A 8 3		
Vul: E-W	♥ A 10 5		
	♦ J		
	♣ A K J 10 7 6		
♠ 6 5		♠ J 10 9 2	
♥ Q 6 2		♥ K 7 3	
♦ 6 4 3		♦ Q 9 8 7 5	
♣ 9 5 4 3 2		♣ 8	
	♠ K Q 7 4		
	♥ J 9 8 4		
	♦ A K 10 2		
	♣ Q		

WEST	NORTH	EAST	SOUTH
Me	*Mosca*	*Wolff*	*Lauria*
			2♣ (1)
Pass	2♦ (2)	Pass	2♥ (3)
Pass	2NT (4)	Pass	3♣ (5)
Pass	3NT	All Pass	

(1) Limited opening with six or more clubs or a hand with any three suits.

(2) Asking for further description.

(3) 4-4-4-1 hand.

(4) Asking for the short suit.

(5) Clubs.

The Italians' system actually worked against them. Mosca couldn't tell his partner had the singleton ♣Q – a rather big card on this deal – so 3NT seemed the right way to go. Declarer took all 13 tricks after Wolffie led the ♠J. At the other table, Weichsel and Sontag were much more aggressive.

WEST	NORTH	EAST	SOUTH
Garozzo	*Weichsel*	*Belladonna*	*Sontag*
			1♦
Pass	3♣	Pass	4♣
Pass	6♣	All Pass	

Weichsel's bid of 3♣ promised a good suit, so Sontag had no problem raising on his singleton honor. Peter played it carefully and ended up plus 920 for a 9-IMP gain. The Aces were 1 IMP ahead.

Two deals later, the Italians went back in front when they made three overtricks in 1NT for plus 180 while I played 2♠ on a 4-3 fit and barely scrambled home with plus 110. We went back in front on the very next deal, however. Bobby and I stopped in 1NT on a deal that had only seven tricks while Garozzo and Belladonna propelled themselves into 3NT and went minus 200. The 7-IMP gain put us back in the lead by 6 IMPs.

Two more pushes followed, then we gained 5 IMPs when Lauria and Mosca bid too much on Board 169. On Board 170, we gained another 2 IMPs – Weichsel and Sontag bid and made 6♠ while Mosca and Lauria bid the slam in clubs. We were 13 IMPs up with six boards to go.

Italy clawed back, however. Garozzo and Belladonna got to 4♠ after a strong 1NT opener by Weichsel – making five. Bobby and I didn't bid the game. 6 IMPs to Italy. Another 5 IMPs went their way when Weichsel and Sontag got to 2NT, down one, when Mosca and Lauria stopped in 1NT, making on the nose. We were ahead by 2 IMPs with four boards to go.

There were four boards to be played in the Open Room when Bobby and I stood up from the table in the Closed Room. Remember, we had started a little ahead of them so the vugraph commentators would have some comparisons. Also remember: we didn't know any of these scores. Bobby and I felt that we had had a good set, but you never know what's happening in the other room.

We stretched a bit, shook hands with Mosca and Lauria and walked out the door of the small room where we had been playing.

Moose was right there. "How'd it go?" he asked, wide-eyed. "What did you do on the last four boards?"

I ran over the boards mentally.

The fourth hand from the end, you've got 11 opposite 12. We played 3♥ making four. There's no way to stop four but no way to bid it. On the next board, Mosca and Lauria bid a 40 percent slam and made it. It's possible a momentum auction will get you to slam.

The next board was a 5♠ hand, somewhat in jeopardy. It's hard to stay out of five, but there's no way to get to six since you're off two aces. The last board was a ma and pa 3NT.

Now came my question: "Where do we stand?"

"We're up 2 IMPs," Moose said.

All three of us – Bobby, Moose and I – raced to the vugraph room.

The long, narrow ballroom was wall-to-wall, standing-room-only with people. I knew that Susie and her kids and Chris were in there somewhere, but I couldn't see them for the crowds. I could, however, see the vugraph screen. It showed USA 400, Italy 398. Garozzo and Belladonna versus Sontag and Weichsel.

Board No. 173 was up right then.

```
Dlr: North        ♠ J 4
Vul: Both         ♥ 9 6 5
                  ♦ 6 3 2
                  ♣ A K J 4 3
♠ A Q                          ♠ 9 7 5 2
♥ K 10 8 7                     ♥ Q 4 3 2
♦ J 10 9 5                     ♦ A K Q
♣ Q 10 8                       ♣ 7 5
                  ♠ K 10 8 6 3
                  ♥ A J
                  ♦ 8 7 4
                  ♣ 9 6 2
```

At our table, I had opened 1♥ in fourth seat and Wolffie had raised to 3♥, invitational. Even the wildest bidders in the game wouldn't consider game with that piece of cheese opposite a passed hand. I had to pass. We got plus 170.

We watched as Garozzo and Belladonna conducted the exact same auction. Plus 170 to Italy. No swing. We were still ahead by 2 IMPs.

The crowd was restless waiting for the next board to be put on the screen. Except for Bobby, Moose and me – I didn't see Mosca or Lauria anywhere – no one in the room knew what had happened on

any of the coming boards. For all they knew, there was a huge swing
in the offing for the beloved Italians. Finally, Board No. 174 came up.

```
Dlr: East            ♠ K Q 7 4 2
Vul: None            ♥ 10 4
                     ♦ A K 7 5 4
                     ♣ 6
♠ 9 5 3                                    ♠ 10 8 6
♥ 8 3 2                                    ♥ K Q 7 6
♦ J 6                                      ♦ Q 8
♣ A Q J 10 2                               ♣ 9 5 4 3
                     ♠ A J
                     ♥ A J 9 5
                     ♦ 10 9 3 2
                     ♣ K 8 7
```

This had been the auction at our table.

WEST	NORTH	EAST	SOUTH
Me	*Mosca*	*Wolff*	*Lauria*
		Pass	1♥
Pass	3♦	Pass	4♦
Pass	4♠	Pass	4NT
Pass	5♦	Pass	6♦
All Pass			

The 3♦ bid showed a two-suited hand with diamonds and spades,
at least 5-5. 4♠ was a cuebid and 4NT a general slam try – not
Blackwood, as it appears. 6♦ isn't the worst slam ever bid, but when
Bobby led a club and we got our trick on the go, Mosca clearly was
not pleased to be at the six level needing good luck in trumps. As you
can see, his luck was all good – they quickly scored up plus 920.

It appeared that the match had come down to whether Peter and
Alan would bid the slam. They were up.

WEST	NORTH	EAST	SOUTH
Garozzo	*Weichsel*	*Belladonna*	*Sontag*
		Pass	1♦
Pass	1♠	Pass	1NT(12-14)
Pass	. . .		

Weichsel could have bid 2♣, an artificial bid asking Sontag about spade support (Alan could have had a singleton spade in their system). Finally, he settled for 3♦, which was forcing. Sontag bid 3♥ (a cuebid?) and Weichsel bid 4♦, denying the ♣A (he would have cuebid 4♣ if he had it).

. . .	3♦	Pass	3♥
Pass	4♦	Pass	4♠
Pass			

Sontag's 4♠ bid was nebulous. Was it another cuebid? Delayed support for spades? Were diamonds firmly set as trumps? Don't forget, Weichsel and Sontag were playing Precision, so the 1♦ opening could have been made on a doubleton.

The tension was unbearable. It didn't seem possible that Alan and Peter could stay out of slam. Or could they? Weichsel was deeply troubled. What was he thinking about? Finally, after long thought, he *...passed*!

I could see Sontag's face on the vugraph camera. You could see him sag, not because either he or Weichsel had done something bad, but because he could hear the roar of the crowd in the ballroom where I stood. It was that loud. Sontag knew it was a pro-Italian crowd, so he knew the noise was bad news for the Aces.

The cheer that arose in the ballroom the instant that Weichsel passed was so stunning that for a moment I lost perspective. It seemed as if the whole scene was in slow motion and I was a distant observer. The nightmare had become reality.

Back to earth, all I could think of was, "He passed! He passed! How could he pass?!?" It didn't make sense to me. I didn't know the particulars of their system, and perhaps my thinking was colored by the situation, by wanting to beat the Italians so badly, but I was terribly disappointed. It looked like we were going to lose another world championship to these bastards.

Weichsel made five for plus 450, but we lost 10 IMPs. We were behind by 8 IMPs with two flat boards to go. There was no way we were going to win. I wanted to push my fist through a wall.

Bobby and Moose were disconsolate. Bobby couldn't stand to watch the Italians win another world championship off of us, so he left. He went up two flights to his room on the fourth floor and lay on the bed in the fetal position until his wife Debby found him. "You've got to go back downstairs and congratulate them," she said. Bobby didn't move.

Meanwhile, Moose and I stood at the back of the ballroom to watch the last two boards. Were we gluttons for punishment? Too stupid to know we had lost? I don't know. I guess I'm one of those guys who doesn't want to leave a game even though one team is down by a huge margin. What if I missed the greatest comeback ever? And what was it Yogi said?

The people in the jam-packed vugraph room were even more restless now. Only two boards to go before the Italians would be the proud possessors of another Bermuda Bowl title. The place was alive with the excitement.

This was the next-to-last deal. When it went up on the screen, you could hear the buzz through the crowd. It looked like a "safe" hand — one where there was little danger of the wheels coming off.

```
          Dlr: South    ♠ 7 4
          Vul: N-S       ♥ 6
                         ♦ A J 10 8
                         ♣ Q J 7 6 4 3
      ♠ Q 10 8 5 3                      ♠ A K J 9 6 2
      ♥ A J 5 4                         ♥ K 7 3
      ♦ 5                               ♦ K Q 3
      ♣ K 10 2                          ♣ 8
                         ♠ —
                         ♥ Q 10 9 8 2
                         ♦ 9 7 6 4 2
                         ♣ A 9 5
```

In our room:

WEST	NORTH	EAST	SOUTH
Me	*Mosca*	*Wolff*	*Lauria*
			Pass
1♠	Pass	4NT	Pass
5♦	Pass	5♠	All Pass

Yes, I know. Opening bids were getting hungrier and hungrier. We landed in a precarious spot at the five level. If both minor-suit aces were offside I would need to guess hearts to avoid going down. Luckily, both aces were right for me and I chalked up plus 450 rather swiftly.

It was depressing to see that deal on the screen, but I guess I'll never give up hope while there's anyone breathing on my side. The auction started on vugraph.

WEST	NORTH	EAST	SOUTH
Garozzo	*Weichsel*	*Belladonna*	*Sontag*
			Pass
1♠	Pass	2NT	Pass
3♠	Pass	4NT	Pass
5♦	Pass		

Belladonna's 2NT showed a spade raise with a singleton somewhere in the hand. Garozzo could have asked where the singleton was with 3♣, but he was beginning to regret opening the hand, so he tried to discourage Belladonna by bidding 3♠. It was speculated later that Garozzo's decision not to relay with 3♣ was confusing to Belladonna, who thought the 3♠ bid was a trump asking bid. His 4NT bid, therefore, was intended to show two top honors in trumps with extra length. Garozzo's 5♦ bid was a response to Blackwood, showing one ace.

At the point that Belladonna bid 4NT, I thought, "Turn out the lights, the party's over. There's no way they're bidding slam when they find out they're off two aces."

I almost turned away in disgust. I didn't want to actually see our championship go up in smoke. Suddenly, there was a strange feeling in the pit of my stomach – Belladonna was taking much too long to sign off in 5♠. What in the hell was he thinking about? Was it possible that his 4NT bid was not Blackwood, or was he somehow confused? Had the 12-plus days of play taken their toll on the old war-horse? I glanced down for a second. Just then I heard Moose shout, "He bid it! He bid it!" I looked back at the screen and I could hardly believe my eyes. There, big as life, was that wonderful, beloved SIX SPADE bid right there for everyone to see.

Silence descended on the room like a pall. Just moments before, the room had been full of people rockin' and rollin' and ready for the coronation of the Italians as world champions. Now there was silence, except for Susie, her kids and my son Chris, risking life and limb by cheering their hearts out up in the front.

Meanwhile, Bobby had come downstairs at Debby's urging. The first person he met getting off the elevator was Weichsel's girlfriend, who informed Wolffie that the Italians had just bid a slam off two aces. Bobby turned right around and went back to his room.

Back in the arena, Weichsel led the ♣Q and Sontag grabbed the ace. He returned the ♥10, momentarily raising my anxiety level. I could see, however, that no matter what Garozzo did he couldn't shake the diamond loser in his hand. Down one. Plus 50 for the Aces, who had gone from minus 8 IMPs to plus 3 *with one hand to go.* Could we get this one right? Could we shake that old Italian magic?

The crowd was still deathly silent as Board No. 176 went up. The Aces were ahead, 411-408.

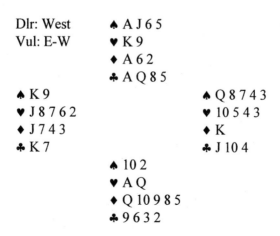

```
Dlr: West        ♠ A J 6 5
Vul: E-W         ♥ K 9
                 ♦ A 6 2
                 ♣ A Q 8 5
♠ K 9                          ♠ Q 8 7 4 3
♥ J 8 7 6 2                    ♥ 10 5 4 3
♦ J 7 4 3                      ♦ K
♣ K 7                          ♣ J 10 4
                 ♠ 10 2
                 ♥ A Q
                 ♦ Q 10 9 8 5
                 ♣ 9 6 3 2
```

At our table:

WEST	NORTH	EAST	SOUTH
Me	*Mosca*	*Wolff*	*Lauria*
Pass	1♣	Pass	1NT
Pass	2♣	Pass	2♦
Pass	2♠	Pass	2NT
Pass	3NT	All Pass	

Mosca and Lauria were playing a forcing club system and Lauria did well to respond positively in notrump rather than in diamonds. I led a heart against his game and he made the percentage play in diamonds – low to the ace. Eventually he made nine tricks via the club finesse. Plus 400 to Italy. If Sontag and Weichsel could bid and make game, the Bermuda Bowl would be ours.

WEST	NORTH	EAST	SOUTH
Garozzo	*Weichsel*	*Belladonna*	*Sontag*
Pass	1♣	Pass	2♦
Pass	2♥	Pass	3♣
Pass	3♦	Pass	3NT
Pass	?		

My stomach did a few flips when Sontag chose to make a positive response in diamonds – they were playing Precision. Weichsel's hand was quite good and he had a diamond fit. This could lead to another slam swing if we weren't careful.

Weichsel's 2♥ bid was a relay and the 3♣ showed a second suit. I was thinking the rot was setting in as Sontag showed his great second suit – four to the 9. Weichsel's 3♦ was another relay and 3NT showed a 2-2-5-4 pattern with a minimum positive response. Still, Weichsel was over there thinking again. He was probably selecting the weapon with which he was going to murder the genius who came up with the idea of using 2♥ as an inquiry, an inquiry which was going to cause 3NT to be played from the wrong side. Meanwhile my heart was in my throat. Science and discipline were about to cost us 10 IMPs and another loss to the goddam Italians. The slam swing on the penultimate hand was just a way for the fates to tantalize us before they squashed us.

Immersed in self pity, I glanced at the TV monitor in time to see Peter pull out that beautiful green pass card. At last we had the bastards, I thought.

Then it dawned on me – even though we were in the right spot, there was a plausible, though inferior, line of play that would fail. Weichsel's decision to play 3NT had not locked it up. The Italians might still snatch victory from the jaws of defeat – again. All they needed was for Sontag to win the heart in his hand and lead a diamond honor.

Garozzo led a heart. Sontag won it in the dummy and quickly called for the ♦A. *Now* I could happily sing *Turn Out the Lights* – for the other guys. Belladonna tried some razzmatazz by playing the ♣J as Sontag ran the diamonds after knocking out the jack. Since Alan needed the club finesse to make his contract, he ended up taking four club tricks for plus 460. The 2-IMP gain gave us the world championship by 5 IMPs.

It was an incredible feeling to get the monkey off our backs. There has been better bridge played in world championships, but we had nothing to be ashamed of. It might have been a Pale Blue Team we knocked off, but I don't know anyone who would turn down a world championship trophy under similar circumstances.

This might have been the sweetest victory of my career. I wish Ira had been there to savor it with us.

18

Close calls

MANY MOONS AGO, Victor Mitchell and Sam Stayman were partners in a rubber bridge game in New York. At the time, Vic suffered from migraine headaches, and he was having a doozy that day. Stayman, sensitive to this, was being very solicitous of his partner and friend.

"Are you feeling okay, Vic?" Sam asked during a break.

"No, I'm not feeling okay, Sam," Vic said.

"Vic," said Sam, "is there anything I can do? Can I play faster? Slower? Can I get you some water? Can I adjust the lights?"

Vic lifted his head and looked his friend in the eye. "Well, you might try playing better."

Sometimes, playing well isn't enough. There are occasions when you need luck – maybe just a smidgen. It also helps to be in the right place at the right time.

Bobby and I ended up on the team that won the 1985 Bermuda Bowl because, in essence, we were in the right place at the right time. It didn't hurt that we made a few right moves.

The place was Memphis. The time was May of 1984. It was the team trials for the Seventh World Team Olympiad that fall in Seattle. Our team was an Aces reunion squad: Wolffie and me, Bobby Goldman-Paul Soloway and Malcolm Brachman-Ron Andersen. To the bridge press, we were the Texas team. With Brachman bankrolling the squad, we had won the Spingold the previous year.

In the semifinal, we beat Chip Martel's team by 72 IMPs to advance to the final. Our opponents included a pair of young men we had seen quite a lot of recently – Meckstroth and Rodwell. They had been added to the Kaplan team for the trials.

Bobby and I had done well against Jeff and Eric in the trials for the 1983 Bermuda Bowl and in the Bermuda Bowl semifinals in Stockholm. In fact, over those two events, it almost seemed like a set game between us and them. I think we played them seven out of 10 sets in the trials and the semifinals. We won both rather handily.

In the 1984 trials final, Meckwell – as Jeff and Eric are sometimes called – came out with guns blazing, as though they were trying to end the match early. It was actually pretty tight late in the match, but we poured it on over the last 32 boards and won rather comfortably.

What worked to our future advantage at the 1984 trials was that Martel, after losing to us in the semifinal, stuck around to kibitz the championship match. He had a good long look at everyone who was playing.

The following year, Chip's team earned two qualifications to the trials for the 1985 Bermuda Bowl by winning the Vanderbilt and the Grand National Teams. Until very recently, the trials consisted of the winners of those two events plus the winners of the Spingold and Reisinger. Bobby and I hadn't won so much as a local duplicate, but we got to play in the trials anyway.

Martel's four-man team – with Lew Stansby, Hugh Ross and Peter Pender – needed another pair for the trials. They had pretty much decided on Meckstroth and Rodwell, but Martel had seen how we did in the 1984 trials. Considering that we had won the trials for both the 1983 and 1984 teams and had prevailed against Meckwell in the semifinals of the 1983 Bermuda Bowl, Martel convinced his teammates to offer us the open slots.

Don't get me wrong, now. I'm not putting Jeff and Eric down. They were super players then and they're better now. They have also been teammates of mine recently and I can't say enough about their standard of play and their team spirit. But in 1985, Bobby and I were the logical choices to be the add-ons to the Martel team. It probably would not have happened that way if Martel had not decided to stick around for the final of the trials. The fact that we were defending Bermuda Bowl champs didn't hurt.

The upshot of our selection to the team is that Bobby and I became involved in one of the all-time best matches in ACBL history – the 1985 Bermuda Bowl trials.

Our almost-Aces team – Bobby and I, Soloway and Goldman, Brachman and Andersen – had played in the World Team Olympiad in Seattle in the fall of 1984. In the round-robin, we were second in our bracket, but we lost to Austria in the quarterfinals.

In March of 1985, the same team again lost in the quarterfinals of the Vanderbilt. Being tied for fifth through eighth was getting to be a drag.

In May, Bobby and I – now with Martel's crew – checked into the Hyatt Regency Hotel in Memphis for a long weekend of bridge. Since this team had a double qualification for the trials, we got an automatic bye to the final, while two other teams fought it out for the right to play us.

Our NPC was Freddy Sheinwold, who was making a comeback of sorts after being drummed out of the non-playing captain business after the 1975 Bermuda Bowl. Remember, Lew Mathe and some of the other ACBL board members had been unhappy with some of Freddy's actions during the foot-tapping incident. As a result, Sheinwold had been removed from ACBL's approved list of NPCs. I was glad to have him back on our team.

The semifinal and final were two-day matches – 128 boards each. That's a lot of bridge: four 16-board sessions a day. That much bridge, with all the intense concentration you have to muster, can wear you down. That may be why it's a *requirement*, not an option, that teams in the trials have six members. I don't care how much stamina you have, if you played every set in a long trials match like that you would be brain-dead before it was over – making you a liability to your team.

Anyway, the semifinal winners were our pals Jeff and Eric, Marty Bergen-Larry Cohen and Mark Lair-Eddie Wold. George Rosenkranz was non-playing captain.

A word about our opponents. You've already heard about Jeff and Eric – quite formidable opponents. With each year that passes, they become more and more capable of carrying a team. They are super aggressive, incredibly active in the bidding and relentless competitors.

Bergen and Cohen were also mix-it-up players, principally because of Bergen's bidding style. Marty, who lives in the New York City area, has an uncanny knack – at least in certain settings – for finding just the right moment for an off-the-wall action, wreaking havoc on the opponents' auction. That kind of stuff can also be hard on partner. Marty's reputation as a player has suffered somewhat because of his "creativity," but he is a fine player.

Cohen, by contrast, is a mild-mannered, soft-spoken guy with collegiate looks and a baby face. To look at Larry, you would never guess the truth about him – that he is tough as nails. At one time, Bergen and Cohen were about the hottest pair going. They won seven major championships playing together, including two Blue Ribbon Pairs, and were sought after as teammates.

The partnership ended in the early 1990s on friendly terms. They've published a couple of books together and have played as teammates on occasion. But while Cohen formed a highly successful partnership with Dave Berkowitz, Bergen has more or less dropped out of tournament bridge. For the time being, anyway, he is concentrating on book publishing and teaching in the New York area.

Then there were Lair and Wold, highly skilled bridge pros and veterans of the tournament circuit. Lair and Mike Passell have one of the most successful partnerships in North America and Lair is third on the list of all-time masterpoint holders. Wold has also had considerable success and annually rakes in tons of masterpoints.

There's one thing to understand about the touring pros, however. Most of the time when they go to tournaments – mostly regionals – they are by far the best players in the field and they don't have to extend themselves to win. That can soften you for really tough competition such as the team trials. Also, many pros play a lot with bad players as clients, which can result in bad habits.

Anyway, we were the betting favorites. Bobby and I had won the previous Bermuda Bowl and the other four on our team had won two of the four qualifying events – the Vanderbilt and the Grand National Teams – and lots of other major events.

Martel and Stansby are kind of like Mutt and Jeff. Martel is a college professor. He teaches computer science in the San Francisco area. With a bushy mustache and longish hair, he looks a bit like a hippie. Chip is a little guy – he can't weigh much more than 120 pounds – but he has the heart of a lion and the tenacity of a bulldog.

Stansby, by contrast, is tall – well over six feet – and looks like a banker or some other kind of businessman. Lew is also a very good player, but he needs a partner like Chip to do some growling. Luckily, Chip growls at just the right times. Their partnership is one of the best. Besides the many ACBL championships they have won, Chip and Lew took the World Open Pairs title in Biarritz, France, in 1982 and came in second in the Rosenblum Cup Teams at the same tournament.

Pender and Ross were another odd couple. Ross used to be in the computer business. He is a transplanted Canadian who now lives in Oakland. Despite the rigors of high-level competitive bridge, I don't think I've ever seen Hugh in a bad mood. He's a tall, rangy fellow with a shock of hair often hanging in one of his eyes. An inveterate smoker, Hugh sat at the table in the trials with a big cigar sticking out of his mouth most of the time.

Ross is a tough competitor who has proven himself through the years at the highest levels of bridge play. He has won two Bermuda Bowls and several national championships, including back-to-back wins with Zia in the Life Master Open Pairs at the Fall Nationals in 1990 and 1991.

Pender was originally from Canada, and grew up in Philadelphia. He inherited a pile of money, so he didn't have to work, but he liked to busy himself with various projects. One of them was a resort for gays in the San Francisco area. Peter could be fussy and he was definitely impatient with fools, but he was a solid player. In 1966, he helped Jeremy Flint of England become a Life Master in 11 weeks. That same year, Peter won the McKenney Trophy for earning the most masterpoints. When Pender died of AIDS in 1991, he left a legacy to bridge with a grant for the development of a computer vugraph show that has been highly successful.

No one could have known how wild and crazy it would get when we sat down to play for the right to go to Brazil for the 1985 Bermuda Bowl. It was an amazing contest.

The Rosenkranz team had polished off Russell, 298-167, so they seemed to have momentum going into the final. We quickly reversed that trend as we jumped out to a 51-25 lead after the first of the eight 16-board segments.

This was one of the deals that got our team off to the right start.

```
Dlr: North      ♠ A 9 8 6
Vul: Both       ♥ 10 8 7 6 5 2
                ♦ 6
                ♣ K 8
♠ Q 10 7 2                      ♠ K 4
♥ 9 3                           ♥ A Q J
♦ A J 10 5 3                    ♦ K Q 8 4
♣ 10 2                          ♣ J 9 6 5
                ♠ J 5 3
                ♥ K 4
                ♦ 9 7 2
                ♣ A Q 7 4 3
```

At one table, Rodwell opened 1NT with the East hand and eventually landed in 3NT. Stansby led a low club and Martel defended accurately after winning the king by switching to a low heart – a beautiful play. Rodwell now had no chance. When he finessed, the ♥K became the fifth trick for the defense, to go with three clubs and a spade.

At the other table, Bergen opened the North hand with a weak 2♥ bid – consistent with his wacky style. Bergen's opening was supposed to give his opponents fits. What it did was induce Cohen to lead the ♥K against East's 3NT contract. All Pender had to do after that was knock out the ♠A for his ninth trick. 12 IMPs to our side.

Bobby and I came in for the second set, replacing Pender and Ross, and things got bloody. We hit them with a 56-26 pounding over those 16 boards and our lead grew to 56 IMPs. This deal, which swung 7 IMPs to our team, was widely reported.

```
Dlr: South      ♠ Q 8 2
Vul: Both       ♥ 10 9 8 7 4 2
                ♦ J 8 5
                ♣ 7
♠ K 10 7 6                      ♠ A J 9 5 4 3
♥ Q J 3                         ♥ A K 5
♦ 4 3                           ♦ 10 9 2
♣ K Q 10 8                      ♣ 2
                ♠ —
                ♥ 6
                ♦ A K Q 7 6
                ♣ A J 9 6 5 4 3
```

In the other room:

WEST	NORTH	EAST	SOUTH
Wold	*Martel*	*Lair*	*Stansby*
			1♣
Pass	1♥	1♠	2♦
2♥	Pass	4♠	4NT
Pass	5♦	Pass	Pass
Dbl	All Pass		

Wold, knowing that Stansby was going to need to ruff clubs in dummy, led a trump, hoping to cut down on the ruffs. Theoretically – and, on this deal, in practice – it is better to play a forcing defense against a freak two-suiter (as this obviously was) when declarer is playing in his shorter suit.

After that lead, Stansby could have gotten out for down one (minus 200) by winning in hand, cashing the ♣A and ruffing a club with the jack, followed by two more rounds of trumps. Then he could concede two club tricks to West. Stansby, however, put up dummy's jack and ended up getting overruffed twice by Lair. He also had to concede a club trick and went down 500.

Here's what happened at our table:

WEST	NORTH	EAST	SOUTH
Wolff	*Cohen*	*Me*	*Bergen*
			1♣
Pass	1♥	2♠	3♦
4♠	Pass	Pass	4NT
Pass	5♦	Dbl	All Pass

Bobby led a spade and when Bergen ruffed my jack, he was already in trouble – down to four trumps with lots of work to do. He then played the ♣A and another club, ruffing in dummy with the 8. I thought about this a long time before I decided not to overruff. I tried to picture Bergen's hand. He was most likely 7-5 in the minors, and if his clubs were all that great he would have pulled trumps before playing on clubs. He was going to have to get back to his hand to ruff more clubs, and he couldn't do it with trumps because he needed those babies in dummy to handle his losing clubs. So he had to ruff something to get back to hand.

After the ♦8 held, Bergen played a heart. I won the trick and forced him again in spades. He ruffed a club with the ♦J but once again had to ruff to get back to his hand. Now he was down to two trumps. I had him outnumbered. He ruffed the fourth round of clubs with the ♦5. *Now* I overruffed and forced him again with a spade. Marty finished with only eight tricks – five trumps in hand, two club ruffs in dummy and the ♣A. Plus 800 for our side – a 7-IMP gain that would loom very large later on.

In set three, we picked up another 34 IMPs, 72-38, and were up by 90. It looked like a cakewalk.

At that point, Bobby and I made a serious mistake. We went out to dinner. What we should have done was go right back in for set four and finish them off. The other team was mentally beaten, and Bobby and I are pretty good at making sure the other guy doesn't get up off the floor and get back into the fight. We might not be as good as some pairs at getting the lead, but once we've got it, we can finish them off as well as anyone.

Pender and Ross, on the other hand, were a flighty pair – subject to getting pounded, capable of inflicting pain but very much a momentum pair.

By the time we got back from dinner and saw what was happening, the momentum had changed. The other guys had won the fourth set 60-24 and were back in the match. They kept on pouring it on in the first set of the second half, winning that one 65-25. Suddenly, our 90-IMP lead was down to 14.

Unbelievably, they crushed us again in segment six, 80-22. What a turnaround! Now they were *ahead* by 44 IMPs. We were hanging on the ropes and in a desperate state. The other team had outscored us by 134 IMPs over three sets. *We* were the ones who were going to have to fight back – and time was running out. Only 32 boards to go. How were we going to stem this tide? Could we?

The way to do it, I've found, is to play one board at a time. As far as I know, there isn't a 40-IMP play in bridge – and if you go looking for one on every hand, you'll only bury yourself deeper. You've got to knuckle down and grind it out.

We sat down against Eric and Jeff for the start of the seventh set. Pender and Ross played Bergen and Cohen at the other table. Nothing much happened for most of the set, but near the end, the pendulum swung back in our direction. There were two key deals. First:

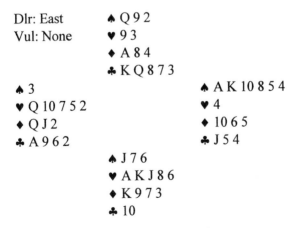

```
Dlr: East        ♠ Q 9 2
Vul: None        ♥ 9 3
                 ♦ A 8 4
                 ♣ K Q 8 7 3
♠ 3                          ♠ A K 10 8 5 4
♥ Q 10 7 5 2                 ♥ 4
♦ Q J 2                      ♦ 10 6 5
♣ A 9 6 2                    ♣ J 5 4
                 ♠ J 7 6
                 ♥ A K J 8 6
                 ♦ K 9 7 3
                 ♣ 10
```

At the other table:

WEST	NORTH	EAST	SOUTH
Ross	*Bergen*	*Pender*	*Cohen*
		2♦ (1)	Pass
2♠ (2)	Pass	Pass	3♥
Dbl	All Pass		

(1) Multiple meaning bid: weak two-bid in either major, an intermediate two-suiter or a strong balanced hand.

(2) Signoff if West has a weak two in spades; encouraging if partner's suit is hearts.

Ross had an easy double of 3♥, but Cohen played well to go down only one for minus 100. Things went quite differently at our table:

WEST	NORTH	EAST	SOUTH
Meckstroth	*Me*	*Rodwell*	*Wolff*
		2♦ (1)	2♥
Pass	2NT	Pass	3NT
All Pass			

(1) Weak two-bid in either major.

This auction was in keeping with our philosophy of bidding game – just do it. Remember, on the occasions when you're not cold for it, the opponents may find it difficult to figure out how to beat you. Sure, we were in a 23-point game and, as you can see, it has no legitimate play, but watch what happened.

Rodwell, East, hit on the unfortunate – for his side, anyway – lead of a low club. Meckstroth won the ace and switched to a spade. Rodwell cashed the top spades and played a third round, on which Meckstroth threw a club. All of a sudden, I had four club tricks. If I had been left to play the suit myself, it's doubtful I would have taken more than one trick. Anyway, I scored up plus 400 and our team gained an 11-IMP swing.

This deal, the next to last in the seventh set, completed the swing of the momentum back to our side.

```
Dlr: South      ♠ J 9 7 3 2
Vul: N-S        ♥ A 7 4 3
                ♦ 8 5 2
                ♣ 5
♠ —                         ♠ A K Q 5
♥ K J 8                     ♥ Q
♦ A K J 10 7 4 3            ♦ 6
♣ A 6 2                     ♣ K Q J 8 7 4 3
                ♠ 10 8 6 4
                ♥ 10 9 6 5 2
                ♦ Q 9
                ♣ 10 9
```

At our table, Jeff opened a strong 1♣ as West and thus became declarer at 6♣. I cashed the ♥A and that was that. Plus 920 for them. At the other table:

WEST	NORTH	EAST	SOUTH
Ross	*Bergen*	*Pender*	*Cohen*
			Pass
1♦	Pass	4NT	Pass
5♥	Pass	6♣	Pass
7♣	All Pass		

Pender launched straight into Blackwood with his powerful hand, signing off when he discovered the partnership was missing an ace. Ross, not knowing whether his void was a positive asset, took a chance that it was and bid the grand slam. Bergen had cause to regret not doubling the 5♥ response to 4NT because Cohen had no clue on the auction for his opening lead. He did have a negative inference regarding hearts, however – partner did not double 5♥ when he had the opportunity. So Cohen selected a spade for his opening lead and Pender quickly claimed his grand slam. Another 11 IMPs to us. We had cut their lead to 21 IMPs. There were 16 boards to go.

In the final set, Bobby and I played against Lair and Wold while Stansby and Martel faced Meckstroth and Rodwell.

The first two boards were pushes. Then the other guys widened their lead to 33 IMPs when I was doubled in 3♦, down 500, while

Chip played in 4♥ at the other table, down one. But we got back 25 IMPs on the next two boards. First, Chip and Lew bid to 6♦, which was cold, while Lair and Wold stopped in 3NT at our table – 13 IMPs for us. Then Lair and Wold took a 4♦ save against our 3NT that went for minus 300 while, at the other table, 3NT went down three vulnerable tricks. Plus 300 for our team at both tables – 12 IMPs to our side.

We took the lead after Board 121 when Bobby and I stopped in 4♠, making on the nose, while Jeff and Eric bid to 5♠ trying for slam and went down one. We were up by 5 IMPs with seven boards to go.

This was the killer board for our opponents.

```
Dlr: South      ♠ —
Vul: None       ♥ Q J 7 6 5 3
                ♦ 9 8 7 6
                ♣ 10 9 2
  ♠ 10 8 6 5 4                 ♠ 7 3 2
  ♥ 9 2                        ♥ A K 10
  ♦ A K J                      ♦ 10 5
  ♣ K 4 3                      ♣ A Q J 7 6
                ♠ A K Q J 9
                ♥ 8 4
                ♦ Q 4 3 2
                ♣ 8 5
```

WEST	NORTH	EAST	SOUTH
Lair	*Me*	*Wold*	*Wolff*
			1♠
Pass	1NT	2♣	2♠
2NT	Pass	3NT	All Pass

I couldn't lead a spade, so it was pretty easy for Mark to score up plus 430. He could finesse in diamonds safely, knowing I couldn't hurt him with a spade return even if I won the ♦Q. At the other table:

WEST	NORTH	EAST	SOUTH
Stansby	*Meckstroth*	*Martel*	*Rodwell*
			1♠
Pass	1NT	2♣	2♦
2NT	Pass	3NT	Dbl
All Pass			

I think Eric may have panicked after bidding 2♦, fearful that partner might lead a diamond rather than a spade. So he doubled to be sure partner led his first suit. Stansby took the same 10 tricks that Eddie did. Lew scored up 650, however, a 6-IMP gain. Our lead had grown to 11.

Thank goodness, there were only minor swings on the last five boards. Two were pushes and they gained 1, 2 and 3 IMPs on the other three boards.

When Bobby and I emerged from the room where we had been playing, Frank Stewart, who was writing for the ACBL *Bulletin*, rushed up and asked how we did. Bobby, ever the pessimist, told Frank we had probably lost. It turned out that Chip and Lew had had a monster set over the last 16 boards, however. We had prevailed, 339-334.

I'm sure we all felt as though we had done 15 rounds toe to toe with Joe Louis or Rocky Marciano. I know I was physically and emotionally drained, and I'm sure the other guys were, too. There's a natural tendency, of course, to reproach yourself when you lose a close match. *I could have done this on board so-and-so, or that on board thus-and-such. Then we wouldn't have lost.* As I've said before, that's losing practice. Still, I can appreciate the depth of the other guys' disappointment to come out on the short end of such a battle royal.

In the post-game hand-shaking phase, Rodwell was particularly gracious. Although he lost, he appreciated the magnificent effort put forth by both teams. "It was," he said, "the most exciting match ever."

In late October of 1985, our team made its way to São Paulo, Brazil, to compete in the Bermuda Bowl. We had an automatic bye to the semifinals, along with European champion Austria, so we were able to rest while the other teams fought it out in the round-robin.

It turned out that our semifinal match with Brazil was a lot more interesting than the final.

Brazil and Israel had come in first and second respectively in the round-robin. Our team drew the South Americans since Israel and Austria – both from Europe – were an automatic match because of the rule prohibiting two teams from the same zone meeting in the final.

The Brazilians were naturally the hometown favorites, and in fact we found the vugraph audience to be just as rabid in support of their heroes as the crowds that had favored Italy in previous world championships. By now, I was used to being on the "bad guy" team in these events. All I wanted was for someone to point me to a table.

Brazil's team was two pairs of brothers, the Brancos (Marcelo and Pedro) and the Sampaios (Claudio and Fabio) and Gabino Cintra and Sergio Barbosa. This team performed well enough to win the round-robin comfortably, but it had a glaring weakness – the absence of Brazilian superstar Gabriel Chagas.

Gabriel and his partner, Jose Barbosa, had been suspended by the Brazilian Bridge Federation for making a ruling at their own table without calling the tournament director during Brazil's equivalent of the team trials. Chagas had persuaded his opponents that Barbosa, apparently down in a slam he had misplayed, had made it after all. Gabriel and Jose Barbosa had been replaced by the 21-year-old Sampaios, who were still wet behind the ears. In Brazil's match against us, the Sampaios didn't pick up a card, so the Brancos and Cintra-Barbosa played all 160 boards. It had a telling effect.

Brazil took an early lead and kept building on it through five sets (16 boards each). After 80 boards, they were up by 45 IMPs. We rallied slightly in set six, cutting the lead to 22, but they ended set seven up by 25. We had a crusher in the eighth set, winning 49-3, as the Brazilians began to show the effects of playing every hand. We were up by 21. Brazil cut the margin to 2 IMPs going into the last set and, in fact, with two boards to go, they had come back to lead by 6 IMPs. We didn't know this, of course, but the vugraph audience was practically foaming at the mouth as they watched their underdog countrymen on the verge of knocking off the American invaders.

The final two boards show how the difference between winning and losing can be razor-thin – and how close some of our matches have been. In fact, in many cases if someone had been breathing against us at the end we would have been losers instead of winners. I've been on both sides. Fortunately, I've been on the winning side more often than not. I'll let others judge whether it was skill or luck or a combination of both. I know this, though: winning is a helluva lot better than losing, no matter how it comes about.

On the next-to-last board, Brazil could have put the match away.

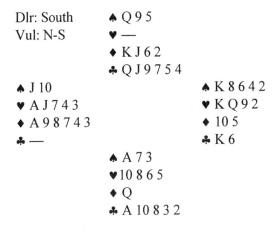

Dlr: South   ♠ Q 9 5
Vul: N-S   ♥ —
           ♦ K J 6 2
           ♣ Q J 9 7 5 4

♠ J 10   ♠ K 8 6 4 2
♥ A J 7 4 3   ♥ K Q 9 2
♦ A 9 8 7 4 3   ♦ 10 5
♣ —   ♣ K 6

           ♠ A 7 3
           ♥ 10 8 6 5
           ♦ Q
           ♣ A 10 8 3 2

Brazil's result in the Open Room was somewhat soft.

WEST	NORTH	EAST	SOUTH
Cintra	*Martel*	*Barbosa*	*Stansby*
			Pass
Pass	Pass	1♠	Pass
2♥	Pass	4♥	Pass
5♣	Pass	5♥	All Pass

Barbosa's blast into game is somewhat suspect, but I'm sure he didn't dream that his passed-hand partner was going to go sniffing for slam. Cintra did his best, but he couldn't handle the 4-0 trump split and he finished down one for minus 50. When Bobby and I played the deal against the Brancos, it didn't seem like the same hand.

WEST	NORTH	EAST	SOUTH
Me	*Marcelo*	*Wolff*	*Pedro*
			Pass
1♥	2♣	4♥	5♣
5♥	Pass	Pass	6♣
Pass	Pass	Dbl	All Pass

Can you believe it? North-South are cold for 6♣ but our teammates at the other table weren't even in the auction. There's a risk associated with vulnerable overcalls with hands like North's, but sometimes they pay off – as it might have on this deal. As you can see, South's decision to "save" at the six level could have reaped a huge reward – plus 1540 for Brazil – but it wasn't to be.

Bobby led the ♥K and Marcelo Branco ruffed. He immediately led the ♣Q. Bobby followed low smoothly and, as the vugraph audience shrieked, "Finesse! Finesse!" – it's a good thing for us you couldn't hear the audience in the playing areas – Branco called for the *ace*! Down one. A net of plus 250 for our side and a 6-IMP gain. Now it was dead even with one board to play. I'm glad I didn't know it at the time. These photo finishes have a way of putting the years on you in a hurry.

The final deal of the match shows dramatically what it means to be in the right place at the right time in a bridge setting.

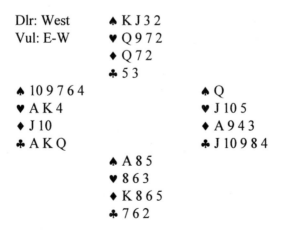

```
Dlr: West     ♠ K J 3 2
Vul: E-W      ♥ Q 9 7 2
              ♦ Q 7 2
              ♣ 5 3
♠ 10 9 7 6 4              ♠ Q
♥ A K 4                   ♥ J 10 5
♦ J 10                   ♦ A 9 4 3
♣ A K Q                  ♣ J 10 9 8 4
              ♠ A 8 5
              ♥ 8 6 3
              ♦ K 8 6 5
              ♣ 7 6 2
```

We played the board first.

WEST	NORTH	EAST	SOUTH
Me	*Marcelo*	*Wolff*	*Pedro*
1NT	Pass	Pass	Pass

Although Bobby and I play a strong club system, I decided that 1NT was a better choice because of the bad spade suit and the fact that the doubleton ♦J probably wasn't pulling its full weight. This put our partnership in the right place – with West as declarer – at the right time. Since my maximum was 17 high-card points, Bobby decided not to move over 1NT. Perhaps he should have been more aggressive since we were vulnerable, but it worked out just fine. Marcelo Branco made the normal lead of a low heart, giving me nine tricks right off the bat. I ended with 10 tricks for plus 180. There was concern, obviously, that we would lose 10 IMPs if the Brazilians bid and made game at the other table. But it was too late to worry about it and, as it happened, it didn't matter – look what occurred at the other table:

WEST	NORTH	EAST	SOUTH
Cintra	*Martel*	*Barbosa*	*Stansby*
1♣	Pass	1♦	Pass
1♠	Pass	2NT	Pass
3NT	All Pass		

When the four hands were flashed on the vugraph screen, it was obvious this board could win or lose the match for Brazil – remember, the vugraph audience knew the match was tied. Everyone knew that Bobby and I had not reached game. If Brazil could bid game and make it, the team would be in the final against Austria, who had defeated Israel.

A hush fell over the crowd at the Hotel Maksoud Plaza as the auction began. Cintra and Barbosa were playing a strong club system, so Cintra began with 1♣. Barbosa's 1♦ bid showed 0-8 high-card points. Cintra might have disregarded his feeble spade suit and bid 1NT, making him declarer, but he decided on a natural 1♠.

The pro-Brazilian crowd, sensing what was coming, grew even more still. It was Barbosa's turn to bid. He knew game was a good prospect and he wanted to let his partner know. He could have kept the auction going by bidding his five-card club suit, but that would have been merely forward-going, not the highly invitational bid he wanted to make. 2NT seemed to describe his hand well – a maximum for his 1♦ bid, no spade support. Cintra was happy to raise to game.

Not a sound could be heard in the vugraph ballroom as Stansby considered his opening lead. Finally he placed the ♦5 on the table. The Brazilians in the audience issued a collective groan. They knew it was curtains for Barbosa unless Stansby and Martel screwed up royally. Although the diamond lead does not generate a lot of tricks for the defense, it takes the only entry out of the East hand before the club suit can be unblocked. 3NT has no chance with a diamond lead. North will put on the queen and continue the suit if declarer ducks. If declarer wins the first trick, his hand is dead.

Lew and Chip defended carefully to defeat the contract two tricks. That was plus 180 and plus 200, a gain of 9 IMPs. Had either Brazilian chosen to bid differently and placed West as declarer, I would be writing that Brazil had defeated us by 10 IMPs in the semifinal of the Bermuda Bowl – another disappointing tournament. Same story if Marcelo Branco finesses in clubs on the doubled slam instead of playing for the drop.

Instead, I can report that we went on from there to trounce Austria in the final. It was an anticlimax, to be sure. Bobby and I had won our fifth Bermuda Bowl. All I could think was, "When is the next one?"

19

Sure things

FOR YEARS, I've been offering people a bet – and nobody's taken me up on it yet.

Here's the deal. I will take a non-bridge player off the street and train him for a month. At the end of the month, I and my new partner will play against any pair in the world for any stakes, subject to one condition: before anything happens, I get to look at my right-hand opponent's hand.

I submit that no one would have a chance against us.

So, you ask, do I have a point? Yes – that when a player gratuitously gives information about his hand to his opponents – say, through an elaborate auction – he's going through a minor modification of my wager scenario.

When you do this against people who can play – not just some total off-the-street novice – you're really skating on thin ice.

There is a lead convention that falls into this category. It's called "jack denies." It means that whenever you lead a jack against a no-trump contract, it's the highest card you have in the suit. The idea is that, when you lead a jack, partner doesn't have to guess whether you've led from J1098 or KJ109. That's wonderful, but you know what? Declarer doesn't have to guess, either!

I think "jack denies" is the stupidest lead convention ever invented. I hope all my opponents play it. You think I'm exaggerating? Overstating? Well, come with me to the 1987 Bermuda Bowl Team Trials, and I'll show you what I'm talking about.

Just about two years after the donnybrook we miraculously survived in the Bermuda Bowl Team Trials in 1985, the very same team was back in Memphis for another try. We had a new non-playing captain – Dan Morse – but the team itself was intact.

Once again, Bobby and I had been added to Chip Martel's team. It wasn't a double qualification this time – they had won the 1985 Grand National Teams – so we were going to have to play a full tournament. At least, we hoped we would.

Our opponents in the opening round were led by playing captain Malcolm Brachman, who had put together a formidable group – Mike Passell, Mark Lair, Ron Andersen and former Aces Bobby Goldman and Paul Soloway.

It turned out to be one of the wildest – and closest – matches I've ever played in.

Malcolm's team started off like gangbusters. They were up 29 IMPs after the first 16 boards. We got some back in the second set and tied them in the third. We went back and forth in the match, like two heavyweights pounding on each other. Then things turned bizarre.

Bobby and I were defending a 3NT contract against Lair and Andersen. Lair was declarer. At one point, I showed out of a suit. Now in those days, you weren't allowed to ask partner whether he had any of a suit if he showed out. Although the rule has been changed by the ACBL since, it's still *verboten* in many other countries. If you ask when you're not supposed to, it's an automatic established revoke.

(For those not familiar with the rules, if you fail to follow suit when you could have, it's a revoke. If you correct your mistake before either you or partner plays to the next trick, it's a simple revoke and the first card played becomes a penalty card – usually no big deal. If the revoke becomes established, however, you usually have to pay with tricks to the other side. That can be much more serious.)

Well, when I showed out of the suit, Bobby said, "What's going on here?" At the same time, Lair called for a card from dummy. I actually had a card of the suit I had shown out of, and I had the proper card ready to play. In the confusion, I sort of flipped the card, not really playing it. If I had been playing it, I would have done so in a much more methodical fashion.

Anyway, now I had two cards on the table. We called the director, naturally, and eventually got a ruling that there had been an established revoke. It was pretty serious in this case because the trick penalty allowed Lair to make his contract, which would have been defeated otherwise (it *was* defeated at the other table). At first I thought the director's ruling was based on Bobby's comment. I later learned that he had decided I had been following to the next trick when I was actually attempting to follow suit from the previous trick.

Our 10-IMP loss on this board loomed very large in the match. When it was all over, Malcolm's team was on top, 274-271.

But wait! The directors also determined that Soloway and Goldman had taken more than their fair share of time. They were hit with a slow-play penalty of 3 IMPs. After 128 boards, it was a dead heat.

We appealed the revoke ruling and they appealed the slow-play penalty. Both appeals were rejected. Someone made the observation that it wouldn't have looked too good for Wolffie, who was president of the ACBL that year, to win both appeals. Over the years, I've found that people who serve on appeals committees bend over backwards to be fair, even if they go against a big name in bridge. Some committee decisions have been real stinkers, but by and large they're on target.

Many people think committees are biased in favor of the professionals or big-name players. I've seen many a ruling go against the big guys, though. In the 1994 Vanderbilt, Paul Soloway and his team went to committee over a director's ruling that had gone against them on a key board. If the director's ruling had been overturned by the committee, Paul's team, which lost the match, would then have won.

Lots of people thought Soloway's team would win the appeal just because of who filed it. Paul figured different. He predicted the committee would let the result stand and his team would be out of the event. He was right.

But back to 1987. We started our 12-board semifinal playoff at just about the time the final was supposed to begin.

Bobby and I played against former Aces teammates Soloway and Goldman. Chip and Lew were at the other table against Lair and Andersen.

Late in the playoff, it looked bad for us. Soloway and Goldman had played well. Bobby and I thought they were leading by too much for us to catch them. Then came my favorite lead convention: "jack denies."

Dlr: South	♠ Q 8 6	
Vul: E-W	♥ 10 7 4	
	♦ J 10 8 7 4	
	♣ K 3	

♠ J 10 9 7 4		♠ A 2
♥ K Q		♥ J 9 6 5 3
♦ 9 6		♦ K 5 3 2
♣ Q 10 9 5		♣ J 7

	♠ K 5 3	
	♥ A 8 2	
	♦ A Q	
	♣ A 8 6 4 2	

This is what happened at the other table:

WEST	NORTH	EAST	SOUTH
Martel	*Lair*	*Stansby*	*Andersen*
			1NT
Pass	Pass	Pass	

The auction was perfectly reasonable. Lair had no reason to bid with his 6-point hand.

Chip led the ♠J. Andersen played low in dummy and won the king in his hand. He played the ♦A and ♦Q, ducked by Lew. Ron then turned to clubs, playing the king, ace and a third round, hoping the suit was split 3-3. Chip won the third round of clubs and put the ♠10 on the table.

Now Ron had to guess. Chip's lead of the ♠J could have been from the holding he actually had – or it could have been from the AJ109(x). If Chip had led from the ♠AJ, Ron should go up with dummy's queen. If not, he should duck, hoping Chip had led from a five-card suit headed by the jack. The point is that, since Chip and Lew weren't playing "jack denies" leads, Ron had to guess. On this occasion, he went wrong, putting up the queen. Martel and Stansby chalked up plus 50.

At our table:

WEST	NORTH	EAST	SOUTH
Soloway	*Me*	*Goldman*	*Wolff*
			1♣
Pass	1♦	Pass	1NT
Pass	3NT	All Pass	

Bobby's 1♣ opener was strong and artificial and the 1NT rebid supposedly showed 18-20 high-card points (he really liked his hand, didn't he?). After that, I didn't see any point in messing around. There was clearly no slam on this deal, but we were sure getting to game. I practice what I preach.

Luckily for Bobby, Soloway's lead of the ♠J denied a higher card in the suit. Goldman knew Wolff could not go wrong, so he went up with the ♠A at trick one and switched to a heart. Bobby ducked to the queen and ducked again when Paul played the ♥K. With no more hearts to lead, Paul continued the attack on spades. Bobby won in hand and played the ♦A and ♦Q. Goldman did the best he could by ducking, but Bobby played a club to the king and drove out the ♦K. He got back to dummy with the ♠Q. Nine tricks in the bag. Plus 400.

Think about it. At one table, the declarer in *one* notrump *goes down*, while at the other table, they get to *three* notrump and *make it*. Does that tell you something about "jack denies" leads? That's not even the best part. We won 10 IMPs on this board – and we won the playoff by one – count 'em, one – IMP, 22-21. Without "jack denies," Bobby might not have come close to making that shaky game – and if he goes down, we're out of the trials. I won't deny it was a lucky hand – the blockage in hearts was very helpful, to be sure – but when the opponents are kindly giving you so much information, your "luck" seems to increase tremendously.

We played the Cliff Russell team in the final, which wasn't very interesting after the nail-biter we had just survived. We won handily. It was on to Ocho Rios, Jamaica, for the 1987 Bermuda Bowl.

Even before we left for Jamaica the following October, we knew an adventure awaited us.

In a world championship event, the contestants are required to submit detailed descriptions of their systems so that the other teams can prepare defenses to the really unusual stuff. Through this process, we learned that the British, one of the favored teams, were going to be playing what is known as a "strong pass" system, sometimes called the "forcing pass."

That means that when they said "pass" in first or second seat, it showed the values for an opening bid. If they actually bid something in either of those seats, it denied the values for a traditional opener. The basic idea is that the pass gives more bidding room for good hands. Of course, there's another factor: it's difficult to cope with such unusual methods. It's not uncommon in tournament bridge for pairs and teams to adopt unusual methods strictly because their opponents will have trouble with them.

My fundamental objection to all the weird stuff you encounter in tournaments nowadays is that, at the point where you remove restrictions on methods, bridge becomes a game of language rather than logic – and it loses a lot in the exchange.

The World Bridge Federation, which runs the world championships, does enforce restrictions on what people can play in pair games. It would be an absolute zoo if you had to try to come up with defenses to dozens of weird systems on the spot, and for just two hands. Players would go nuts and the game would die.

For long matches, where teams have a chance to prepare defenses for all the homemade junk they encounter, the WBF is more lenient. Thus we were saddled with the job of figuring out what to do if and when we encountered Great Britain in the Bermuda Bowl. The six-man British team was mixing and matching players in several partnerships, two of which played the strong pass system.

All this brought to mind an occasion in the 1970s when the Aces were preparing to play against Poland in a world championship. At the time the Polish were introducing the world to the strong pass system. In their methods, most first- or second-seat bids showed hands in the 7- to 12-point range. Very bad hands were opened with a special "bid of misery," often 1 ♦.

Before the match with Poland, the team talked about how to defend against the strong pass. Here were some suggestions:

"If it goes pass by them and pass by me, that's a takeout double."

"If it goes pass by them and 2NT by me, that's still the unusual notrump."

"For the two lower unbids?"

"No, top and bottom."

"No exceptions?"

"Well, maybe if they later bid spades and I don't double."

Ira Rubin, a real stickler for sound opening bids, loved to play against the forcing pass system – there is never a passed-out hand. Think about it: if either Pole had passed, that showed an opening bid and was forcing since it might be a gigantic hand. If neither player had an opening hand, they had to bid something! Said Ira: "Against them I can relax and play my style. I can pass my cruddy 13 pointers with assurance and confidence that somebody is going to find an opening bid."

By the time we got to Jamaica for the 1987 Bermuda Bowl, our team had changed. Peter Pender had become ill and was replaced by Mike Lawrence, who was playing with Hugh Ross. Both are from the San Francisco area, so they had a chance to get used to each other before the tournament.

As defending Bermuda Bowl champs, we had a bye to the semifinals along with Sweden, which won the European championship. As expected, Great Britain made it to the semifinals, along with the upstart team from Chinese Taipei, which came in first in the round-robin.

Great Britain and Sweden, both from Europe, were required to play in one semifinal, leaving us to face the Chinese. We murdered them, 421-290, while the British knocked off Sweden, 358-311.

As expected, the Brits' system contributed heavily to their win. There was one deal where the Swedes, confused by a British 2NT opening which showed a two-suited hand with 7 to 10 high-card points, landed in 3NT redoubled. That went for 2800, believed to be the largest minus score ever recorded in a Bermuda Bowl.

In the final, we also had our difficulties against the strong passes and "fert" bids. "Ferts" – short for fertilizer – are the bids the Brits were opening with when they didn't have opening hands. This hand caused consternation for both sides:

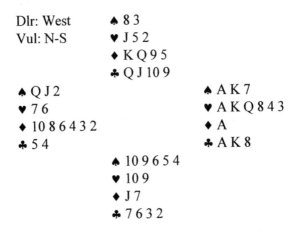

```
Dlr: West        ♠ 8 3
Vul: N-S         ♥ J 5 2
                 ♦ K Q 9 5
                 ♣ Q J 10 9

♠ Q J 2                        ♠ A K 7
♥ 7 6                          ♥ A K Q 8 4 3
♦ 10 8 6 4 3 2                 ♦ A
♣ 5 4                          ♣ A K 8

                 ♠ 10 9 6 5 4
                 ♥ 10 9
                 ♦ J 7
                 ♣ 7 6 3 2
```

West opened 1♣, a bid that showed a bad hand – just what East wanted to hear. Far from helping, the confounded system got in their way and they struggled to the inelegant contract of 5♥ on a hand where they were cold for a grand slam.

Unfortunately, a blasted fert at the other table messed us up, too. Mike Lawrence (West) passed with that horrid collection. North, however, opened 1♦, showing less than an opening bid. Our players had agreed to ignore the fert bids and make the bids they would make if the fert hadn't been made. Thus, if the Brits opened 1♣, a 1♠ overcall would show a normal 1♠ opening bid; a 2♣ bid would be just as if you had opened a strong, artificial bid.

Well, Hugh Ross remembered that agreement but Lawrence forgot, so when the Brit opened 1♦ and Ross bid 2♣ with the 27-point monster, Mike passed! North, sensing that something had gone very wrong for our side, was happy to sign off. Ross was playing 2♣ on a 3-2 fit instead of the frigid 7♥. Actually, Hugh played it well to come to eight tricks, but it was still a big loss for us. This loss had nothing to do with bridge skill, system technical merit or anything other than the advantage that comes from playing methods which increase the probability that the opponents will forget their systemic defenses.

In the 1993 Bermuda Bowl semifinals, a similar forget by Bobby Levin-Peter Weichsel was much more costly – they ended up in a doubled grand slam down 800 – a loss of 16 IMPs. This disaster was followed by others, and the U.S. team lost by 3 IMPs to the Netherlands. Systems and conventions which rely primarily on lapses due to opponents' misunderstandings should not be part of the game.

All in all, however, we handled the British system pretty well and, of course, they managed to shoot themselves in the foot a few more times. Still, the championship was in doubt – our lead was only 14 IMPs – as we sat down to start the final 16 boards on the third day.

It wasn't close. We blew them out 58-8. Fittingly, one of the big swings in the match occurred when a fert bid caused the British pair to play a 4♥ contract from the "wrong" side. Martel and Stansby defeated the contract with normal defense, while Bobby made 10 tricks in hearts from the "other side."

At the victory banquet, we shared the spotlight with the American women's team, who won the Venice Cup (the Bermuda Bowl for women players). Their team – Kathie Wei, Judi Radin, Beth Palmer, Lynn Deas, Juanita Chambers and Cheri Bjerkan – was even more excited about the victory than we were, if that was possible.

All but Wei and Radin were winning their first world championship, and they were flying high. I knew how they felt. In fact, although I had just won my sixth Bermuda Bowl, I felt the same way they did. It's what keeps me coming back. There's nothing like winning, and it never gets old.

1986 was a new start for me. I had a new girlfriend, soon to be my wife – Petra. I had known her for a long time. We first met at the Spring Nationals in Cleveland in 1969, when I was a brand-new member of the Aces. We had been friends from that point until we got together more and less permanently at the World Championships in Miami in 1986.

Petra has been an avid player almost from her first experience with the game. Despite her training in five-card majors and forcing notrumps, she was able to convert to the four-card majors that I love. Talk about willing to make accommodations.

Another benchmark in 1986: Wolffie, Jacoby and I got Seymon Deutsch's big-league bridge career launched by winning the Grand National Teams. Also that year, Jimmy Cayne decided to retain an expert team on a continuous basis. We hoped to get Aces-type results.

Seymon is an interesting character. He and Bobby went to school together in San Antonio and played a little bridge. Seymon dropped out of bridge, however, when he started his business career and didn't play for 22 years. In the mid-1980s, he decided he had time to play. He got back into the swing of things by sponsoring teams.

Seymon lives in Laredo, Texas, right on the Mexican border in the lower Rio Grande Valley. He's a wealthy man – he owns a distinctly upscale retail clothing business – but you wouldn't know it to talk to him. He's a hyperactive, tough competitor who has a hard time believing it is possible to lose. Although Seymon is not an expert player, he is always ready to play and is oblivious to pressure. He is a great teammate with the ability to inspire his troops. Seymon's record in the Vanderbilt and Spingold is really outstanding. In seven starts, he has two wins, three seconds and one loss in the semifinals. In the 1994 Vanderbilt, Seymon performed very well as his team won.

Winning the GNT, as with so many other victories, involved some close calls. In the quarterfinals, we played a tough team from New England and trailed by 38 IMPs going into the final quarter. This was a critical hand for our side.

```
Dlr: West        ♠ 10 9 6
Vul: Both        ♥ 7
                 ♦ A Q J 5 3
                 ♣ A 10 8 5
♠ K Q J 5 2                      ♠ 8 7
♥ Q J 6                          ♥ 9 8 5 4 2
♦ 7 6 4                          ♦ K 10 8 2
♣ 4 2                            ♣ K 6
                 ♠ A 4 3
                 ♥ A K 10 3
                 ♦ 9
                 ♣ Q J 9 7 3
```

WEST	NORTH	EAST	SOUTH
	Jacoby		*Me*
Pass	1♦	Pass	2♣
Pass	3♣	Pass	3♥
Pass	4♣	Pass	4♠
Dbl	5♥	Pass	6♣
All Pass			

West's double of 4♠ was like a clap of thunder, and his opening lead of the ♠K was swift and confident. It had the look of KQJ to me. Looking at dummy, it didn't take a genius to see I was in deep trouble. I cashed the ♥A and the ♥K, pitching a spade from dummy. On the second heart, West played the jack. I was beginning to see some hope. If West, who passed as dealer, had the ♥QJ and the ♠KQJ, he was very unlikely to have either minor-suit king.

Accordingly, I played the ♦A and the ♦Q. I ruffed when East covered and led the ♥3, on which West played the queen. I cashed the ♣A, the first time I had played trumps, and played the ♦J, pitching a spade. I ruffed a diamond with the 9 and played the ♥10, forcing West to ruff. I overruffed in dummy and led the good diamond. The only trick for the defense was the ♣K, which East could take whenever he chose. That was a 13-IMP gain in a match we won by a single IMP. Whew! We blew out our semifinal opponents and defeated a good team from Chicago in the final for a very satisfying victory.

The 1986 GNT win qualified us for the team trials to represent the U.S. in the Olympiad in Venice, Italy, in 1988. We added Meckstroth and Rodwell, making us the favored team. In the opening round of the trials, we got a great draw, a rather weak team that we absolutely destroyed. The beauty of it was that, with our team so far ahead, Seymon could get in lots of extra boards, a big boost to his confidence.

Our opponents in the final were our former teammates – Pender, Ross, Stansby and Martel – plus Peter Boyd and Steve Robinson, a very tough pair from the Washington DC area. They were doubly qualified by winning the Reisinger and Vanderbilt. This was an entirely different kettle of fish.

We started slowly, but we rallied to pull dead even about halfway through. When Seymon was in, he played with Wolffie while I played with Jacoby. The fact that we had played even with them was a huge psychological edge for us. All players are required to play at least one quarter of the match, so when Seymon completed his requirement in the first 48 boards, it was going to be Bobby and me and Meckwell for the duration. The other team could reasonably expect to take the lead with an inexperienced player like Seymon in our lineup. The fact that we had pulled even with them while Seymon was still in was a severe setback for them and a bonus for us.

There was another huge factor in our favor – Pender's illness. Although he lived for two more years, AIDS had taken a severe toll on his energy and playing skills. Although he had as much grit as anyone I've seen, he wasn't up to the rigors of the team trials in his condition. No one can play his best when he's sick, and Pender had to get in his share of the boards. In his final set, he was so spent he could hardly see the cards. We picked up a ton of IMPs while Pender was in and playing quite miserably. Peter could be a pain in the butt at times, but it was still sad to see such a competitor struggling as he did.

Martel-Stansby and Boyd-Robinson played well over the final 32 boards, but we prevailed by 16 IMPs and found ourselves planning a trip to Venice.

Venice was great. Our team was loose and ready to play. The United States had never won a World Team Olympiad and this was the eighth time it was to be played. We felt that our chances were as good as any other team in the field, and if Seymon continued to play with the kind of confidence he had shown in the trials, we could bring home the trophy for the first time.

We made it through the round-robin to the quarterfinals, where we drew the one team we didn't want to play: Denmark. Their pairs played very strange systems and they were wild bidders. We were fearful that their unusual methods might cause big problems for Seymon, who obviously lacked experience at the international level. Our team was down by 19 IMPs with 16 hands to go, but Bobby and I had a huge set to go with a solid one from Meckstroth-Rodwell and we won by 15.

Our reward was a very significant piece of luck – our opponent in the semifinals was India. The Indians were capable players, but the

Indian psychology worked strongly to our advantage. Through centuries of tradition, the Indians are very much attuned to acceptance of one's station in life. It's part of their culture – it's ingrained in them. They are very tough if they believe themselves to be the favorites in a match. You don't want any part of them under those circumstances. If they perceive themselves as underdogs, it's a different matter. My experience with teams from India is that they tend to lose more often than one would expect when they think they are underdogs and they win more often when they consider themselves favorites.

The Danes, on the other hand, don't think about such things. They just go out and play fearlessly. Of course, they occasionally shoot themselves in the foot and lose some matches they shouldn't, but they also come through with some big upset victories.

As predicted, we clobbered India in the semifinals. One of our huge swings resulted from Seymon's exuberance – and an incredible dose of luck. Just take a look:

```
Dlr: West        ♠ Q
Vul: N-S         ♥ A 10 5 3
                 ♦ 10 6 4
                 ♣ A K 6 4 3
  ♠ 10 9 6                    ♠ A J 7 5 4 3 2
  ♥ J 9 8 4                   ♥ 6
  ♦ 9 8 3 2                   ♦ K 5
  ♣ Q 7                       ♣ 10 9 2
                 ♠ K 8
                 ♥ K Q 7 2
                 ♦ A Q J 7
                 ♣ J 8 5
```

Against Jacoby and me, North-South played a sane 4♥. At the other table:

WEST	NORTH	EAST	SOUTH
	Wolff		*Deutsch*
Pass	1♥	3♠	4NT
Pass	5♥	Pass	6♥
All Pass			

Seymon's bid of 4NT with three possible quick losers in clubs was a bit much, but the proof is in the pudding. Bobby blanched when he saw the dummy after East led the ♠A, but I've never seen Wolffie quit on a hand. As you can see, the fact that the ♦K and ♣Q are doubleton allows this 8% slam to come home. That's Seymon for you, though – always positive and optimistic. Of course, it never hurts to be lucky, too.

We beat the demoralized Indian team by 64 IMPs to advance to the final against a team from Austria that had less talent than might be expected for the final of a world championship. In fact, in the championship round, the team's overall performance was pretty bad.

Austria didn't put up much of a fight. We jumped out in front by 55 IMPs after the first set. Although it was closer by the finish, and there were some scary hands against Bobby and me in the final 16 boards, the opponents went off the rails at the other table. We were never really in danger and we won by 42 IMPs.

Seymon was practically jumping out of his skin. In a way, he reminded me of Ira Corn – so enthusiastic, so thrilled to win. Ira would have been proud to have put his partner in an 8% slam that just happened to make. I could just hear him saying to Bobby: "That's what makes it so great!"

I thought we were going to have to tie Seymon to a chair to keep him from waking up all of Venice. "It's fantastic," Seymon cried. "It's unreal – the thrill of a lifetime."

I had to agree. It was a special thrill for me, too: America's first win in the Olympiad, and with a team that included an inexperienced player. It was also my last win in a world championship – at least through the summer of 1994.

The long winning streak against Meckstroth and Rodwell ended in Memphis in May of 1991.

The event was the United States Bridge Championship – what the ACBL was calling the Bermuda Bowl team trials at that time. I was playing with Wolff on a team bankrolled by Jimmy Cayne, a fine player who is president of a Wall Street firm in New York. We had been playing with Cayne and his partner, Chuck Burger, a player from Michigan who was one of Corn's and Wolff's original choices for the Aces. Our fifth and sixth were Martel and Stansby.

We had qualified for the trials by winning the Spingold. I thought we were the favorites, but experience has taught me that the best team doesn't always win.

Meckstroth and Rodwell, along with Alan Sontag, had been added to the Grand National Teams winners because one of their players wasn't eligible. Before Meckstroth and Rodwell were added, the team was reasonable enough, but not one you would regard as a threat to make it to the Bermuda Bowl.

Jeff and Eric proved just how dynamic they are – and how much they can influence the course of a match. They played all 256 boards in the semifinal and final. Most players would be exhausted and brain-dead if they even tried it. Jeff and Eric were still going strong at the finish. Their teammates, of course, deserve credit for the victory, too, but Jeff and Eric were the major reasons for the win.

In the semifinals, we had them down by 30 IMPs with 16 boards to go, but they beat us by 41 in the final set. They went on to win the trials and play in the Bermuda Bowl in Yokohama, Japan, that year. I hated to lose with what I considered to be a superior team – and I really hated for the streak to end – but I had to acknowledge Jeff's and Eric's fine play. They deserved the victory. I'm quite happy to list them as teammates now.

The defeat in the trials pretty much signaled the end of our association with Cayne. He wasn't too happy with the way things worked out in Memphis, and Stansby and Martel weren't the ideal match for Cayne. I wouldn't consider Chip and Lew anyone's drinking buddies, and Jimmy likes to hang around with his teammates to a certain extent. *No simpatico* might be the best way to describe that situation. It was also time for me to call it quits with Cayne, not because of any animosity but because of my association with Nick Nickell.

Nick had become involved in my prize promotion business and I felt an obligation to play with him in major events – some pair games and all the major team events.

Nick is fun to be around. He's the president of Kelso and Company, a small securities firm that has been very successful in the leveraged buyout business. He moved to New York from North Carolina several years ago. He looks like the quintessential Ivy Leaguer, and he clearly enjoys life to the fullest. He loves to talk bridge hands and swill Heineken until all hours of the morning. He's also an excellent player. He and Richard Freeman form a very strong partnership. At the Fall Nationals in Indianapolis in 1991, Nick and I won the Blue Ribbon Pairs. That sort of made up for the poor showing our team had in the Reisinger.

Since then, however, we have won the Spingold twice (at the 1993 and 1994 Summer Nationals) and the Reisinger (fall 1993). We stubbed our toes in the 1994 Vanderbilt, but our current lineup is the closest to a truly dominant team since the vintage days of the Aces.

My last appearance in a world championship was in 1992 in Salsomaggiore, Italy, a little resort town in northern Italy. Remarkably, I played there as a member of the defending champions in the World Team Olympiad – and our team was nearly the same as in 1988. Jim Jacoby, who died in 1991, had been replaced by Michael Rosenberg. Michael, a top-notch player originally from Scotland, now trades options in New York. Our team was a much more functional unit than in 1988 because Michael would play with Seymon.

We earned the trip to Italy in another of those nail-biting trials in Memphis. The issue was in doubt until the final board – Richard Pavlicek went down in 4♥ against Bobby and me while Eric made it at the other table.

The hand itself was very interesting and instructive – and I wrote about it in the BOLS Tips competition. This was the full deal:

```
Dlr: West          ♠ 10 8 6 5
Vul: None          ♥ K 9
                   ♦ J 4 2
                   ♣ Q 6 4 3
   ♠ J 7 4 3                      ♠ K
   ♥ A 8 4                        ♥ Q J 7 5 2
   ♦ K Q 8                        ♦ A 9 6 5 3
   ♣ K J 8                        ♣ 5 2
                   ♠ A Q 9 2
                   ♥ 10 6 3
                   ♦ 10 7
                   ♣ A 10 9 7
```

WEST	NORTH	EAST	SOUTH
Root	*Wolff*	*Pavlicek*	*Me*
1♦	Pass	1♥	Pass
1NT	Pass	2♦ (1)	Pass
3♥	Pass	4♥	All Pass

(1) Checkback for three-card heart support.

I led the ♦10, and Pavlicek won with the king in dummy. Obviously, Pavlicek could have played the ♥A and another heart, going after trumps to prevent a ruff and hoping to make the right guess in clubs if it came to that. But Pavlicek tried to steal a trick by leading a spade right away. That sealed his fate. I won the ♠A and played another diamond. Now I could always get a diamond ruff. The ♣A would be the setting trick.

Pavlicek won the diamond in his hand and played the ♥J to Bobby's king. Now Bobby started thinking – and my mental energy became misdirected. We can still defeat 4♥ even without the diamond ruff, but I was rooting so hard for Bobby to return a diamond that I'm afraid I might have blown the defense if I hadn't gotten the ruff.

Say Bobby had returned a spade, the only logical alternative to playing a diamond. After ruffing the spade, Pavlicek would have had no option but to play a club immediately – and he would have had to play me for the ace. If Bobby had the ♣A and got in again, he would surely find the diamond return then.

So, after making the correct guess in clubs, Pavlicek would pull trumps, unblock diamonds and get back to his hand with a spade ruff. Making four.

But I could still defeat 4♥ even without the diamond ruff. The winning defense is for me to rise with the ♣A and force declarer with the ♠Q, deliberately setting up the ♠J. Pavlicek would have been down to two trumps in each hand (while I also still had two) and would not have been able to untie the diamond suit and pull trumps, too. He would still have gone down.

Fortunately, Bobby gave me the ruff and I wasn't put to the test. The very important point of this hand is that if I had let the disappointment of not getting a diamond ruff interfere with my thinking, I would have had no chance to do the right thing later. Defense of this type is difficult to find under the best of circumstances. I surely would not have found it had I sat there pining for partner to return a diamond. I had been wasting my time rooting for a diamond back rather than thinking about how to beat the contract if Bobby had played some other suit.

The reality of bridge is that partners vary from great to bad – and even the great ones will not always see the defense that is obvious to you. The same thing applies in other settings. When your opening lead turns out to be a bad one, don't sit there saying, "Gee! I wish I had made a different lead." Spend your mental energy searching for ways to recover. There may still be time – and ways – for your side to prevail.

Beating 4♥ was a 10-IMP gain, and we won the match by 3 IMPs. It was a hard-fought and intense contest – just the kind I like. Winning a match of that kind is much more satisfying than blowing someone out. When you're in gut-check mode at the very end, you feel as though you've accomplished something and you've toughened yourself for the next test. In the games I prefer, there are no easy marks.

Salsomaggiore was full of surprises.

For one thing, there was hardly any air conditioning at the hotel where the Olympiad was played – a truly unfortunate circumstance since the temperature during the day averaged about 95. The only cool place was the vugraph room. Naturally, I didn't plan on spending a lot of time there. I wanted to be playing – not watching.

Another unexpected development was the play of Egypt, a team of young players with little international experience.

There were 57 teams split into two groups. The top four finishers after the separate round-robins would play quarterfinal matches. Scoring was IMPs converted to Victory Points, and we easily led our group. We scored more than 100 IMPs in two of our first three round-robin matches. The unheralded Egyptian team, meanwhile, was third in their group behind Israel and an experienced team from Poland.

As the winners of the round-robin, we got to pick our opponents. We chose Egypt. With an easier opponent, Seymon could get more playing time, building his confidence and thereby strengthening the team. The other matches were all among European teams: Israel vs. the Netherlands, France vs. Denmark and Poland vs. Sweden.

As expected, we handled Egypt with little trouble, 225-154, while Sweden slugged Poland, 173-98. The other two matches were close all the way. The Netherlands defeated Israel, 130-121, and France won their match with Denmark on the last board when a Danish declarer butchered a 3♥ contract to go minus 300 for a 4-IMP loss. France won, 145-143. We drew Sweden in the semifinal while France played against the Netherlands.

Once again, system became an issue in a world championship. One of the Swedish pairs – Björn Fallenius and Mats Nilsland – was playing something they called a "Minimajor" system, the cornerstone of which was some sort of rubbish about 1♣ and 1♦ openers "emphasizing" corresponding majors suits (♣ for ♥, ♦ for ♠), although the major might be only two cards long. I ask you, can we realistically hope to sell bridge to the public with stuff like that in the showcase?

Anyway, because this system was so unusual, we were able to invoke a WBF rule that allowed us to choose who we would play against the Minimajorettes. That is, the pair playing Minimajors had to seat themselves first. Our designated hitters against them were Meckstroth and Rodwell.

The unusual methods had little effect. We knocked off the Swedes 202-136.7 (the fraction came from carryover). France disposed of the Netherlands, 148.7-115. We were back to defend our title.

I was pleased to note that the French team played all natural methods, as they did in 1980. Two members of that team from 12 years previous – Michel Perron and Paul Chemla – were back. Paul looked almost the same – gray around the temples, but still with that hang-dog, world-against-me look. And still a helluva card player.

We were the heavy betting favorites, even though France started with a 9.7-IMP carryover, the result of their 29-IMP win against us in the round-robin. That didn't seem like much of a spot to me and, indeed, it wasn't significant in the overall match. They beat us by so much it didn't matter.

Chemla and his buddies jumped out to a 47-16 lead and we never caught up. I'll give them credit. They outplayed us and they deserved to win. There were a few hands I would consider unlucky for our side, but I've been the beneficiary of plenty of luck in my time, so I don't complain about it when I'm on the other side.

Despite the loss, I'm proud of our team for not giving up. In fact, we started a serious rally in the fourth set when Jeff Meckstroth showed up wearing a towel around his head – in the same spirit that baseball teams show when they all put their caps on backwards. They call them "rally caps" to show team solidarity. Well, we all put on the towels and shot a 62-29 fourth segment to pull to within 27 IMPs with 32 boards to go. Unfortunately, that set was the last of the day and going to bed seemed to take our momentum away. We lost the fifth set by 22 and then lost tons more IMPs in the final 16 boards trying to create some swings. The final margin was 80 IMPs.

Fortunately, in bridge there is often another day. Nickell, Freeman, Meckstroth, Rodwell, Wolff and I are sharpening our teeth in anticipation of inflicting some pain in the World Championships to be held in Albuquerque, New Mexico, in September 1994. I consider myself lucky because my desire to win has not diminished one iota. Competing, matching my best against yours, is what it's all about. I don't crunch the numbers quite as quickly or efficiently as I once did, but experience is very important in bridge. And believe me, when I make mistakes, they are unlikely to be rookie mistakes.

20

A competitive game

A FEW YEARS AGO, I was watching the Pittsburgh Steelers and Kansas City Chiefs one Sunday afternoon. Pittsburgh was ahead by 3 points with barely over two minutes to go – and they had the ball on the Kansas City 25. The Chiefs were out of time-outs and it appeared the Steelers had the game sewed up.

The obvious strategy was for Pittsburgh to down the ball three times, eating up the clock. Then Kansas City would have regained the ball with about 25 seconds to go and with no time-outs, a virtually hopeless situation.

Instead, Pittsburgh called a running play. One of Kansas City's defensive ends, Art Still, got through and hit Steeler quarterback Terry Bradshaw just as he was about to hand off. One of the Chiefs picked up the fumble and ran it back 76 yards for a touchdown.

When Kansas City kicked off a few moments later, one of the announcers said, "We've seen Bradshaw bring the Steelers back many times. Let's see what he can do now."

I'll never forget the comment by the other broadcaster. Bob Trumpy said, "Forget it. Pittsburgh is history. A team cannot recover after taking a shot like that. They don't have enough time to regroup. Kansas City is more likely to score."

Trumpy was right on target. Bradshaw almost immediately threw an interception and there was no drama to the final minutes. Pittsburgh had lost, snatching defeat from the jaws of victory.

In bridge, there's no way to lie down on the ball and play it cozy. The greatest single danger in a match when you're ahead is that you'll get robbed on a series of hands. To keep this from happening, you've got to get into the pot and take risks. You've got to bid as aggressively as you would if the match was tied.

It's great if you get a series of no-brainer hands when you've got a big lead, but you can never tell if and when the no-brainers are coming. You can't run out the clock in bridge. You've got to get the last out. To me, that's one of the very best facets of the game.

Do you want to play better bridge? Are you serious about the game? And I don't mean do you hope one day to win the Vanderbilt or the Bermuda Bowl. You can be serious about bridge by just wanting to play your best each time out. If bridge for you is just a way to pass the time, you probably won't be interested in reading much further. Just skip to the *Postscripts* at the end of this chapter.

But if you love the game and want to hear a little about what I've learned over the years, stay with me.

Combinations of factors bring about improvements in any field of endeavor. It could be analysis, it could be trial and error. More frequently, it's a combination of many forms of review combined with a fair amount of effort in the design stages. Ultimately there is improvement, and the rate of progress has a tendency to accelerate.

Bridge has a few underlying basic conditions. First, the objective is to perform successfully in a real-time environment where your performance has one very important constraint that is present in very few other areas of endeavor.

For example, if you are involved in a lawsuit, you research it, explore theories, check and cross-check. If you do anything of a research nature you test, retest, and check it over one last time before finally coming up with your best shot.

In most games – and bridge is a prime example – you take your shot and, unfortunately sometimes, you have to live with it. Good or bad, that's what you've done. You can't take it back. You can't make a move in a chess game and say, "Oops!" In football, you can't throw a pass to the other team's middle linebacker and say, "I really meant to throw it to the tight end." You can't take it back.

Not many real-life undertakings take place in real time – you're seldom stuck with your first stab. Of course, there are exceptions – crash landing airplanes and police work are two that come to mind. Games are different from most real-life endeavors. You are stuck with what you do.

Second, in games usually the objective is to win. You aren't trying to beat somebody by six touchdowns. You're trying to beat them by one point. Granted, if you can get ahead by six touchdowns you have more margin for error late in the game. But the objective is still to win.

To achieve your goal of winning you must either be lucky or more skillful than your opponents. How much better do you have to perform to be a significant favorite? I would say 32 IMPs in an all-day 64-board match. That's three game swings – a lot, but it doesn't represent a huge skill differential.

You're not going to get beaten very often if you're 32 IMPs better than your opponents. If you have to be a little better than the opponents to have a better than even-money chance of winning, what must you do to increase your chances of winning?

Step 1: Don't screw up the easy ones. There are multiple ways to screw up the easy ones. There are more ways to screw them up than to do them right. You think you won't make a mistake that is well within your capabilities to avoid, but a funny thing happens – you make the mistake.

Why might you make such a mistake? For one reason or another – you're sick or distracted, perhaps – you're not concentrating or you're not in physical shape to play. Maybe you've become tired in the course of the fray. It stands to reason you're a lot more likely to get tired if you have to do more work than you should. If you turn easy problems into hard ones because your difficult methodology has sapped all your energy, the easy ones suddenly become huge boulders and the hard ones become almost impossible.

Maintaining concentration is much more important than working on the electronic three-way notrump or any other convention. We're not talking about a factor of 1.01 – we're talking about a factor of 20. Having the right mindset is of ultimate importance because you're dealing with a real-time event. People are used to thinking and dealing with problems that are subject to review. You can write a computer program, run it, test it, rework it several times until you're happy with it. You can't do that in bridge.

You improve concentration by working on good table habits – as in keeping your mouth shut. Now, if something comes up where there was a clear-cut misunderstanding, five seconds to get a quick clarification is okay. One player or the other should say without debate what it's going to be for the rest of the session. Just get it over with quickly – don't spend any energy on it.

Conjecture is destructive. "Could you have made the hand if you had done this?" You don't want to even think about it. The hand is over. If you're going to needle anybody, needle the opponents. Don't pick on your partner.

Now I know that emotions are not entirely a voluntary process, and being on an emotional edge can be useful because it keeps the adrenaline flowing and increases the energy level. But if emotion gets out of control, it can sink the ship.

Keep this in mind: in a game like bridge where you're making real-time decisions, you're going to look like a fool a certain percentage of the time – count on it. It's going to be embarrassing. Don't let it bother you. Don't say anything. Get on to the next hand.

Concentration means avoiding distractions. There is more than one element to winning, but first and foremost is concentration. You're not going to learn how to pull off a compound squeeze between the third and seventh deals of the set. If something is beyond your level of skill at the start of a session, chances are it's not going to become part of your repertoire before the session is over.

Step 2: Ask yourself a series of questions. This part of the equation applies mainly to playing and defending but also to a degree to bidding. *What is going on? What is this picture I'm looking at? Where is the ball?* If you don't know where the ball is, it's pretty hard to pick it up.

Asking yourself questions is part of the concentration process. You have to do this until you do it automatically or subconsciously. Take stock, and remember that you're dealing with a moving picture. You pick up a hand. What do you know? You know the hand you're looking at – that's all. As events progress, you obtain additional information.

Bidding is a declarative-interrogative process – mainly declarative. You're constantly telling or asking or switching back and forth. At the end of the process you stamp "paid" on the ticket and place the final contract or take the final action.

To use the computer programming analogy, don't start developing applications before you know the problem or the language. You can't do it, but that's what lots of people try to do when they play bridge.

Bridge players – and this includes some pretty damned good ones – often make the mistake of asking themselves, "What should I do now?" That is seldom the right question. The right question is, "What in the hell is going on?" Unless you know what's going on, it's very hard to figure out what to do.

Occasionally you need certain conditions to exist in order to achieve your goal on a given hand. Well, if you need certain conditions to exist, you have to assume that they do. If they don't, you can't achieve your larger goal, so just get on with it.

Say you're on a desert island where there's no water. You're fading fast. There are two canisters in front of you. One contains an instantly fatal poison, the other contains water – enough to last you until the next boat arrives. Nobody knows you're on this island and the chance of anyone rescuing you before the boat arrives is less than 1%. If you have no way of determining which canister is which, you might as well make an assumption. Choose one and pour the other one out so that you don't get deluded and drink from both of them. Take your best shot and good luck.

Well, when the bridge equivalent of that occurs, make your choice. Assume it's going to work. There's no way to hedge your bets. Granted, a little more effort crunching the numbers might yield a better plan. But bridge is a timed event – at a certain point the conditions of contest stipulate that you must make a decision or suffer some penalties.

Let's assume you have the capacity to make the necessary decision in some reasonable time frame. Your assumptions may be somewhat flawed, you may miss something, you may make a mistake. If so, go back after the fact and review it. See if you can learn from the situation. But don't try to save face and don't flog yourself. Try to figure out what really happened.

But not right now. Figure out what really happened later – at your leisure. Right now, concentrate on the next hand – that's all that matters at this point in time. The hand on which you made a mistake is history – put it out of your mind for now.

Every player can improve. Even the very best players can improve by focusing harder on mechanics.

If you're paying attention to what's going on and not screwing up the easy ones, it's much easier to get the hard ones right. As a result you use less energy for the hard ones. If you don't screw up the easy ones, you can afford to get a hard one wrong once in a while.

I talk about system a lot, but I don't attach much weight to system in general. Most serious players spend way too much time and effort tinkering and refining. As a result they have trouble remembering what their last understanding was. Among my many partners, Kantar was the worst in this regard. He was keenly interested in the theory of the game. He believed there was a solution to every bidding problem, and he had a need to fix everything on the spot. He had a patch for every bad result, and we had great difficulty remembering the many system changes.

In May of 1994, *Sports Illustrated* had a cover story entitled, "Is Tennis Dying?" Much of it dealt with the sorry attitudes of the big-name players, but there was also a strong suggestion that the souped-up graphite rackets have made tennis a boring sport. In short, the author's view was that technology is killing tennis. Big servers using high-tech rackets have taken all the drama out of the game. It's just *Boom! Boom! Next point!*

A major problem for the game of tennis is that the companies producing the super-hot rackets have a huge monetary stake in keeping them in the game – probably hundreds of millions of dollars.

Looking at bridge from that standpoint, all the high-tech systems and strange methods you see nowadays have created just one more barrier to entry for new players. Bridge, even at its simplest level, is already perceived by much of the general public as overly compli-cated. When bidding becomes so complex that even experienced players can't understand what's going on, forget about attracting new faces. They don't want any part of it.

Bridge is lucky, however, because there aren't any multi-million dollar companies out there with a stake in the high-tech and/or bizarre systems. We can affect changes if we deem them to be in the game's best interests. I'm here to say that some changes are needed.

Now I'm not opposed to innovation and/or improvement. In fact, improvements in methods and the expansion of knowledge about the game over the decades have made bridge that much more exciting and appealing. For example, my level of play with the Aces when they were at their peak wouldn't be good enough to win as often as I win today. The progression of knowledge is such that the best players of the 1930s and 1940s would be blown out by good amateurs today.

My objection in the high-tech area concerns the advantage gained because a system or method is completely foreign to the opposition. Full disclosure – mandatory if you're to have a fair contest – is impossible in many cases.

Pair games are an incredible mine field. Usually you're playing two boards a round. If your methods are so complex that you have something to explain on a high percentage of the hands, that's a bar to full disclosure. You have an unfair advantage against everyone.

Let's say, however, that I somehow have become familiar with what you are doing to the point that I can cope with it. That's fine for me for the two boards I play against you, but I can't make all the other pairs in the event become equally familiar with your methods. So when you face the other pairs, you're back to having an unfair advantage against them and, by extension, against me. You may not be trying to conceal what you're doing, but your methods are so difficult to explain that you don't have time during a round to meet your responsibilities adequately.

That leaves me a choice: come up with my own brand of unfathomable crap, or get beat. I would rather have total non-disclosure – and every man for himself – than what we've got right now.

Complicated methods create other problems. One of the most offensive conventions is the so-called Smith Echo. It is used primarily against notrump contracts. This is a defensive convention where, after the opening lead is made and declarer starts playing on a suit, either member of the defensive partnership can signal *in the suit played by declarer* whether the opening leader's suit should be continued by the next defender who gets in.

In other words, say partner leads a spade. Declarer wins and begins playing on hearts. Now either defender can say he liked the opening lead by playing a high card. Either defender can play a low card to suggest that the suit not be continued.

My problem with this convention concerns the information that can be passed by either player's tempo. Here's an example. Say the bidding goes 1NT (15-17) on your left, 3NT on your right. You're looking at:

♠J 8 7 6   ♥8 4 3   ♦K 7 6   ♣9 6 2.

Partner leads the ♠4 and dummy hits with:

♠9 2   ♥A 9 4   ♦Q 10 2   ♣Q J 10 5 4.

Partner's ♠4 goes to your jack and declarer's king. Declarer immediately plays the ♣K and another club. You don't have to give count in this situation because declarer has the ♥A for a dummy entry. Your club plays will be interpreted by partner in the Smith Echo framework – you liked the spade lead or you didn't.

If partner has led from ♠A10543, you should signal high so he'll lay down the ♠A, dropping declarer's queen. The defense will then take four spade tricks to go with the ♣A. But suppose partner has led from the ♠A1054 and has the ♦A on the side. Now it's necessary for him to get you in so you can lead a spade through declarer's remaining spades (Q-3) to defeat the contract. To complicate matters, your side card might be the ♥K, and a diamond shift could blow the hand.

You've got to make a split-second decision here – to hesitate for even a millisecond will pass information to partner. Think about it. If you don't play a smooth card on the ♣A, partner will know you have some kind of problem. What problem could you have? If you started with three spades to the Q-J, you wouldn't have a problem – you'd drop the ♣9 without a hitch. If you started with only three spades to the jack, you'd play your ♣2 – no problem. The only holding you could have where you would have doubt about your signal would be the holding you actually have – *and your tempo has just relayed this information to your partner.*

With conventions like the Smith Echo, such situations are plentiful, and they're just murder. They are particularly lethal in the hands of someone who knows all the ramifications and doesn't mean well.

This is the very same reason that the ACBL forbids odd-even signaling – as opposed to odd-even *discards*, first discard only. There were too many situations where defenders were dealt no odd or even cards in a suit. As a result, too much information was being passed by slow, tortured even (discouraging) or odd (encouraging) plays.

Lest you think I'm preaching that bridge is on the brink of ruin, let me say that I still think it's the greatest game ever invented. There's a reasonable blend of skill and luck needed for success, and the underdog has a chance in many settings. Bridge has excitement, drama, pathos – and players can function at high levels even as they advance in age.

I'm 56 years old, and I feel incredibly lucky to be playing a sport where old geezers like me can be competitive – perhaps more than competitive – with the best players in the world. Oh, to hell with the false modesty – I am still ready to take on any opponent, at any time, for any stakes. In what other sport is such longevity even remotely possible?

There's a need for more young blood in the game, though. Consider how few young players have demonstrated that they have truly arrived as competitors at the national level. There are probably others, but only a few come to mind immediately – youngsters like Brad Moss, Ravindra Murthy and Geoff Hampson.

Here are some ideas for helping bridge grow:

• Remove the perceived barriers to entry: that there are too many languages (bidding systems), that it takes too much time to learn the languages, that being smart and putting in a lot of effort aren't enough by themselves.

• Make bridge comprehensible to the general public – another way of addressing the language issue. Golf is a good example. I don't play golf, but I know what the objective is. I can watch golf on television and understand what's going on because it's simple – players are trying to knock the ball into the hole.

The same is not true with bridge. Can you imagine trying to broadcast a match involving teams playing forcing pass systems? People would recoil in horror. *Why are they opening the bidding with bad cards and passing with good cards? What's going on here?*

• Eliminate devices such as the Smith Echo, which can be utilized reprehensibly, and put restrictions on other conventions ripe for abuse, such as super-weak 1NT openers and the Multi 2♦. I'm not saying get rid of them, but some controls should be established since the potential for abuse is so great.

• Establish a commissioner of bridge – someone like the commissioner of baseball, who has the power to take action and make decisions for the good of the game and who has a talent for promotion. We need a Larry King (who put women's tennis on the map) or a David Stern, NBA Commissioner.

• Establish a system for flighting events based on current performance. The technology is certainly there for the ACBL to rate players in that fashion.

Let's face it, lots of players with more than 1500 masterpoints have no business in a Flight A event, nor do they have any desire to be there. What happens? These people eventually stop playing. You would see more of them at tournaments if they knew they could play against people of the same skill level. That's one reason why Senior tournaments are so popular.

Using a more advanced rating system, the ACBL could "promote" a player who consistently performs well to the next higher level. At the same time, the ACBL could allow a player who is doing poorly in his class to move down to a less competitive level. Players in lower levels would have something to shoot for – moving up – while the players who aren't quite as competitive would enjoy playing against their peers.

I would love to play in a game where all the players were tough. It would be a kick to compete in a game where 53% was a good score. Not everyone wants that, however. That's why the ACBL should consider a different way of rating players rather than counting the piles of masterpoints, many of which probably were won in the distant past or against weak competition.

In 1994, I'm one of the few current top competitors who has a link to the players who were dominant in the early days of bridge. I've played against nine of the 10 original Life Masters. P. Hal Sims, LM #5, had the discourtesy to die before I took up the game. I cut my bridge teeth in an incredibly tough atmosphere at the L.A. Bridge Club. The only other top experts in this country with similar backgrounds who are still major threats in national championships are Grant Baze and Paul Soloway. The other top guns learned their trade at tournament bridge.

In my opinion, 95% of those who enjoy a competitive challenge and pursue the game seriously will derive much exhilaration from bridge. The highs from competitive success compensate for the pain of defeat, and it sure as hell beats solving crossword puzzles.

My wife Petra (we married in 1987) is the most successful bridge teacher in Dallas and the greatest enthusiast for the game I have ever seen. Despite the questionable judgment she showed in associating with me, she has become an excellent player. I coached her team last year in the Women's Team Trials (for the Venice Cup in Santiago, Chile) and they nearly upset the eventual winners.

My son Chris, who is developing into a fine bridge player, is also a strong enthusiast. We have played a few national events together and, although we haven't won one, I'm confident we will. Chris and I played in the 1994 Grand National Teams, representing District 16 in the San Diego Nationals. Our team tied for third.

The fates have been good to me. In 1986, after being in the insurance business for 20 years, I started a business called SCA Promotions. SCA accepts prize risk for sponsors of contests and promotions – hole-in-one contests for golf tournaments, direct mail campaigns, lots of other things. It's a terrific business and my 24 employees – including Chris – keep me busy practically all the time.

Somehow, though, I keep finding time to make it to the Nationals three times a year. The last one I missed was the 1963 Spring Nationals in St. Louis – when I had mononucleosis.

I've had good times and bad times in bridge. You know what? The disappointments are kind of hazy in my mind. The triumphs are crystal clear – along with the memories of the great people I've met and made friends with through the years. What a great game! What a great place to be – *at the table*, butting heads with my opponents to see who's the best.

Postscripts

In the course of doing research for this book, I had occasion to talk to many friends of Bob Hamman. What these people expressed about Bob he would never say about himself -- either out loud or on paper.

There was such a unanimity of opinion about Hamman's goodness, character and honesty that it is appropriate to record some of the accolades here. The following are some of the comments about Bob Hamman, the man, from people who know him well and are truly happy they do.

Brent Manley

Mike Lawrence, who played with Hamman on the Aces in the early 1970s: Bob was a very upbeat person. I played with him when things were going badly and he'd say something like, "Well, we've got these guys right where we want them – we're 60 IMPs down. We'll beat them now." Sometimes we would.

Fran Tsacnaris, a regular at the L.A. Bridge Club when Hamman first started playing: He was a terror at bridge. You just knew the talent was all there. The old guys couldn't keep up with him. Playing bridge was as natural as breathing for Hamman. He had a lot of heart, too, although he won't admit it. One time he came into the bridge club and was about to cut into a game when he noticed I was stuck badly. Someone said, "Hey, Hambone, don't you want to cut in?" He said, "No, I think I'll just watch." He wanted to give me a chance to get even, which would have been a lot tougher with him in the game.

Bruce Keidan, the reporter who broke the story of the cheating scandal during the 1975 Bermuda Bowl: Bob Hamman is a man's man – and a gentleman.

Don Krauss, Hamman's partner in winning the 1963 Pair Trials for the World Bridge Olympiad: When we came out of the pair trials, Bob was talking about three hands, and it was obvious his level of thinking about bridge was way above most other players. He has an incredible analytical mind. At the same time, he's not afraid to admit to a mistake, something Lew Mathe could never do. And if you beat him, Bob congratulates you.

Ron Andersen, former teammate of Hamman, many-time North American champion and frequent vugraph commentator: Bob is one of my favorites on vugraph. He looks like he should be in a football uniform instead of sitting at a bridge table. Hamman is the Mike Singletary of the bridge world. The intensity in his eyes is unbelievable.

After we lost the trials to his team in a 12-board playoff, Bob said, "Nobody should lose in overtime. They should declare two winners." That was about the only thing an opponent could have said where somebody wouldn't have thrown a chair at him.

Al Okuneff, owner of the L.A. Bridge Club when Hamman started his bridge career: Bob has a strong killer instinct at the table. Away from the table, he's one of the nicest people you'd ever want to meet. Bill McWilliams, who was an alcoholic, one time fell on lean times and was in poor health. Bob went out of his way to help. He was always that way.

Bobby Goldman, former member of the Aces and currently one of the top professional players in North America: In analysis of card play (during Aces' meetings) Hamman was far and away the leader. His intellect on card play was so far in excess of everyone else's . . . he strengthened everybody. I wish I still had him in my life. I would play my cards a little better.

Joe Musumeci, coach of the Aces: When Bob joined the Aces, he helped me. He didn't believe in any horseplay. He wanted to work. Bob was great. He and Wolff are just fantastic players.

Garland Ergüden, law student at the University of Memphis and a former professional player: In 1984, I was involved in a movement to try to improve conditions for women players and get the powers that be to recognize the legitimacy of women's bridge. I approached Hamman at the Fall NABC in San Diego, asking if we could use his name. Without hesitation, Bob agreed. He also pulled $100 out of his pocket and told me to come back if we needed more. He understood what we wanted and viewed us as bridge players, not *women* players. He was wonderful. Bob's support helped our cause tremendously.

Bobby Wolff, Hamman's regular partner for more than 20 years: Bob has a great analytical mind. He's far and away the best analytical player who's ever played. He loves the beauty of the game more than anybody else. Bob is very well liked among the top players for his approach to the game, his ethics and the fact that he's not a snob.

Brent Manley, ACBL Bulletin managing editor and co-author of this book: In 1993, my wife, Donna, and I had the pleasure of playing against Bob Hamman and his teammates in the second round of the Vanderbilt Knockout Teams. It was the thrill of a lifetime despite the drubbing we took. Later in the tournament, we discussed the match with Hamman briefly. Naturally, we commented on his team's huge margin of victory. With typical class and no hint of condescension, Bob said, "Well, you weren't very lucky."

Bob has given tremendously to the game of bridge simply by playing. His spirit, integrity, indomitable will and love for the game have made bridge a better sport. No hall of fame is big enough for Hamman and, anyway, it's not where he wants to be. Look for him where the toughest, most competitive bridge games are being played. In those settings, you'll find Bob Hamman, as always, *at the table*.

ᘓhe skins on the wall

1959 Commercial & Industrial Pairs in Coronado w/Ralph Clark (1st)

1962 Reisinger (then Open Teams) in Phoenix w/Don Krauss (1st)

1964 U.S. Team Trials (11/63) in Miami Beach w/Krauss (Qual. 1st)
1964 World Team Olympiad in New York w/Krauss (2nd)
1964 Vanderbilt in Portland w/Krauss (1st)
1964 Blue Ribbon Pairs in Dallas w/Lew Mathe (1st)

1966 U.S. Team Trials (11/65) in San Francisco w/Mathe (Qual. 2nd)
1966 Vanderbilt in Louisville w/Mathe (1st)
1966 Bermuda Bowl in St. Vincent w/Mathe (2nd)

1968 Vanderbilt in New York w/Eddie Kantar (2nd)
1968 Reisinger in Coronado w/Kantar (2nd)

1969 U.S. Team Trials (10/68) in Atlantic City w/Kantar (Qual. 3rd)
1969 Spring NAC Men's Teams in Cleveland w/Mike Lawrence (2nd)
1969 Spingold in Los Angeles w/Lawrence (1st)
1969 Fishbein Trophy for most masterpoints won at the Summer
      NABC

1970 U.S. Team Trials (10/69) in Phoenix w/Lawrence (1st)
1970 Vanderbilt in Portland w/Lawrence (2nd)
1970 Omar Sharif Bridge Circus – 840 boards (1st)
1970 Bermuda Bowl in Stockholm w/Lawrence (1st)
1970 Spingold in Boston w/Lawrence (2nd)
1970 Reisinger in Houston w/Billy Eisenberg (1st)

1971 Vanderbilt in Atlanta w/Eisenberg (1st)
1971 Bermuda Bowl in Taipei w/Eisenberg (1st)

1972 U.S. Team Trials (10/71) in New Orleans (1st)
1972 World Team Olympiad in Miami Beach w/Paul Soloway (2nd)

1973 Vanderbilt in St. Louis w/Bobby Wolff (1st)
1973 Bermuda Bowl in Guaruja, Brazil w/Wolff (2nd)

1974 U.S. Team Trials (10/73) in Milwaukee w/Wolff (1st)
1974 World Open Pairs in Las Palmas w/Wolff (1st)
1974 Bermuda Bowl in Venice w/Wolff (2nd)
1974 Pan American Invitational Pairs in Mexico City w/Wolff (1st)

1975 Grand National Open Teams in Miami w/Charlie Weed (1st)
1975 Bermuda Bowl in Bermuda w/Wolff (2nd)

1976 Pan American Invitational Pairs in Mexico City w/Wolff (1st)

1977 Grand National Open Teams in Chicago w/Wolff (1st)
1977 U.S. Team Trials in Houston w/Wolff (1st)
1977 Pan American Invitational Pairs in Mexico City w/Wolff (1st)
1977 Bermuda Bowl in Manila w/Wolff (1st)

1978 Herman Trophy for most masterpoints earned at a Fall NABC
1978 Reisinger in Denver w/Wolff (1st)

1979 U.S. Team Trials in Cherry Hill NJ w/Wolff (2nd)
1979 Spingold in Las Vegas w/Wolff (1st)
1979 Reisinger in Cincinnati w/Wolff (1st)

1980 U.S. Team Trials (12/79) in Memphis w/Wolff (1st)
1980 Men's Board-a-Match Teams in Fresno w/Wolff (2nd)
1980 Life Master Pairs in Chicago w/Eric Rodwell (1st)
1980 World Team Olympiad in Valkenburg w/Wolff (2nd)
1980 Life Master Men's Pairs in Lancaster w/Paul Swanson (2nd)

1981 Vanderbilt in Detroit w/Wolff (2nd)
1981 Life Master Pairs in San Francisco w/Krauss (2nd)

1982 Spingold in Albuquerque w/Wolff (1st)

1983 U.S. Team Trials (11/82) in Minneapolis w/Wolff (1st)
1983 Spingold in New Orleans w/Wolff (1st)

1983 Life Master Pairs in New Orleans w/Kantar (1st)
1983 Fishbein Trophy for most masterpoints earned at a Summer NABC
1983 Bermuda Bowl in Stockholm w/Wolff (1st)

1984 U.S. Team Trials in Memphis w/Wolff (1st)
1984 Men's Board-a-Match Teams in San Antonio w/Wolff (2nd)

1985 U.S. Team Trials in Memphis w/Wolff (1st)
1985 Bermuda Bowl in São Paulo w/Wolff (1st)
1985 Men's Pairs in Montreal w/George Mittelman (2nd)

1986 Men's Pairs in Portland w/Paul Swanson (1st)
1986 Grand National Teams in Toronto w/Wolff (1st)
1986 Blue Ribbon Pairs in Atlanta w/Ron Von der Porten (1st)
1986 World Mixed Pairs in Bal Harbour FL w/Kerri Shuman (2nd)

1987 Master Mixed Teams in Baltimore w/Rama Linz (1st)
1987 U.S. Team Trials in Memphis w/Wolff and Jim Jacoby (1st)
1987 Bermuda Bowl in Ocho Rios, Jamaica w/Wolff (1st)

1988 Open Pairs in Buffalo w/Paul Lewis (2nd)
1988 U.S. Team Trials in Memphis w/Wolff (1st)
1988 Men's Board-a-Match Teams in Nashville w/Wolff (1st)
1988 Reisinger in Nashville w/Wolff (1st)
1988 Herman Trophy for most masterpoints earned at a Fall NABC
1988 World Team Olympiad in Venice w/Wolff and Jacoby (1st)

1989 Spingold in Chicago w/Wolff (1st)
1989 Men's Board-a-Match Teams in Lancaster w/Wolff (2nd)

1990 Open Swiss Teams in Fort Worth w/Bart Bramley (1st)
1990 Spingold in Boston w/Wolff (1st)
1990 World Par Contest in Geneva, Switzerland (2nd)
1990 ACBL Player of the Year – for most masterpoints earned in National events

1991 Blue Ribbon Pairs in Indianapolis w/Nick Nickell (1st)

1991 Named Honorary Member – for contribution to bridge

1992 Open Swiss Teams in Pasadena w/Wolff (2nd)
1992 U.S. Team Trials in Memphis w/Wolff (1st)
1992 Life Master Pairs in Toronto w/Hemant Lall (1st)
1992 World Team Olympiad in Salsomaggiore, Italy w/Wolff (2nd)

1993 Spingold in Washington w/Wolff (1st)
1993 Reisinger in Seattle w/Wolff (1st)
1993 Blue Ribbon Pairs in Seattle w/Michael Rosenberg (1st)
1993 ACBL Player of the Year – for most masterpoints earned in
     National events

1994 Spingold in San Diego w/Wolff (1st)

♠ ♥ ♦ ♣

Vanderbilt – 1st four times, 2nd three times.
Spingold – 1st eight times, 2nd once.
Reisinger – 1st six times, 2nd once.
Blue Ribbon Pairs – 1st four times.
Grand National Teams – 1st three times.
Life Master Pairs – 1st three times, 2nd twice.
Master Mixed Teams – 1st once.

U.S. International Pair Trials – 1st once, qualified three times.
U.S. International Team Trials – 1st eleven times.

Pan American Invitational Pairs – 1st three times.
Bermuda Bowl – 1st six times, 2nd four times.
World Team Olympiad – 1st once, 2nd four times.
World Open Pairs – 1st once.
World Mixed Pairs – 2nd once.
World Par Contest – 2nd once.